The Child & Society

Pg 1-53

Consulting Editor:
CHARLES H. PAGE
Professor Emeritus
University of Massachusetts

The Child & Society

THE PROCESS OF SOCIALIZATION

Third Edition

FREDERICK ELKIN
York University, Toronto

GERALD HANDEL
*The City College and Graduate School
of the City University of New York*

 RANDOM HOUSE • NEW YORK

Third Edition
987654321
Copyright © 1960, 1972, 1978 by Random House, Inc.

Library of Congress Cataloging in Publication Data

Elkin, Frederick.
   The child and society.

   Bibliography: p.
   Includes index.
   1. Socialization.   I. Handel, Gerald, joint author.
II. Title.
HQ783.E43   1978   301.15'72   77-15953
ISBN 0-394-32074-3

Manufactured in the United States of America
Typography by Deborah Payne

Permissions Acknowledgments

Grateful acknowledgment is made to the following authors and publishers for permission to reprint selections from copyright material:

From William A. Caudill, "Tiny Dramas: Vocal Communication between Mother and Infant in Japanese and American Families," Chapter 3 in William P. Lebra (ed.), *Transcultural Research in Mental Health*. Copyright © 1972 by The University Press of Hawaii. Reprinted by permission of the publisher.

From Ernest G. Schachtel, *Metamorphosis: On the Development of Affect, Perception, Attention, and Memory*. Copyright © 1959 by Basic Books, Inc. and Routledge & Kegan Paul Ltd.

From Philippe Aries, *Centuries of Childhood*, translated by Robert Baldick. Copyright © 1965 by Alfred A. Knopf, Inc. Reprinted by permission of Alfred A. Knopf, Inc. and Jonathan Cape Ltd.

From Margaret Mead and Martha Wolfenstein, *Childhood in Contemporary Cultures*. Copyright © 1955 by The University of Chicago. All rights reserved. Copyright 1955 under the International Copyright Union. Published 1955.

From Harry M. Caudill, *Night Comes to the Cumberlands: A Biography of a Depressed Area*. Copyright © 1962, 1963 by Harry M. Caudill. Reprinted by permission of Little, Brown and Co. in association with the Atlantic Monthly Press.

From John U. Ogbu, *The Next Generation: An Ethnography of Education in an Urban Neighborhood*. Copyright © 1974 by Academic Press. Reprinted by permission of the author and the publisher.

From M. Kay Martin and Barbara Voorhies, *Female of the Species*. Copyright © 1975 by Columbia University Press. Reprinted by permission of the publisher.

Dedicated to Madge *F. E.*
and to
Ruth, Jonathan, and Michael *G. H.*

Preface To The Third Edition

The first edition of this book was published in 1960, the second in 1972. Since 1972 there has been an enormous amount of research and thought about socialization, clearly necessitating an updating of this book. One topic especially has come into greater prominence—the differential socialization of girls and boys. We have given particular attention to this topic in preparing the revision and have also incorporated the results of new research and thinking bearing on virtually every topic we discuss.

The goal of this edition is unchanged from that of the first two: to provide a coherent treatment, from a sociological standpoint, of how children are socialized into modern society. Some of the matters we discuss are highly controversial among specialists; we have sought to present these issues clearly and to present the main evidence on all sides as fairly as we have been able. We have taken seriously the sometimes passionate arguments that have been advanced, and we have tried to do justice to the diverse evidence that has been presented.

Inevitably, as in previous editions, we have had to be selective. The materials in anthropology, human development, political science, psychiatry, psychology, sociology, and the other disciplines concerned with socialization are far too voluminous and diverse to be fully represented in a brief, introductory treatment. Indeed, the rapid spurt of research in the history of childhood alone has added an intriguing new facet to the study of socialization, but we have been able to note only a few of its highlights. We have, then, tried to offer the reader a comprehensive synthesis of the main ideas and evidence concerning socialization; we have not tried to be encyclopedic.

Except for a new chapter on sex roles and socialization, the basic plan of the book is unchanged from the earlier editions. The section on ethnic groups has been almost completely revised. Other sections have been amplified, enlarged, and updated. More attention has been given in this edition to research on early stimulation, primate communication, socialization in families with working mothers (both female-headed and male-headed), sports as a factor in socialization, and the controversy over the relationship between television violence and violent behavior.

Gerald Handel assumed the major responsibility for the new chapter, "Sex and Socialization," and the new material on family variations and on television. Frederick Elkin assumed the major responsibility for the revised section on ethnic groups and the new section on socialization in specialized communities. The general plans for the revision and the final review of the manuscript were collaborative.

Frederick Elkin was the sole author of the first edition. Gerald Handel became coauthor and assumed major responsibility for preparing the second edition.

We express our thanks and appreciation to Charles Page and Ann Beuf who made helpful suggestions for revision and then read the revised manuscript; to Evelyn Kallen and Ellen Baar whose ideas contributed to the discussion of ethnic groups; and to Brigid Marcuse whose thoughtful reading of the chapter on sex and socialization enabled us to improve it. Finally, we are indebted to Madge Elkin who prepared the index for this third edition.

F. E.
G. H.

Contents

The Child & Society

1 Socialization Defined

A s children grow they develop in many ways. Physically, they become taller, heavier, stronger, and capable of such activities as walking, talking, writing, riding a bicycle, and, later, having sexual relations. Mentally, they become capable of such activities as memorizing poems, working out problems in algebra, imagining love scenes, and acquiring the knowledge necessary to carry through a job. Each child also acquires a more or less consistent personality structure, so that he or she can be characterized as ambitious, shy, sociable, cautious, and so on. However, these descriptions, useful as they may be, are of limited value in explaining how someone functions in society, because they do not reveal the interactions and relationships that a child has with others in the society. They do not tell us, for example, how a child learns what to expect from a doctor or a store clerk or learns the difference between behavior that is acceptable at a hockey game and behavior acceptable in church. In the course of growing up, a child must acquire varied knowledge and skills, such as what utensils to use when eating specific foods; how to greet strangers; how to show or conceal emotion in different settings; when to speak and when to be silent. As children grow they move into a widening world of persons, activities, and feelings—all shaped by encounters with others who help define a socially organized world. These others will establish standards of right and wrong, and as a result children will come to have certain feelings if they are inadvertently rude, fail an examination, consider taking drugs, or in some other way do not measure up to their own expectations or the expectations of others.

Babies, of course, know nothing of these ways of the society; but they have the potentialities to learn them. The potentialities are in fact wide and varied. In one setting, children will speak English, in another, Russian; in one they will eat rice with chopsticks, in another with a fork; in one, they will be taught to emphasize self-interest, in another to focus on the interests of the group. In one setting a boy will be deeply respectful of his father, in another he will speak to him as a "pal." In one setting, a girl will be taught that her future inevitably will involve being a wife and mother; in another, that she will have the freedom to choose her life style and commitments.

It is with such matters that the socialization of the child is concerned. Socialization may be defined as *the process by which we learn the ways of a given society or social group so that we can function within it.* As the examples above illustrate, many kinds of learning are encompassed within this general process. Some of what is learned is overt and visible, such as wearing appropriate clothes for different kinds of occasions. But even these overt behaviors can be understood only if we recognize that they come to be guided by more generalized learning, the effects of which are not directly visible but must be inferred. Put otherwise, children learn to be concerned with appropriateness as a general guide to their conduct. They develop a "sense of propriety," which not only governs their behavior in situations comparable to those they have already experienced but which also guides them in dealing with new situations that they encounter for the first time. Thus, when they enter a new group they do so with some sense of how to act, because they have learned to be concerned with acting appropriately in a group. When they take their first job, they are not at a total loss, because they have had experience in other situations that have the quality of "being supervised by someone with authority to supervise." Of course, people then go on to learn the specific requirements for membership in a new group or the requirements for being supervised as employees, which are different from the kind of supervision they received as children from their parents or as pupils from their teachers.

In addition to learning specific overt behaviors and a general sense of appropriateness, children also learn to experience certain specific emotions in specific kinds of situations. They may learn to feel possessive with property or feel indifferent to it. They may learn to feel proud at winning a fist fight or ashamed for having gotten into one.

Some of what children learn in the course of being socialized is explicitly taught by people who have the obligation to teach them, as when they learn to use eating utensils or to feel patriotic. Parents and teachers are specifically entrusted with the task of preparing the young to become qualified participants in society. But some of the learning that is included in socialization is self-motivated, and children develop and build on a constantly changing base. Having first become responsive to their parents, they have been prepared to be responsive to others. Early on, children begin to see in other people models for what they might like to become, and at home they are apt to take their parents as models for behavior in which they have not been instructed. If father brings home a briefcase, his five-year-old son may pick it up and carry it around "like daddy." Police officers and fire fighters are early heroes of many young children, and children see them, at least for a time, as models for their own later behavior.

Socialization is, then, a process that helps explain two different kinds of phenomena. On the one hand, it helps to explain how a person becomes capable of participating in society. For it is clear that the newborn infant is not a social being. Most of the qualities we regard as human are present in the child only as potentialities. In the early days of life, the infant experiences hunger pangs, cries, gains satisfaction by sucking on a source of nourishment, experiences visceral tension, and gains relaxation by excretion. In short, the newborn's capacities for functioning with other human beings are exceedingly minimal. They are developed through socialization.

On the other hand, socialization helps to explain how society is possible at all. While certain species of animals lower in the evolutionary scale function in rudimentary societies, none of these approaches the complexity of human society, which takes so many different forms and is elaborated with infinite subtleties. Consequently, looking at our species from the perspective of evolution, it is necessary to explain how vast numbers of organisms called human are able to attune their actions to one another in such a way as to make possible an ongoing social order. While a full explanation, insofar as one is possible, would take us far beyond the subject matter of this book, the socialization process is one key element of such an explanation. Social order is possible because human infants encounter adults who teach them and from whom they can learn to regulate their actions in accordance with various standards of appropriateness.

As implied in some of our earlier examples, the process of socialization is not confined to infancy and childhood. It continues throughout the life of the individual. The term "socialization" refers to learning the ways of any established and continuing group: an immigrant becomes socialized into the life of his or her new country, a recruit into the life of the army, and a new insurance agent into the patterns of the company and the job. The recognition of the continuing nature of socialization has led to the concept of *adult socialization.* The term takes account of the fact that adults are obliged to go through certain experiences and developments somewhat similar to those undergone by infants and children, although there is a basic difference in that later socialization is built upon an already acquired capacity to evaluate one's own behavior and function as a social being.

Having thus delineated the basic nature of socialization, it will be useful to indicate some problems that are not encompassed by this concept. First, it is not a problem of socialization to explain or speculate upon how a society or social group began. The society into which the child is born, with its common expectations, ways of doing things, standards of right and wrong, and current trends and issues, is the result of a unique historical evolution and exists before the child enters it. Socialization begins with the assumption of this ongoing preexisting society.

Second, socialization is not concerned with the impact of new members on the society or on given groups. Socialization is not strictly a one-way process. The entrance of a new member into a family, or into any unit, changes the group. It is not just the old group with one added person; it is a *new* group with new relationships and a new organization. But only insofar as the interrelationships affect the socialization process is this new reorganization directly relevant to our interests in this book.

Third, socialization does not try to explain the uniqueness of individuals. Although it is true that no two individuals are alike and that each person has a singular heredity, distinctive experiences, and a unique personality development, socialization focuses not on such individualizing patterns and processes, but on similarities, on aspects of development that concern the learning of and adaptation to the culture and society. In the course of development children go through two major processes simultaneously: individuation and socialization. In their earliest years children do not experience this distinction, but at later ages they do become capable of recognizing such a distinction in their life experience. They are able to do so, however, only if they have been socialized in a way that permits the kind of individuation that allows them to perceive distinctions of this kind.

This study deals with the process of socialization, with the problem of how the child becomes a functioning member of the society. We shall use a wide range of illustrations, but generally they will come from North American society and from the middle-class groups with which we are most familiar. However, we shall also give some attention to socialization patterns that differ from the most familiar, as well as to socialization in later life. Chapter 2 discusses the basic preconditions for socialization and is followed by a consideration in Chapter 3 of the processes, mechanisms, and techniques by which it occurs. Chapter 4 considers socialization patterns of certain basic subdivisions in our society:

social class, ethnic group, and community. Chapter 5 is concerned with the primary socializing agencies in our society: family, school, peer group, and media of mass communication. Socialization is intimately related to family life, and although the family is treated as such only in Chapter 5, ramifications of this relationship are discussed at various points throughout the book. Chapter 6 examines the many issues related to sex and socialization. The final chapter discusses later socialization and its relation to childhood.

2 Preconditions for Socialization

For children to become adequately socialized, three preconditions are necessary. First, there must be *an ongoing society,* the world into which they are to be socialized. Second, children must have the *requisite biological inheritance.* If a child is feebleminded or suffers from a serious organic mental disorder, adequate socialization will be impossible. Certain other biological deficits do not make socialization impossible but cause it to be beset by serious difficulties. Children born blind, deaf, or mute encounter special obstacles and are necessarily excluded from certain kinds of opportunities available to others. Nevertheless, such children —and those with such other disabilities as the malformed arms and legs suffered some years ago by children of mothers who took the drug thalidomide during pregnancy—can, with special training, achieve levels of socialization that permit them to function more or less satisfactorily in the society.

Third, a child requires *human nature.* This concept is not readily given a compact definition, but some of its fundamental components can be specified. Of particular significance is the ability to establish emotional relationships with others and to experience such sentiments as love, sympathy, shame, envy, pity, and pride. Scarcely less important is the ability to transform experience into symbols, which makes possible speech, writing, and thought. Although writing is not, of course, necessary for adequate socialization—some societies have no writing at all, and in earlier periods of our own history a person could be adequately socialized without being able to read, let alone write—human socialization is not possible without speech; and speech depends upon the capacity to symbolize.

Each of these necessary preconditions is significant insofar as it points up basic background material for an understanding of socialization.

AN ONGOING SOCIETY

Children are born into a world that already exists. They are "raw recruits" into the world, involuntary recruits, with no wish to be there and no knowledge of how to get along in it. From the point of view of society, the function of socialization is to transmit to new members the culture and motivation to participate in established social relationships. The society has a patterned consistency, so that one can predict, *within limits,* how people will behave, think, and feel. We may view this society from several perspectives, each of which points up certain distinctive features.

First, there is the perspective of *norms* and *values.* A norm is an implicit rule defining the appropriate pattern of behavior in a recurring situation. "Being clothed" is the norm when presenting oneself in a public place. This example indicates that a norm is both a standard by which behavior is judged and also a prediction as to what behavior is likely to occur. People are supposed to be clothed in public, and one may predict that in any public place the people one encounters will probably be clothed. Such convergence of the two meanings of "expected" (what should happen and what is predicted to happen) is never fully realized. Students are expected to study throughout the term—that is, they should do so. But it is also expected that some will do no more than cram before an examination—that is, one may predict that this is how they will study. The two meanings of expectation are not always carefully distinguished, and for many purposes it is sufficient to make the rough assumption that what should be done is what is generally done. Many social problems, however, arise from divergence of what happens from what is supposed to happen, and it is then necessary to distinguish ideal norms from behavioral norms.

Values are more general than norms. They are best thought of as conceptions of the desirable that serve as criteria for norms. A society in which freedom, for example, is a salient value will *tend* to develop norms consistent with that value in its economic practices, its educational methods, the relations between the sexes, the way it rears its children, and in other areas of life. This is not to say that all the norms in these situations are entirely consistent with freedom, for they are not. Other values tend to generate norms inconsistent with those of freedom, so that the norms governing any situation are not simple derivatives from a single value.

A second perspective is that of *status* and *role.* A status is a position in the social structure, and a role is the expected behavior of someone who holds a given status. We can cooperate with others because we know the rights and obligations associated with each status. The taxi driver has the right to ask you for your fare and the obligation to drive you to your destination; the physician has the right to ask about your symptoms and, in some instances, to ask you to remove your clothes; and the physician has the obligation to try to cure you. Similarly, role behavior is expected of the teacher, student, mother, father, daughter, grocery clerk, Roman Catholic, taxicab passenger, and doctor's patient. Each person has many statuses that define his or her expected behavior in given situations.

A third perspective is that of *institutions,* each of which focuses about a segment of life and consists of many norms and statuses. One such institution is the school, whose primary function is to transmit, in a more or less formal way, a large share of the intellectual heritage of a society. Within the school there are norms relating to attendance, sports events, courses, and holiday celebrations; and there are patterned status relationships among the teachers, students, principal, and custodians. The church, hospital, stock market, and congressional system are other institutions that are the foci for the organization of many activities. Despite a regular turnover of personnel these institutions continue to

over a period of many years, in great part because
_w generation is socialized into the appropriate pat-
_.

A fourth perspective focuses on cultural and group subdivisions within the larger society. One major subdivision is
social class. Individuals in our society vary in the amounts
of wealth, prestige, and power they possess; and associated
with these variations are differences in values and ways of
life. Social-class rankings may partake of all of these elements. At one extreme may be the upper-class individual
who is wealthy, has an important business position, lives in
a luxurious home, sends his or her children to private
schools, and vacations in Europe. At the other extreme may
be the lower-class individual who works at an unskilled job,
left school at the age of fourteen, lives in a slum area, and has
"crude" table manners. Between these extremes there are
other rough rankings, from the professional to the lesser
business executive to the white-collar worker to the skilled
laborer. It is evident that no single characteristic clearly
differentiates class groups, that the lines between them are
blurred, and that there is interclass movement. But a stratification system of a kind does exist.

Another major subdivision in our society, one which over-
laps considerably with social class, is the *ethnic group.* The
population of North America has been built up of migrants
from many countries. In coming here they have kept some
of their old-country characteristics or responded distinctively in the new setting and thus may be thought of as
"different" both by others and by themselves. Thus, we find
Italians, Greeks, Jews, Mexicans, Puerto Ricans, Chinese, and
French Canadians, who are distinguished from others by
their names, language, traditional foods, holiday rituals, occupations, folklore, patterns of child rearing, and loyalties. A
related division is the *racial minority,* which is also likely
to be thought of as "different" both by others and by themselves. The most prominent racial minority in our society
are the blacks.

Still another perspective is that of *social change,* especially
important today because of the rapidity with which it oc-

curs. The society into which a child is born is not static; there are conflicting pressures, a diffusion of materials and ideas, and general trends that shift direction. New technology, new experiences, and new decisions reverberate in many directions, generating changes in values, norms, institutions, statuses, roles, and intergroup relationships. The reader will readily identify some of the familiar changes that have been under way for some time: the movement of families to the suburbs; the increasing activism of blacks; the development of new careers in new industries; the tendency to professionalization of teachers, morticians, social workers, insurance agents, pharmacists, and other groups. Among the most dramatic have been the recent upsurges of social action and citizen participation groups, especially the growth of the women's movement. In these, as in the other changes, socialization, inasmuch as it involves a receptivity to modification as well as given patterns of thought, feeling, and behavior, has a part to play.

There is, then, a complex and variable world, which may be approached from many perspectives, into which the children are to be socialized. In order to function within it, whether it be primarily as conformist, rebel, or compromiser, they must have at least a minimum of knowledge about this world and a minimum of what the culture defines as appropriate behavior and feelings. They must know what to expect from people of given statuses, how they themselves fit in with the various groupings, what is considered proper and improper in given situations, and the range of alternative behavior possible in those segments of social life that are rapidly changing. This is the world that the socializers, knowingly or unknowingly, pass on to the newcomer.

BIOLOGICAL INHERITANCE

A second precondition for socialization is an adequate biological inheritance, or original nature. It is apparent that those who have certain serious hereditary deficiencies either cannot be socialized or will have distinctive problems in the process. Socialization depends, for example, upon memory. An adequate memory can develop only if the parts of the brain governing memory are sufficiently intact. A child born with serious injury to that area of the brain may be unable to develop the necessary level of memory. Thus, certain serious deficits in the biological organism preclude adequate socialization. Other organic deficiencies create problems but may be somewhat less fateful. Children born deaf will not learn to speak in the same way other children learn, since they cannot hear their own voices; but with special intensive training they can learn to speak. It is worth noting at this point that the extent to which biological deficit precludes adequate socialization does not depend entirely on the defect itself but on society's response to it as well.[1] The deaf can be more adequately socialized today than formerly because our institutions chose to discover (with some success) ways of modifying deafness and its consequences. Intensified efforts have also been initiated in recent years to find ways to modify the deficit imposed by biologically induced mental retardation, so that this condition, too, may yield to the power of social organization. New norms and new institutions for coping with biological deficit yield new outcomes in socialization.

Although abnormal biological conditions present special problems in socialization, problems that may be recast by social advances, socialization is also intimately involved with biology for the organically normal individual. Certain biological characteristics set the context for socialization. First, human organisms are *helpless* and completely dependent at birth. They cannot survive without the intervention of persons who give them care. Now it is evident that physical survival depends upon the provision of nourishment and protection against temperature extremes; but there is also evidence, to be cited shortly, that these necessary rudiments of care may not be sufficient for the infant's survival, let alone for his or her adequate socialization. External stimulation and responsiveness from other people appear to be necessary for survival itself.

The newborns of many species are helpless and dependent

at birth, but the human offspring has the *most prolonged dependency* of any. Lower forms of life—animals, birds, and insects—can often function well merely by following inborn patterns of goal-directed activity that have persisted relatively unchanged for thousands of years. No comparable built-in mechanisms exist in human beings, and in order to function within society, we must learn from others how to build homes, earn a living, and take care of our children.

A third basic biological fact is *maturation.* The human organism develops according to a fairly set timetable, which varies within rather narrow limits. This timetable helps to shape the course of socialization. The newborn infant cannot immediately be trained to use eating utensils, whether these be chopsticks or knife and fork; a minimum level of eye-hand coordination must be achieved first. And, although a six-month-old infant may be "possessive" of a rattle, the social importance of "respect for property" can be communicated only when neuromuscular development allows walking and permits the toddler to reach for fragile lamps and other breakables.

The evolutionary development of certain specific organs is particularly important as a foundation for socialization. The development of the outermost layer of the human brain—the cortex—is a prerequisite to socialization. Vocal organs capable of highly varied speech (rather than merely a few grunts or tweets); the fact of being two-footed rather than four-footed; the fact that sexual drives are not restricted, as in many other animals, to a periodic mating season—these are some of the organismic characteristics of the human that serve as determinants of or (looked at in another way) resources for socialization.

Although the biological character of the organism and the timetable of maturation set certain outer limits to human variation, a no less significant factor is the psychobiological *plasticity* of the human body. Thus, children inherit certain "mass movements," impulses that are expressed in random undefined directions. For example, they make numerous different sounds and move their fingers in a variety of ways. Whether these sounds are eventually organized into the English, Spanish, or Chinese language, or whether the finger movements come to include the ability to write, manipulate Ping Pong paddles, or play musical instruments, are functions of the specific definitions and guidance given by people in the surrounding world. Drives such as hunger, thirst, sleep, and sex can be satisfied in many ways. The need for food may be satisfied by eating meat, vegetables, insects, or even people. Sex needs may be expressed directly or sublimated in dancing, art, or religious ceremonies; they may be directed toward people within or outside certain groups; they may be suppressed before marriage or encouraged and directed to certain specific outlets. Which foods or which forms of sex expression are preferred will reflect social and psychological influences. Such influences can be meaningful only because the body allows variation.

Not to be overlooked are other types of variation. Children are born with certain temperamental tendencies toward passivity or activity, perhaps toward restlessness; and they are also born with certain sensitivities. Such tendencies are evidenced from birth in a baby's movements, sleeping and crying habits, frustration tolerance, and responses to food. These temperamental tendencies gain some of their significance from the interpretations of those who react to them. An "active" baby will receive one kind of response if his or her parents enjoy an active baby and quite another response if they would be more comfortable with a placid and docile child.

Similarly, the development of intelligence and particular talents cannot be separated from the surrounding world. Indeed, in no aspect of human development is it more futile to ask what proportion derives from original nature and what proportion from experience. Since *all* intelligence is "experienced" intelligence—that is, an indeterminate blend of native potentiality and experience—there is no known way to measure "native intelligence." Whether a particular potentiality is actually developed and what direction development takes depend upon the possibilities that are available, the encouragement that comes from others, and the growth of the personality structure. A society without paints would not know Picasso, and neither Mozart nor Marx would have become what they did in Mozambique. Neither would they have succeeded if their personalities were so disturbed that they could not focus their attention long enough to develop their talents and abilities.

Clearly then human biological nature—the form and transformation of the body through time—both allows and requires socialization; and certain biological requisites are necessary for adequate socialization. For purposes of analysis it is necessary to identify the biological substratum underlying socialization, but in actual situations biological factors become so closely linked with elements of the social world that it is often impossible to isolate empirically the hereditary from the environmental and to weight the importance of each.

HUMAN NATURE

A third precondition for socialization is what Charles H. Cooley, an early American sociologist, called human nature. What he wished to emphasize by this term is something distinctive to humans as compared to other animals and yet something universal among humans, not a product of only some societies. According to Cooley, a fully developed human nature is a product rather than a precondition of socialization. Yet infants must have certain prototypical capacities out of which their full human nature can develop. In the following discussion we shall briefly delineate Cooley's concept of human nature and then specify the capacities that underlie it.

To Cooley, human nature consists of sentiments. He regards sympathy as the most basic sentiment, one which enters into such other sentiments as love, resentment, ambition, vanity, hero worship, and the "feeling of social right and wrong." He writes:

> Human nature in this sense is justly regarded as a comparatively permanent element in society. Always and everywhere men seek honor and dread ridicule, defer to public opinion, cher-

ish their goods and their children, and admire courage, generosity, and success. It is always safe to assume that people are and have been human.[2]

From our present perspective, more than sixty-five years after Cooley, and with much intervening experience and research, we know that the situation is more complex than he described it. Some people will brave ridicule rather than dread it; not all defer to public opinion, nor do all cherish their children. But certain of his fundamental observations are durable: Such sentiments as honor and ridicule, courage and generosity are distinctively human and possible in all human societies and thus are not limited to certain cultures, although they receive varying emphasis and are expressed differently in different cultures.

Such complex sentiments as pride, embarrassment, cruelty, and envy are based on two human capacities. One is *the ability to empathize* with others, to place oneself imaginatively in their positions and to be aware of their feelings. Although the lower animals have the ability to form emotional attachments, they do not, as far as we know, have the capacity to empathize. We assume, for example, that a cat that toys with a mouse is unaware of the feelings of the mouse and therefore is not, in Cooley's sense, "cruel"; nor is a large dog that attacks a small one and takes his bone "unkind." However, an older child who takes and refuses to return a younger child's toy is very much aware of the younger one's unhappiness.

The second capacity on which such sentiments rest is *the ability to symbolize*—that is, to give meaning, both cognitively and emotionally, to sounds, gestures, and signs of various kinds. Our symbolic capacities are often described as though they were only intellectual in nature. The capacity for intellectual symbolization is certainly important, but it is not the whole of symbolization by any means. We shall cite a few familiar examples.

If a person clenches and shakes a fist at someone, the recipient understands that the person is angry and wants him or her to feel threatened and afraid. The gesture is a symbol; it stands for something other than itself. It stands for a threat and feeling in the one who makes the gesture and for an anticipated response in the one who receives it.

As another example, the prison guard who inflicts torture wishes to see the prisoner suffer; that is, the guard wishes to bring about certain responses which, when they occur, will give him or her satisfaction. This kind of satisfaction, unlike that of animal hunger or sex, can only be understood in terms of our ability to symbolize. The prisoner's behavior—screaming or pleading or whatever—represents for the guard a symbolization of him or herself, perhaps as strong or tough or in authority. (Perhaps also the guard's state of mind, with its complex of meanings and gratifications, may be found in the other guards as well and be part of an institutional norm.) The prisoner, in turn, might refuse the guard's sought-for self-image by remaining stoic and expressing no pain.

Still another example: A teacher awards a student an "A" for a term paper—intending it to be a cognitive symbol representing academic success. But the "A" obviously can symbolize more. The student may feel pride and see in the "A" an image of his or her potentialities. The student's friends may see still other meanings in the "A" and feel admiration or envy or scorn or a host of other possible sentiments.

The capacity to symbolize, to give meanings, cognitive and emotional, which we see in all of these illustrations, has long been regarded as a distinctively human capacity. Recent research on birds and on primates, especially research indicating the ability of chimpanzees to learn American Sign Language (language of gestures used by the deaf) and even to learn an activity that has (perhaps overenthusiastically) been called "reading," has shown that animals have greater capacities for symbolization than had been believed. Nevertheless, the differences between human nature and the nature of other animals, so far as these are revealed in symbolic activity, remain significant. After a careful review of sixteen features of human language, some of which are found in the communication systems of other species, ethologist W. H. Thorpe concludes:

Perhaps the most reasonable assumption at present is that, however great the gulf which divides animal communication systems from human language, there is no single characteristic which can be used as an infallible criterion for distinguishing between animals and men in this respect. Human speech is unique only in the way in which it combines and extends attributes which, in themselves, are not peculiar to man but are found also in more than one group of animals. We have evidence that animals can use conceptual symbols, but to a limited degree; and that here, as in so many other instances, the difference between the mind of animals and men seems to be one of degree —often the degree of abstraction that can be achieved—rather than one of kind. But man can manipulate abstract symbols to an extent far in excess of any animal, and that is the difference between bird "counting" and our mathematics. I think we can sum up this matter by saying that although no animal appears to have a language which is propositional, syntactic, and at the same time clearly expressive of intention, all these features can be found separately (to at least some degree) in the animal kingdom. Consequently, bearing in mind the work on chimps discussed above, we can say that the distinction between man and animals, on the ground that only the former possess "true language," seems far less defensible than heretofore. Yet, as argued elsewhere in this book, there comes a point where "more" creates a "difference."[3]

The capacity to create and communicate complex meanings, cognitive and emotional, which we find among human beings everywhere, is without equal elsewhere in the animal kingdom. Similarly, the wide range of human sentiment is without equal in other species.

It was Cooley's significant insight that the sentiments that he saw as the core of human nature were not inherited. Rather, human nature develops in primary groups,

> those simple face-to-face groups that are somewhat alike in all societies; groups of the family, the playground, and the neighborhood. In the essential similarity of these is to be found the basis, in experience, for similar ideas and sentiments in the human mind. In these, everywhere, human nature comes into existence. Man does not have it at birth; he cannot acquire it except through fellowship, and it decays in isolation.[4]

Although Cooley's insight (based in part on observation of his own children) perhaps outran the evidence then available to support it, several lines of more recent evidence tend to support and amplify his view. In various ways, they indicate that human nature is a product of involvement with other human beings.

Early Activity and Stimulation

Increasingly, modern research is demonstrating that the newborn infant is not an entirely passive creature, simply waiting to receive and absorb experiences. While the newborn is not equipped to do very much of what is expected of a socialized person, the indications are that it participates actively in the processes of acquiring a true human nature. The activities of which it is capable are preliminary to developing empathy and symbolization. Perhaps the first activity of the infant is receptivity: "The infant has been proven to be receptive to sensory stimulation from birth."[5] Newborns are not only receptive, however, but also *selective*. For example, in one study, eighteen infants under five days of age were shown in several brief sessions six different visual stimuli; the length of time they looked at each was recorded by photographing eye movements. Eleven of the eighteen looked longest at a schematic drawing of a face; none looked longest at a white, a yellow, or a red stimulus that contained no pattern.[6]

Other research supports the notion that newborn infants selectively fixate their eyes on some stimuli in preference to others. Indeed, not only do newborns show preferences for different kinds of stimulation, they also show evidence of several capacities that underlie or are related to this selectivity, including alertness, visual discrimination and acuity, visual scanning in which they selectively respond to different aspects of the stimuli, and visual pursuit or following of a moving stimulus in order to keep it in view.[7] Thus, one investigator concludes that the studies of newborns' visual preferences show that "infants from birth have the capacity to receive and discriminate patterned stimulation, that they do attend selectively to parts of the environment, and that, therefore, *the acquisition of knowledge about the environment begins at the first look.*"[8]

Responsiveness to stimulation is not restricted to the visual domain; the sound of another infant crying promotes crying in a newborn,[9] and babies born blind will smile in response to a human voice.[10]

In brief, the newborn is ready to receive sights and sounds from the outer world and shows preferences from birth for some of these over others. The stimulation that the world provides is, of course, not the same for all newborns. Even in a fairly homogeneous group of families there is considerable variation. "Thus one baby's first home might be quiet, with a low level of stimulation, while another baby might enter a complex, noisy, even hilarious and overstimulating household . . ."[11] Furthermore, it is necessary to distinguish not only between one household and another in terms of level of stimulation but also in terms of particular kinds of stimulation. "If one watches mothers with their babies and measures the sort of obvious things which people seem to regard as stimulation, like talking, smiling, touching, and so on, one is lumping things together under one global heading that do not necessarily belong together. A mother may show a lot of talking but little touching, and vice versa."[12]

It seems evident that these multiple capacities for stimulation, which equip the newborn for contact with a complex and diversely stimulating world, are prerequisite to the development of later abilities to empathize and symbolize.

Isolated Children

As far back as the late Middle Ages reports have appeared from time to time of children who have been isolated from society and who, in one fashion or another, have lived in a wild state. In some cases, supposedly, they have been reared by or at least lived in the company of wild animals.[13] One of the few authenticated and the most celebrated of these cases is that of "the wild boy of Aveyron," discovered in south central France in 1797. Recently, psychologist Harlan

Lane has come across some long lost documents about the case and has written a review and analysis.[14]

The boy was first sighted running naked through the woods. Then, from time to time over a period of more than a year, he was seen digging up potatoes and turnips in fields and searching for acorns and roots. After being captured in a tree by some hunters, he was passed through the hands of several local governmental authorities and finally sent to Paris at the order of Lucien Bonaparte, Minister of the Interior and brother of Napoleon, to be placed in a school for deaf-mutes. In those years, just before and after the French Revolution, issues concerning the relationship of individuals to society were at a new peak of interest, and the study of "savages" was believed to offer important clues to understanding human nature. The *sauvage de l'Aveyron* was closely studied as a case in point.

He was judged to be about eleven or twelve years old when found. His body showed various scars, but he was apparently free of any serious physical deformity. Of particular significance was the fact that he was "entirely without the gift of speech and makes himself heard only by cries and inarticulate sounds,"[15] although later evidence showed he was not hard of hearing. A committee of leading experts, including Philippe Pinel, who is sometimes spoken of as the first psychiatrist and is famous for removing the chains from inmates of insane asylums, delivered an extensive report to the Society of Observers of Man, a leading scholarly association of the time, in which they concluded that the boy was mentally retarded and ineducable. Pinel thought that the boy "was not an idiot because he was abandoned in the woods; he was abandoned in the woods because he was an idiot . . . recognized by heartless parents for what he was."[16]

However, Jean-Marc-Gaspard Itard, a former student of Pinel's who had been appointed resident physician at the school for deaf-mutes, disagreed, and set out to train the boy, to whom he later gave the name Victor. He hoped to achieve five objectives: (1) to interest the boy in social life; (2) "to awaken his nervous sensibility by the most energetic stimulation, and occasionally by intense emotion"; (3) to give him new, more social needs and thus extend the range of his ideas; (4) to teach him to speak; (5) to develop his ability to reason, at least in a rudimentary way.[17] Itard reported some progress. At the outset,

the boy was indifferent to temperature and rejected clothing even in the coldest weather; he would put his hand in a fire; his eyes did not fixate; he reached alike for painted objects, objects in relief, and the image of objects reflected in a mirror; he did not sneeze, even with snuff, nor did he weep; he did not respond to loud voices; he did not recognize edible food by sight but by smell; he preferred uncooked food and had no taste for sweets or hard drink; he had no emotional ties, no sexual expression, no speech; he had a peculiar gait and would occasionally run on all fours.[18]

After three months of Itard's regimen, Victor removed his potatoes from the fire with a spoon instead of by hand; he liked to stroke velvet; he began to wear clothes; he would get up at night to urinate instead of sleeping in a cold, wet bed. He also evidently learned to sneeze; Itard says that "I judged by the fright that seized him the first time this happened that this was a new experience for him. He immediately ran away and threw himself on his bed."[19] Victor later learned to sit at a table, wait for food to be served, and eat with utensils. He developed emotional expression, at times embracing Itard and the woman housekeeper who took him for walks and cared for him in many other ways. He gave evidence of having developed sentiments such as gratitude, remorse, pleasure in pleasing others, but he failed to show any evidence of pity.[20]

Itard worked with Victor over a period of six years. His greatest disappointment was that Victor never learned to speak despite Itard's strenuous efforts and specialized training program. (Itard is considered the founder of what is known today as "special education.") Various explanations for the failure have been proposed by diverse experts from Itard's time to our own. Following an evaluation of these explanations and a review of the evidence, Lane himself

concludes that Victor was probably neither mentally retarded nor autistic.

> Victor's symptoms, then, including his mutism, may overlap
> with those of congenital retardation or autism, but are explained
> by neither; instead they are the result of his isolation in the wild,
> as Itard maintained all along. This is the view that prevails
> among diverse environmentalists, but it meets with the follow-
> ing challenge. If Victor merely confirmed the adaptiveness and
> plasticity of human behavior, why didn't he readapt to society
> once he returned and, indeed, received intensive rehabilita-
> tion. . . . Why didn't Victor recover language and progress much
> further in his intellectual development and socialization?[21]

Lane's explanation so far accords with what Cooley might
have said: Victor lost his human nature by living in isolation. While some elements of that human nature proved
recoverable with the establishment of a primary-group relationship in Itard's household and with Itard's training program, vocal speech, beyond a few sounds, was not. Thus,
Lane suggests a second explanatory factor in addition to isolation: "The prolonged isolation deprived him of the crucial
skill by which children and adults profit from social experiences that are not explicitly designed for their instruction,
namely, the skill of imitation."[22] Whatever the reason, although Victor learned to imitate other actions sufficiently to
communicate in nonspoken ways, and even learned to read
and write simple sentences, he never did learn to speak,
although he lived to an age of more than forty years.[23] Perhaps, as some modern students of language are suggesting,
there is a "critical period" for learning spoken language, and
a child who is deprived, by isolation, of the opportunity to
learn and use spoken language during this phase of maturation is unable to learn it thereafter.[24] Such may have been
Victor's fate, although we cannot be certain of it.

In more recent times the best-authenticated cases are those
of Anna and Isabelle.[25] Anna was an illegitimate child,
confined to one room from infancy. She had very little contact with other human beings. The mother brought her milk

but otherwise paid little attention to her, not ordinarily taking the trouble to bathe, train, supervise, or cuddle her. When Anna was found, at the age of six, she showed few, if any, signs of human nature. She was described as completely apathetic; she lay on her back, immobile, expressionless, and indifferent. She was believed to be deaf and possibly blind. She lived for another five years, first in a country home and later in a foster home and school for retarded children, and in this period developed only to the level of the normal two-year-old. Whether the lack of development was due primarily to mental deficiency, to the deprivations of early life, or a combination of the two is not clear.

Isabelle's circumstances were relatively more fortunate. She, too, was an illegitimate child kept in seclusion. However, her deaf-mute mother was shut off with her, and the two were able to communicate by gestures. When Isabelle was found, also at the age of six, she, too, lacked a manifest human nature. She seemed utterly unaware of ordinary social relationships and reacted to strangers almost as an animal would, with fear and hostility. She made only a strange croaking sound, and in many respects her actions resembled those of deaf children. In contrast to Anna, Isabelle was given a systematic and skillful program of training and, after a very slow beginning, began to develop quite rapidly. By the time she was eight-and-a-half years old, she had reached a normal educational level and was described as bright, cheerful, and energetic. Thus, with an appropriate environment she was able to develop into a girl with normal habits and feelings. That Isabelle attained this level of socialization indicates that she had an adequate intelligence potential, but only intensive and focused social interaction brought it to actuality. It is significant that Isabelle, in contrast to Anna, did have close, although limited, human contact when she was a baby.

Another case, reported from India, tells of a so-called feral child, a child who had been separated from society when still a baby and allegedly reared by wolves.[26] The child was about eight years old when, in 1921, she was discovered in a cave by a British missionary, and she lived for over eight years in the missionary school. When found, Kamala, as she was named, had few human characteristics. She wore no clothing, ate raw meat, lowered her mouth to her food, had impassive facial features, and showed only hostility to human beings. During her stay at the school Kamala never reached a normal level for her age, but she did make considerable progress, especially after she developed an emotional attachment to the missionary's wife. She learned to eat cooked food, to wear a dress, to understand simple language, to like other children, and to express various kinds of emotion. An analysis by Bruno Bettelheim, a child psychoanalyst, strongly suggests that the wolf-rearing part of the story is a myth,[27] but without doubt Kamala had suffered extreme emotional isolation. To use Cooley's term, Kamala had no human nature when she was found; she developed it in the close personal contacts of the missionary school.

Deprivation in Social Relations

Another type of evidence comes from psychiatry. Many instances have been reported of children who, though not literally isolated from society, received as infants little attention and affection and did not establish any strong interpersonal ties or primary relationships with other human beings. In some cases they had a succession of ministering adults; in others they were in custodial institutions in which there were few adults to look after them. A growing body of evidence indicates that these children suffer from fundamental deprivation that prevents them from becoming adequately socialized.

Perhaps the best-known investigation of this problem is that of René Spitz, who reports on an institution in which there were ninety-one children, none older than three.[28] To take care of forty-five infants less than eighteen months old, there were only six nurses. For most of the day these infants lay on their backs in small cubicles, without human contact. Within the first year the average score of all the children on developmental tests fell from 124 to 72. Two years later a follow-up study found that over one-third of the ninety-one children had died, and the twenty-one who were still at the institution were extraordinarily retarded, even though the institution provided adequate nutrition and medical care. Despite the fact that conditions became much more favorable for children when they reached fifteen months, with more nurses and more opportunities for joint play activity, their heights and weights were below average, many could not walk or use a spoon, only one could dress himself, and only two had a vocabulary of more than five words. Spitz concludes that the conditions during the children's first year of life were so detrimental both physically and psychologically that the subsequent more favorable conditions could not counteract the damage.

These studies, as well as many others resulting in convergent findings, are instructive. They show that social isolation affects the biological process of maturation and even biological survival, as well as the socialization process. To grow into a human being—which is to say, to be capable of the sentiments that enable appropriate responsiveness to others—a baby must be treated like a human being; he or she must receive not just medically adequate physical care but "social care" as well.

The clinical investigations of psychiatrists on human children receive some support from two lines of research in related fields. One is Harry F. Harlow's study of rhesus monkeys. Now admittedly, it seems paradoxical to draw support for a view of human nature from observation of monkeys, but such evidence is relevant under certain conditions. If the observed behavior of monkeys has no parallel in human behavior, there is no justification for inferring from monkey behavior to that of humans. If, on the other hand, observations have been made on humans and conclusions drawn from them, then convergent findings on primates lower in the evolutionary scale tend to give support to those on humans. Such is the case with regard to the importance of social contact for development.

Harlow and his co-workers have carried out various experiments involving separation of newborn monkeys from their mothers, sometimes supplying "surrogate mothers." One type of surrogate mother is made simply of wire with a lactating nipple from which the monkey can feed; the other type is similar except that it is covered with cloth. Harlow finds that infants raised with a pair of artificial mothers, one wire and one cloth-covered, spend most of their time in contact with the cloth figure even if feeding from the wire one. When experimental monkeys become adults and mothers themselves, those reared only with a wire mother substitute tend to be either more aggressive or more indifferent toward their offspring than those raised with a cloth substitute. Such "mistreatment" of offspring—a "mistreatment" which may go so far as killing the babies—is also more likely among mothers reared without other monkeys in the same cage, as compared with mothers caged with peers during infancy. Various kinds of isolation make monkeys less "social" in their world. The development of an adequate "monkey nature" requires that the infant be reared in association with others of its species and that it have gratifying tactile experience.[29] This evidence converges with that concerning human infants.

The second line of research deals with "sensory deprivation" in human adults. Various experiments have been carried out to discover the effects of drastically reduced sensory stimulation. For example, one experimental arrangement involved having a person lie twenty-four hours a day on a comfortable bed in a lighted, semi-soundproof cubicle while wearing translucent goggles which admit diffuse light but prevent seeing patterns. Other arrangements involved a darkened room or the wearing of heavy cotton gloves to reduce tactile stimulation. Although this line of investigation is still in its early stages, initial findings tended to converge with what we have already described. When people are subjected to such severe restriction of stimulation as described above, they suffer what psychologists describe as "deterioration of normal ego-functioning." Both emotional and symbolization capacities are impaired. One research group found that:

> Subjects slip into a dream-like transitional state between sleeping and waking which makes coherent thinking difficult; thoughts cannot be anchored in reality and the free flow of fantasy is promoted.... There is little motivation to speak in the absence of a reply, and fantasy about the experimenters is unchecked. It is therefore not surprising that paranoid fears arise, but the extent of such fears *is* surprising, suggesting rapid breakdown of the perception of social reality, that is, in terms of the normal subject-experimenter relationship.[30]

Results such as these suggest that another of the conditions for the attainment and maintenance of human nature is an appropriate level and variety of stimulation. When stimulation is reduced to a bare minimum or is made uninterruptedly uniform for long periods—as occurs during certain types of "brainwashing"—the consequence may reasonably be described as a partial loss of human nature in those who experience it.

Finally, we may note one other relevant line of work. Psychiatric investigation suggests that lack of adequate early primary relations is responsible for many psychopathic personalities. Psychopaths are almost completely self-centered. Their relations with others are superficial; they are quite incapable of caring for others or of establishing emotional ties with them. They seem to have no internalized standards of right and wrong, no feelings of guilt, and often show a general lack of concern in situations that ordinarily arouse some emotional response. When this type of person becomes delinquent, rehabilitation is extremely difficult. In Cooley's perspective such psychopaths have never developed a real human nature, because they have never experienced adequate primary-group relationships.

In summary, then, a third precondition for socialization is an inchoate human nature that develops into abilities to empathize and to symbolize. These abilities, in turn, make possible the development of the complex sentiments that uniquely characterize human nature.

In the ordinary course of events, the preconditions for socialization are taken for granted; only in exceptional circumstances do they come to our attention. Nevertheless, the process of socialization can be understood only as taking place in a context defined by an ongoing society, an adequate biological inheritance, and a characteristic human nature.

3 The Processes of Socialization

Although it is sometimes useful to speak of *the* process of socialization, just as we speak of the process of urbanization or industrialization or bureaucratization or modernization, the fact is that each of these terms is no more than a convenience for certain purposes. Each points in a general direction and identifies certain large-scale effects. When we study these phenomena, we quickly become aware that each of these terms encompasses diverse events. Socialization is not a unitary phenomenon, but rather a term for a variety of processes. The relationships among these specific processes are by no means fully worked out and understood; a unified and comprehensive theory of socialization has yet to be achieved. Nevertheless, we shall try, in this chapter, to identify and discuss the major processes. In so doing, we must approach our topic from several angles of vision, each of which illuminates the subject in a somewhat different way. Our goal here will be to present a general "model" of socialization that is broadly applicable and independent of specific cultures.

To begin, recall our definition of socialization: the process by which we learn the ways of a given society or social group so that we can function within it. By unraveling this definition, we can fashion a framework that helps us locate component processes of socialization. Learning involves change; it sometimes occurs through teaching, which entails communication; learning, teaching, and communicating take place in a medium of emotionally significant relationships. Succinctly, then, we may say that socialization

1. involves developmental change in the organism,
2. through communication,
3. in emotionally significant relationships,
4. which are shaped by social groupings of varying scope.

It will be convenient to begin with the last point and move through the framework in reverse order.

SOCIETY AND SOCIALIZATION

Most commonly, socialization processes have been considered in face-to-face contexts such as the family, school, or peer group. Indeed, we shall focus on these contexts in Chapter 5. Yet it is clear that such groupings are agencies of the larger society. Parents raise their children to function not only in the family but prepare them to leave the family and function in other settings. The school does the same. The values and techniques of peer-group relationships, although less obvious, likewise have their long-run applications. Furthermore, although families, schools, and other social groupings often direct divergent expectations toward those being socialized, they also often have convergent expectations. From this perspective, then, it is reasonable to say that *society specifies certain outcomes or ranges of outcomes of socialization.* For example, every society expends some of its resources to produce children who will become law-abiding adults. Children who do not become law-abiding are likely to be judged socialization failures. Another socialization outcome specified by the society is loyalty. The society seeks to engender loyalty to itself, and its various institutions and groups contribute to this outcome in various ways. Other types of outcomes and the concept of range of outcome will be discussed and illustrated shortly.

Families, schools, peer groups, and other agencies of socialization may vary in how attentive they are to socially desired outcomes, how they go about trying to bring about these outcomes, and how effective their chosen procedures are. Despite these variations, we can say that society—any society—endeavors to bring about certain desired and recognizable results in the socialization of its young. (Indeed, at various times society "gives recognition" when the desired results have been achieved—recognition in the form of titles, badges, diplomas, promotions, and so forth.)

The most basic result sought is a *motivated commitment to sustain responsive participation in society.* Another way to put this is to say that children should become people who recognize and accept legitimate claims made upon them by others. These claims are multiple and diverse, and they differ according to a person's location in the social structure. Some, however, are general. For example, people should accept and function within the limits of communication and emotional expression that are defined as appropriate in different situations. Thus, they may scream at a football game, but not in a supermarket. They may laugh at home, at a movie, at a party, but not at a funeral. Another general type of claim may be expressed in this way: People should accept the obligations of their roles. If they take a job, they should do the work and meet its other legitimate requirements. If they enter into a friendship, they should be friendly according to the norms of that particular friendship, whatever they may be.

Even in those special cases where people are later trained for patterned withdrawal from general society—for example, nuns or monks who take vows of silence—the pattern of behavior is responsive to certain norms. It is not idiosyncratic withdrawal. Such an outcome falls within the range of socially acceptable results of socialization; although it represents a deviant role, it is not defined as a lack of motivated commitment to sustain responsive participation in society. In contrast, the role of "acid head"—the frequent taking of the drug LSD, which induces hallucinations—is one type of "dropping out" of society. By definition, this behavior represents a failure of socialization from the perspective in which we are now viewing socialization.

The difference between the role of the monk who takes vows of silence and that of the acid head can be understood more fully by stating another socially specified outcome. As has been pointed out by sociologist Alex Inkeles[1] and social psychologist M. Brewster Smith,[2] society expects the development of some kind of *competence*. Different societies require different kinds of competence, and any one society requires different kinds of competence for its diverse social roles. Nevertheless, it seems possible to formulate certain general requirements that transcend this diversity. Inkeles does so in the following way:

> Every individual must learn to be reasonably responsive to the pattern of social order and to the personal needs and requirements of the other individuals with whom he is in immediate contact. In other words, he must be basically socially conforming. He must have the ability to orient himself in space and time and have sufficient command of the rudimentary physical requirements of his setting so as not to destroy himself or be an undue burden on others. The requirements of society and of its specific statuses seem usually to involve certain motor and mental skills and techniques, and some kind of specialized knowledge and information; certain ways of thinking about the world, organized in a set of opinions and attitudes and constituting a distinctive idea system; a set of goals or values to guide action, and beliefs about the appropriate and acceptable paths to the goals; a conception of oneself which gives an identity and forms the basis for a system of social relations which include distinctive ways of relating to immediate authority, to intimates and peers, and to the larger community; some pattern for the organization of psychic functioning which favors and facilitates certain distinctive modes of defense or moral functioning; and a particular cognitive, conative, and affective style.[3]

Applying this conception to our example, we may say that our society recognizes certain kinds of "religious competence" and allows the development of institutions in which that competence may be practiced, even when that practice takes the form of withdrawal from verbal communication in order to engage in meditation. In contrast, taking "trips" on "acid"—that is, engaging in drug-induced hallucinations—is defined by our society as willful destruction of a person's social competence and is therefore not generally accepted as a legitimate outcome of socialization in this society.

Now it is necessary here to introduce certain modifications of what has just been said. We have argued that many groups in a society have convergent expectations; that is, in any given society, family, school, church, and youth group, for example, press toward the same general outcomes. Because there is such convergence, we are justified in saying that society specifies certain outcomes. But two important modifications need to be stated: First, the fact that various institutions in a society tend to be mutually supportive in what they expect does not mean that they are entirely so. There is conflict as well as support between institutions. Parents often do not approve of what the school does, and vice versa. The youth group may encourage activities on which the authorities frown. Accordingly, socialization is not a smooth process. The child is subjected to conflicting expectations as well as mutually supportive ones.

Second, in arguing that society seeks to generate a motivated commitment to sustain social participation and certain general forms of competence, we ignored certain phenomena that also are among the processes of socialization. Earlier we spoke of "dropping out" as a failure of socialization. What needs to be added here is that whereas some socialization failures may be attributable to particular socializing agents, other failures may be due to society's own contradictory organization. Thus, society may expect all children to learn certain things but may order its institutions in such a way that some are prevented from learning what they are expected to learn. In the United States, for example, one of the goals of the elementary school is to teach children of diverse backgrounds how to get along with others. But many institutional arrangements have resulted in segregating whites from blacks in their schooling, so that there is a systematically fostered limiting of competence. To take another example: There has been a "rediscovery" of hunger and malnutrition in various sections of the United States. Political and economic institutions do not deliver food to all who need it, and many suffer from malnutrition. These nutritional deficiencies very likely impair mental ability and thus prevent children from learning things they are expected to learn.[4] This again is an example of how the pattern of institutions can generate failures in socialization. More generally, although every society expects various types of minimal competence and seeks to foster more than minimal competence in those activities it most values, no society succeeds in eliciting even minimal levels among all its children, in part because the institutional pattern interferes.

These, then, are the two general goals of socialization: a motivated *commitment* to sustain responsive participation in society and forms of *competence* that the society accepts as appropriate. These goals are generic; they are universally applicable. Of course, when we become more specific, we find that the same kinds of commitment and competence are not expected of all members of society. The artist and the career soldier differ not only in their kinds of competence but also in the kinds of commitment to social participation expected of them. The soldier will participate in a set of relationships governed by rigid rules of obedience to command. The artist will participate in a set of relationships governed by efforts to attract an audience that will appreciate the uniqueness of his or her vision and skill. It is beyond the scope of this book to attempt to explain how the socialization process makes career soldiers of some and artists of others. What can be said here from this example, however, is that society expects the socialization process to enable every new member eventually to find *some* appropriate adult status(es) within some legitimate set(s) of relationships. As we noted in Chapter 2, each status entails a role. On the basis of our present discussion we can add that a role (such as the occupational role of soldier or artist) involves a particular type of commitment to social participation and a particular type of competence.

While socialization is expected to result in the fulfilling of various specialized roles, it must also, as Inkeles points out, make it possible for the person to participate in a variety of ways with others whose statuses and roles are quite different from his own. The late Robert Hutchins, an educator and social reformer, used to deride a certain engineering school that maintained a Department of Engineering English because, as he put it, "nobody else talks engineering English." Whatever the merit of his derisiveness, the point he was making was that socialization can sometimes result in such an intense commitment to a particular form of social participation as to hamper social participation across role boundaries. A similar point had been made earlier by social critic and economist Thorstein Veblen, who spoke of a "trained incapacity."

Any society provides a variety of statuses and roles. Usually it also has more or less explicit rules governing access to at least certain statuses and roles. The social class into which a child is born, for example, may decisively determine the statuses and roles open to that child in later life. As early as 1944, W. Lloyd Warner and his colleagues showed that the type of education young American children receive is determined to a large extent by their social class.[5] Their conclusions have been borne out by much subsequent investigation. Ethnic group membership and religion are often decisive determinants of the kinds of social participation that will be allowed and the kinds of competence that children will be able to acquire. Thus, for example, blacks in the United States, French Canadians in Canada, Slovaks in Czechoslovakia, blacks and other nonwhites in South Africa, Indians in Latin American countries, Catholics in Northern Ireland, and, until recent times, Jews in many countries have been restricted in certain kinds of social participation and often prevented from gaining the kinds of competence the societies value most highly. These groups have, in their respective societies, been depreciated by more dominant groups who have effective control of many institutions including, importantly, the schools, which affect socialization outcomes. With more or less stringency, the children of these depreciated groups have been socialized toward the less valued statuses and roles, often toward those that sociologist Everett Hughes has characterized as the "dirty work" of the society. Conversely, children born into more favored segments of society are socialized toward more favored statuses and roles. Generally, then, we may say that society has criteria for distinguishing among children, often based upon the status attributes of the families into which they are born, and procedures for directing different groups of children into different sequences of experiences which eventuate in different socialization outcomes.

Thus we see that society organizes itself in such a way as to develop in its children both a general commitment to participate in society and a general competence for doing so, and also a variety of commitments and competences that are considered relevant to particular statuses and roles. Our examples of the last point have been drawn from the realm of occupations, but we must now consider an aspect of commitment and competence that is more general than the occupational. One criterion by which every society differentiates socialization outcomes is sex. There is no society that does not expect differences in social participation and competence from males and females, differences that are summed up in the sociological term *sex role.*

Although sex-role expectations are, of course, *based on* anatomy, physiology, and such other biological differences as physical strength and endurance, they are not fully *determined by* these biological factors. Sigmund Freud, the originator of psychoanalysis, once wrote that "anatomy is destiny"; this is true, but not entirely in the way Freud meant it. For, while he saw sexual biology as determinative of the person's psychological outlook and life course, contemporary knowledge gained by anthropology and sociology reveals that society shapes sex roles more than Freud recognized. True, there are at least a few biologically determined universals; no society attempts to socialize males to become mothers. However, contemporary psychoanalyst Bruno Bettelheim argues that this is not because males don't want to be mothers. On the contrary, he argues that males are often envious of women's capacity to bear children and that the rites of puberty for males found in many preliterate societies are in fact not merely socialization into a male role but socialization away from a female role. Such rites often involve inflicting scars, and Bettelheim interprets these as symbolic equivalents of the pains of childbearing.[6] Far-fetched as this interpretation may seem, it affords a curious and subtle support for the sociological interpretation of sex roles. For, along with its insistence on the basic fatefulness of sexual anatomy, psychoanalysis also holds that humans are basically bisexual in their impulses and that socialization must and generally does lead to suppression of impulses that are inappropriate to the societal definition of a person's anatomical sex.

Bettelheim's analysis, which may or may not be correct, is not widely accepted, but it is of interest here in suggesting how significant and far-reaching the socialization process is. In Chapter 6, we consider the topic of sex and socialization in greater detail.

EMOTIONALLY SIGNIFICANT RELATIONSHIPS

Where does socialization begin? We have given one answer to this question by saying that society specifies desired outcomes that are to be brought about by its agencies—its families, schools, churches, youth groups, mass media, and other institutions. From this perspective, socialization begins with the specification of the range of outcomes toward which all newborns will be directed.

But the newborn, of course, knows nothing of this. If we look at the question from this perspective, it receives a different answer: Socialization begins with *personal attachment.* Born helpless, vocal but without speech, with only the potentiality to become human, needing care, infants begin to be socialized by being cared for by one or more persons who are committed to caring for them. At birth, children evoke sentiments of pride, love, tenderness, responsibility, hope, and so forth, in those who receive them as new members of the group. Most important among them usually is the mother. She responds on the basis of the sentiments her child evokes in her. Her response has many aspects. She touches and holds the child in a certain way, perhaps self-confidently, perhaps apprehensively, perhaps with a certain annoyance. She may be diligent or dilatory in responding to its cries. She may breast-feed and sing to her child, or she may routinely give it a bottle and let it feed in solitude.

From the perspective of the individual child starting out in life, the mother-child relationship is where socialization begins. What happens in this relationship that initiates socialization? Many different things.

This is the infant's first relationship with another person. It is therefore his first significant encounter with what it means to be human. Being cared for is one's first experience of social life. As such, and coming before a child can evaluate it, the relationship with the mother is virtually all the social life an infant has and therefore presents his or her first expectation of the social world. The infant whose mother spends much time with it, singing, playing, feeding, will have a different expectation of social life than the infant whose mother gives only minimal care.

Not less important, in this first attachment the child has the beginnings of a sense of self. One fundamental fact of the mother-child relationship is that the adult has far more power than the infant. But this is not to say that the infant is necessarily powerless, as is sometimes incorrectly stated. For in this situation the infant has the possibility of gaining some power. If its cries of discomfort succeed with some consistency in evoking parental response that allays the discomfort, then, we have reason to believe, the infant is launched on a path of experiencing itself as effective. On the other hand, when the infant's cries do not bring a satisfying response, or do so only inconsistently, its sense of powerlessness is intensified.

That the mother-child relationship is important for socialization has long been believed, but efforts to identify the crucial aspects of this relationship have met with uneven success. Psychoanalysis, a bold theory formulated on the basis of closely attentive observation of adults being treated for emotional disturbances, argued that the child's earliest feelings about feeding and excreting were influential—often decisive—in shaping the child's later development. Academic research workers were challenged by this theory presented by nonacademic clinicians and sought to test these ideas in a way that would justify accepting or rejecting them. What was important about feeding? Was it the difference between breast-feeding and bottle-feeding? Was it the suddenness or gradualness of weaning? Since toilet training seemed to be the first clear imposition of society's demands upon the unsocialized infant, did the age at which such training was begun make a difference? And was it better to start early or late? Should the mother be gentle or stern in the way she went about it?

These and numerous related questions prompted a voluminous quantity of research. In a meticulous review of this research—a review which itself fills nearly eighty pages—Bettye M. Caldwell concludes that the results remain inconclusive.[8] The research does not justify the conclusion that feeding and toilet-training practices have no effect, but neither is it clear that the practices as such have definite effects.

A different kind of study, by Lois Murphy, suggests that whether or not the infant was orally *gratified* during the first six months of life is the more important issue.[9] According to her study, children who received much oral gratification during the first six months of life showed greater ability to cope with difficulties and frustrations at later preschool ages. The general explanation is that such gratification minimizes tension in the infant and thereby leaves it free to acquire a firmer sense of self and of environment. We shall return to these questions later. For present purposes it is sufficient to note that although the difference between breast-feeding and bottle-feeding appeared to make no difference to the infant's gratification, whether or not the mother allowed it to reject unwanted foods did make a difference in the child's later effectiveness. Autonomy in the infancy feeding situation was associated with later autonomy in coping with the environment. Since "allowing" is one way of establishing expectations in a relationship, Murphy's study provides some evidence that early experiences in the mother-child relationship give rise to expectations that influence later socialization.

That children form attachments even as early as three or four months is indicated in a study by Leon J. Yarrow. Infants of this age who were moved from foster homes to adoptive homes showed disturbances such as withdrawn behavior, increased apathy, and disturbances of sleep and feeding. "More overt social disturbances—excessive clinging or definite rejection of the new mother—occurred with increasing frequency after six months."[10]

In sum, by being cared for, by evoking response and being responded to, the infant obtains its first sense of self, first sense of another person, first experience of a social relationship. In this relationship the infant develops its first expectations and thus its first sense of social order. A rudimentary temporal order emerges from such experiences as the interval between crying and being responded to; the interval between feedings; the alternation of sleeping and wakefulness. In being cared for, the infant has its first experiences of those sentiments that Cooley identified decades ago as the hallmark of human nature.

We have been assuming that the primary infant-care functions are largely carried out by one person, the mother, which is the usual situation. Some cultures, however, and perhaps increasingly our own, apportion such care among several people; thus the child may form multiple-person relationships. One recent study of father-infant interaction showed that children between the ages of one and two, depending upon the degree to which fathers cared for them, may be equally attached to mothers and fathers.[11] There is some evidence, however, that the infant is likely to form a closer attachment to one among the multiple caretaking figures.[12]

The child's attachment to the earliest caretaking figure is the first of many emotionally significant relationships that the child will form in the course of his or her life with *significant others.* This will be followed by various attachments to a diversity of significant others, who may include other adult figures, siblings, age-mates and older children in neighborhood and school, relatives, teachers, friends, and "enemies." A child will form a somewhat different kind of relationship with each of these people; because of this, and because each has a different status in society and a different role in relation to the child, each will make a different kind of contribution to the child's socialization. These differences will give rise to problems for the child from an early age, with the conflict between parents and age-mates typically being a focus of stress. Four-year-olds encouraged by play-mates to cross the street in pursuit of adventure may experi-ence distress before they follow the suggestion or only after their parents have discovered that they have done so. In either case, they are experiencing an early form of the con-flict of norms and expectations that impinge on them from socializing agents who occupy different statuses.

COMMUNICATION

Now we face a paradox. Society presses toward certain out-comes, yet socialization begins in a two-person relationship of mother giving care to an infant who cannot speak or think or even understand instruction. How can an infant traverse the path from this beginning to that of a participating mem-ber of society? How can he or she be set upon this path?

The relevant facts here are that speechless newborns can feel and can communicate, and these resources can get them started. At the outset infants can feel discomfort and com-fort. When they feel discomfort, they cry. A mother hears the cry, *interprets* it as a sign of discomfort, and *responds* with activities that she hopes will restore the infant to com-fort or at least keep it quiet. She will evaluate, or interpret, her own effort as successful when the child ceases to cry. Her initial efforts may not be "on target" because she may incor-rectly interpret the source of the discomfort and the actions that will be effective in assuaging it. She may assume the child is hungry, only to find that it does not nurse. Further trial and error will lead to a "correct interpretation"—that is, one that leads the child to stop crying and leads the mother to judge that she has responded appropriately.[13]

Symbols, Language, and Interaction

The situation we have just described is the prototype of social interaction from which more complex forms evolve and through which the infant will develop into a person who can function in society. In this rudimentary interaction, the child makes a sound that is not simply a noise to his or her mother. The noise is significant to her—on two bases. First, she accepts the noise as having a legitimate claim upon her attention, because of her relationship to the child. The cry will not go unnoticed as might the noise of an airplane passing overhead, because *for her* it signifies or *symbolizes her* attachment to the child. It does so independently of how she chooses to respond to the cry. But the second meaning of the cry is a responsive or *interactive* meaning. She may decide that the cry should be interpreted as meaning she should attend to the infant right away. Alternatively, she may decide to interpret it as one that allows her to wait until a more convenient moment to respond. Or she may decide not to respond immediately, with the express goal of teaching the child to tolerate more discomfort. Whatever her particular response, she engages in an imaginative process—which may take no more than an instant—in which she represents to herself what the child is probably feeling and what should be done about it. Her overt response to the child's cry occurs only after the process of inner representation.

The capacity to interpret communications from others and to represent to oneself what others may think, feel, and do is fundamental to all of social life. Newborns do not have this capacity, and this is what they must develop. At the outset they experience discomfort but do not know how it can be assuaged. Crying is involuntary; it is not a communication to *the infant*. But in time, as cries succeed in bringing mother and comfort, they begin to be more under the infant's voluntary control. Whether the infant develops, in this preverbal period, the capacity to form mental representations of her is a moot question. Some psychoanalytic writers postulate that preverbal infants do have the capacity to imagine their mothers coming to them. Most scholars, including most psychoanalytic writers, remain skeptical because there is no reasonable way at this time to ascertain whether a preverbal infant does or does not imagine anything. Nevertheless, the child becomes increasingly able to anticipate the mother's appearance. By the time the child becomes able to stand in a crib, the child is also able to look toward the door through which mother will enter and to greet her entry by rocking on the feet, reaching out, and changing his or her vocalization—before she ministers to the child. The child has developed some expectations that are responsive to the mother's expectations as she comes to tend to him or her. The child is on the way to becoming socialized. The child begins to learn how to function in society by learning how to function in the relationship with his or her mother.

There is some evidence that even during this preverbal period of the newborn's life mother-infant interaction varies from one society to another in ways that are already preparing the infant for membership in the particular society. William Caudill, a long-time student of Japan, observed mothers and infants in thirty Japanese middle-class homes and in thirty American middle-class homes. He found in these samples differences between the two societies in mothers' caretaking style and in the infants' behavior, differences that were related to the general organization of the two societies. The American mothers were lively in their caretaking, more often in and out of the baby's room than were the Japanese and, perhaps most important, quick to respond to vocalized unhappiness by the infant. The Americans engaged in active vocal interaction with their infants. The Japanese mothers sought to soothe and quiet their babies while lulling and rocking them. Physical contact was more prominent than vocal interaction. The Japanese mothers were generally slower to respond to their infants' vocalizations, and they did not discriminate between the baby's happy and unhappy sounds by responding more quickly to one type than to the other. The general result that Caudill observed was that the American babies engaged in more happy than unhappy vocalization, while the Japanese babies did the reverse. In explaining why Japanese mothers persisted in a pattern of caretaking that led the babies to be "fussy," Caudill noted that this pattern fitted in with certain general features of Japanese society that contrast with American. He writes:

In America the mother views her baby as a potentially separate and autonomous being who should learn to do and think for himself. For her, the baby is from birth a distinct personality with his own needs and desires which she must learn to recognize and care for. She helps him to learn to express these needs and desires through her emphasis on vocal communication so that he can "tell" her what he wants and she can respond appropriately. She de-emphasizes the importance of physical contact such as carrying and rocking and encourages her infant through the use of her voice to explore and to learn to deal with his environment by himself. In the same way that she thinks of her infant as a separate individual, she thinks of herself as a separate person with needs and desires which include time apart from her baby so that she may pursue her own interests. . . . For this reason the pace of her caretaking is quicker than the Japanese mother's, and when she is caretaking, her involvement with the baby is livelier and more intense. This is true partly because she wishes to stimulate the baby to activity and response so that when it is time for him to sleep, he will remain asleep and allow her time to do other things. . . .

In Japan, the mother views her baby much more as an extension of herself. . . . The mother feels that she knows what is best for the baby, and there is no particular need for him to tell her what he wants because, after all, they are virtually one. Thus, in Japan, there is greater emphasis on interdependence, rather than independence, of mother and child, and this emphasis extends into adulthood. Given this orientation, the Japanese mother places less importance on vocal communication and more on physical contact; also, for her, there is no need for hurry as the expectation is that she will devote herself to her child without any great concern for time away from him. . . . As we know from other research . . . , the Japanese child will ordinarily sleep with his parents until he is approximately ten years of age.

Given the differences in these two styles of care, we believe that the infants have learned to respond to each respective style in culturally appropriate ways by three to four months of age. . . . This learning process takes place well before the development of the ability to use language in the ordinary sense; hence, these infants have acquired before then some aspects of the "implicit culture" . . . of their group—that is, those ways of feeling, thinking, and behaving that go on largely out of awareness and that, in general, characterize the actions of people in a given culture.[14]

With the gradual acquisition of language, socialization accelerates and becomes qualitatively transformed from its preverbal beginnings. Language is, of course, part of the heritage of a society, and facility in the use of its language is one of the kinds of competence toward which society directs its newborns. But while *language facility* is one of the expected outcomes of socialization, *language acquisition* is of enormous importance as one of the component processes of socialization long before full facility is achieved.

Recall our account of mother-infant interaction. When the infant cries, the mother interprets this as a sign of need. But she must discover for herself whether the infant is hungry, wet, cold, has caught its foot in the slats of the crib or is in some other state of discomfort. The infant's cry is an interpretable symbol to its mother but only imperfectly so; and it is not at all a symbol to the infant.[15] As infants acquire the ability to use common gestures and language, they are acquiring the ability to symbolize—the ability to identify and name things, people, and feelings. In place of nonspecific cries, they are able to point or tug or name their wishes to another. But in order to be able to do this, they have to be able to identify wishes to themselves. When children are able to present to themselves the same symbol for an object that they present to others, they have taken a large step toward regulating their own behavior and simultaneously a large step toward participating responsively with others. A qualitative change of great importance has thus taken place when, instead of nonspecific cries, children can designate their wishes with words that communicate specifically: "bottle," "wet," "pick me up," and so on. They now have at their disposal specific symbols whose meaning *they know* and that they know their mothers know. They are entering into a social world of shared symbols. Their capacity for social interaction is thus expanding enormously as they master an expanding array of shared symbols. In this process they are gaining the capacity to move beyond the circumscribed world of the mother-child relationship into a larger social world of widely shared symbols.

Recent research on the acquisition of language indicates that it is a far more complicated process than had previously been supposed.[16] Indeed, like socialization generally, it involves many component processes. Two deserve brief mention here. From one point of view, language consists of words, and learning language involves learning words. Infants begin to speak by making random sounds. When they make a sound that approximates a word in their "native language," their parents and others encourage them by repeating the sound as the "correct word" that they almost hear. By responding in an interested and pleasurable way and by providing the child with "correct pronunciations" of words they imagine the child is struggling to say, the significant others reward and encourage the child's further efforts. Since much of this activity goes on in relation to specific objects and experiences in the child's world, the random sounds develop into both "real words" and into symbols for objects and experiences. Sound and meaning come to be associated.

This view of language learning has been held for some time. It seems satisfactory as far as it goes, but it does not go far enough. A number of linguistic scholars, most prominently Noam Chomsky, have pointed out that language consists not simply of words but of sentences.[17] Further, there is no limit to the number of sentences that can be formed. Even children will, at some point, begin to speak sentences they have never heard before and which therefore cannot be explained simply as the result of their being directly taught in the fashion described in the preceding paragraph. Accordingly, these scholars argue, in some fashion children learn "*productive rules* that enable the speaker to produce the infinite variety of sentences that he produces and to understand the infinite variety of sentences that he hears."[18] How the child learns these rules is not yet understood, but more is involved than learning textbook grammar. The available evidence does indicate, according to James J. Jenkins, that

> the child is very systematic in his approach to language. It may be that he moves from one system to another, testing, changing, testing, trying again, or it may be that he chooses one system and progressively differentiates it into finer and finer portions; but the evidence that he is doing *something* systematic is overwhelming. . . . there is evidence that the child is struggling with a system for generating language at every stage and in very complex ways.[19]

These insights into the child's learning of language emphasize that in the course of socialization he or she is engaged in an effort to develop an inner regulation of behavior, an internal order that in some adequate way corresponds to an external social order.

Language is, then, an example of social order, just as the arrangement of houses on streets or the exchange of money for goods and services are examples of social order. All three regulate the relationships among people in accordance with rules, and the child will have to learn the relevant rules for these and many other aspects of social order.

But language plays a particularly significant part in organizing a social order and in the child's socialization into that order. Language is, among its other functions, a system for classifying objects and events in ways that are socially significant. Thus, if a child sits on a table, he or she may be told "that's not a chair." The table surface lends itself to sitting just as does the seat of a chair; but despite their physical similarity in this respect they are socially defined as completely different objects, and this difference is embodied in a verbal classification that organizes behavior in relation to the objects. The way in which things and events are verbally classified defines their social nature, and these classifications become a fundamental part of our way of thinking and acting. Our very perception is shaped by our language categories. In time the child will not even see the table as offering the possibility for sitting, because his or her knowledge of it as being within the category "table" will preclude the possibility.

Categorization of social reality takes more complex forms. A common example in our society is the disposition to see many situations in "either-or" terms. The child may encounter this at the dinner table in the form of "Either eat your vegetables or go without dessert." Another situation of similar form is "Practice the piano (do your homework, clean up your room) or you can't go out to play." Desired activities are thus often incorporated in an "either-or" way of thinking that makes them contingent on the performance of some undesired activity—"or else."

Finally, one further indication of the way in which language shapes experience is of particular interest. Freud called attention to "the peculiar amnesia which veils from most people (not from all) the first years of their childhood, usually the first six or eight years."[20] He was impressed with the fact that childhood experiences are often vivid and that they include love, jealousy, and other passions. Yet despite the intensity, memories of these experiences in later years are fragmentary at best. Following up Freud's observations, but dissatisfied with his explanation of this massive failure of memory, Ernest G. Schachtel proposed the following explanation: Memory organizes past experiences in the service of present needs, fears, and interests. Adult memory is organized into categories that are shaped by society. These categories "are not suitable vehicles to receive and reproduce experiences of the quality and intensity typical of early childhood," because they are shaped by the biases, emphases, and taboos of adult culture. Adult memory is essentially conventionalized, and therefore early childhood experience —in which everything seems new, fresh, and exciting—is incompatible, hence forgotten. The conventionalization of memory proceeds so far that, as Schachtel puts it:

> the memories of the majority of people come to resemble increasingly the stereotyped answers to a questionnaire, in which life consists of time and place of birth, religious denomination, residence, educational degrees, job, marriage, number and birth-

dates of children, income, sickness and death.... the average traveler through life remembers chiefly ... what he is supposed to remember because it is exactly what everybody else remembers too.... Experience increasingly assumes the form of the cliché under which it will be recalled.... This is not the remembered situation itself but the words which are customarily used to indicate this situation and the reactions which it is supposed to evoke.... There are people who experience a party, a visit to the movies, a play, a concert, a trip in the very words in which they are going to tell their friends about it; in fact, quite often they anticipate such experience in these words. The experience is predigested, as it were, even before they have tasted of it. Like the unfortunate Midas, whose touch turned everything into gold so that he could not eat or drink, these people turn the potential nourishment of the anticipated experience into the sterile currency of the conventional phrase which exhausts their experience because they have seen, heard, felt nothing but this phrase with which later they will report to their friends the "exciting time" they have had.[21]

Thus, Schachtel maintains, language not only shapes memory into conventionalized categories; in extreme cases it even conventionalizes the experience before it passes into memory. But even in ordinary cases, conventionalization is so powerful that most early childhood experience is not accessible to memory.

Although society provides linguistic categories for organizing our thoughts and ideas, conversations themselves may have a problematic aspect for the participants because much of what is said assumes many things left unsaid. Social interaction depends upon interpretive procedures that help the person "make sense of" or "understand" what is going on. To illustrate the constantly ongoing interpretation in social interaction, Harold Garfinkel reproduced a conversation between a student and his wife (left-hand column) together with the meaning that was understood in each statement (right-hand column). We quote it in the same format that Garfinkel used:

HUSBAND: *Dana succeeded in putting a*   This afternoon as I was bringing Dana, our four-year-old son, home from the

penny in a parking me-ter today without be-ing picked up.	nursery school, he succeeded in reaching high enough to put a penny in a parking meter when we parked in a meter parking zone, whereas before he has always had to be picked up to reach that high.
WIFE: *Did you take him to the record store?*	Since he put a penny in a meter, that means that you stopped while he was with you. I know that you stopped at the record store either on the way to get him or on the way back. Was it on the way back, so that he was with you, or did you stop there on the way to get him and somewhere else on the way back?
HUSBAND: *No, to the shoe repair shop.*	No, I stopped at the record store on the way to get him and stopped at the shoe repair shop on the way home when he was with me.
WIFE: *What for?*	I know of one reason why you might have stopped at the shoe repair shop. Why did you in fact?
HUSBAND: *I got some new shoelaces for my shoes.*	As you will remember, I broke a shoelace on one of my brown oxfords the other day, so I stopped to get some new laces.
WIFE: *Your loafers need new heels badly.*	Something else you could have gotten that I was thinking of. You could have taken in your black loafers which need heels badly. You'd better get them taken care of pretty soon.[22]

Such interpretive procedures must be, and evidently are, learned fairly early in the course of socialization, although just when and how are not yet understood. But the point is clear if we apply Garfinkel's procedure to an exchange of taunts between two schoolboys that was reported by Iona and Peter Opie. The conversation is again in the left-hand column; the right-hand column gives our analysis of what might be interpreted by each participant.

FIRST BOY: *If I had a face like yours I'd put it on a wall and throw a brick at it.*

I'm going to insult you and make you feel bad, and I'm going to do it in a smart way. You're ugly; you ought to feel ashamed of how you look. If I looked like you, I'd just as soon end the whole business.

SECOND BOY: *If I had a face like* yours *I'd put it on a brick and throw a wall at it.*[23]

I'm not going to take your insult and just let you get away with it. In fact, I can be even more insulting and more clever than you. Whatever I look like, you look worse. You're the one who should feel bad. You propose a drastic procedure for me; I propose an even more drastic one for you.

Each sentence spoken carries a wider range of meaning than is actually stated. Conversational language therefore must be continually interpreted by the participants. Gregory Bateson and his co-workers have pointed out that all communication involves something said and a modality in which it is said—words are said seriously, jokingly, commandingly, questioningly, and so on. The participant in a conversation must interpret the modality being used as well as what is said. Very young children are sometimes unable to do this. For example, they may not understand that parents are commanding, not asking. Certain kinds of playful comments made by older children or adults may not be understood as playful by the very young child, who may burst into tears. When this happens, the older children or adults may engage in a detailed explanation of what was intended. In the course of socialization, most children develop the ability to interpret (and later to use) modality appropriately most of the time. Still, there are times when anyone may be uncertain and may ask: "Are you serious?" or "Are you kidding?" Adequate socialization makes such occasions infrequent. We are able to recognize the modality by the combination of words spoken, tone of voice, and the social context in which the words are spoken. But even when we understand the modality, we still must continually interpret the words, as our two examples demonstrate.[24]

THE SIGNIFICANCE OF SIGNIFICANT OTHERS

With our discussion of emotional attachments and of communication as background, we are now in a position to identify some additional processes that make significant others significant to the child and that help the child develop from the primarily biological organism he or she is at birth into a person as well.

When we say that the task of socialization is to enable the child to learn to function in society, we refer to a complex type of adaptation that cannot be understood as a kind of mechanical conformity. As our brief sketch of human biological nature in Chaper 2 makes clear, human socialized behavior is not analogous to the behavior of the trained rat running a maze and receiving rewards for making correct turns in correct sequence. (The fundamental dissimilarity is conveyed by the once popular expression "rat race," referring to a pattern of life that is too dominated by pursuit of externally set goals in conformity with rigidly specified rules. To call this life pattern a rat race is to criticize it as departing too far from human nature.)

Socialization is, then, not simply a process of making correct motions prescribed by trainers. Running in a rat race or jumping through a hoop are, when applied to humans, terms for caricaturing certain distortions of socialization.

As suggested by our discussion of learning language rules, the essence of socialization is the person's *internal regulation* of his or her own behavior in ways that are adequate to the interpersonal situations and to the larger social order in which he or she participates. The capability for internal regulation develops as a result of interaction with significant others.

Significant others present themselves to the child in two essential ways:

1. By what they do
2. By what they say (and how they say it)

Doing and saying are, of course, organized in terms of roles. Thus, traditionally, a mother presented herself to her child by feeding, changing diapers, offering toys, addressing the child with words of endearment. Older brother threw a ball, climbed trees, and used a different vocabulary. Father carried a toolbox or a briefcase, watched football games, and used yet another vocabulary.

As infants become aware of the activities going on around them, they become interested in these activities; and because these are the activities of people to whom infants are emotionally attached, infants want to do what those around them do and, indeed, to be as they are. For example, not long after a mother begins giving her child nonliquid food, the child wishes to feed her as he or she is being fed. The child tries to take the spoon from her and feed her. As the range of observation expands, the child tries other activities that seem interesting: turning light switches on and off, opening the refrigerator, and the like. And while the child's significant others are engaged in such activities, they are also engaged in saying things—naming the objects they handle, describing what they are doing ("Here's your doll."), playing word games ("Where's your nose? Show me your nose."). Children begin to repeat the words they hear and to carry out the actions they see others carry out. In short, they perceive their significant others as *role models,* sources of the patterns of behavior and conduct on which children pattern themselves. It is through interaction with these role models that children develop the ability to regulate their own behavior.

The basic fact that the child's regulation of his or her own behavior develops from interaction with role models has been noted by numerous interpreters but explained variously by them. No single account of this process and its consequences is fully satisfactory, nor has anyone yet developed a satisfactory composite interpretation. We shall therefore draw upon several sources that seem necessary for an adequate understanding of this process but which do not yet fit well together.

For George Herbert Mead, an influential figure in American sociology though not himself a sociologist, the principal outcome of socialization that makes self-regulation possible is the development of the *self.* The self, in his view, is the capacity to represent to oneself what one wishes to communicate to others. Language plays a crucial part in development of the self. This is why, from Mead's point of view, the child's change from simply crying to being able to use socially shared symbols such as "I want bottle," "Go outside" (for "I want to go outside") is such a significant transformation.[25] Only humans can self-consciously and purposively represent to themselves that which they wish to represent to others; this, for Mead, is what it means to have a self and what it means to be human. The child who can do this is on his or her way to becoming human, that is, to being simultaneously self-regulating and socially responsive.

In addition to language, which he considers paramount, Mead also recognizes the importance of the child's observations of others' activities. He postulated that children go through two stages of observation toward the development of self. In the first, or *play stage,* children take the roles of others: They play at being the others who are significant to them. They want to push the broom, carry the umbrella, put on the hat, and do all the other things they see their parents do, including saying what parents say. The story is told of the four-year-old playing "daddy" who put on his hat and coat, said "good-bye," and walked out the front door, only to return a few minutes later because he didn't know what to do next. He had taken as much of his father's work role as he could see and hear—the ritualized morning departure. What is noteworthy in this illustration (as in all play) is that the child is now able to govern his own behavior to a certain extent. When he first heard adults say "bye-bye" to him, he did nothing because the sound had no meaning to him. Nor did it mean anything when he first learned to repeat the sound. Now when he says "good-bye," he directs himself to walk out the door.

In the play stage children play at many roles that offer interesting models to them, not only imitating their parents and other children but also playing "cops and robbers," letter carrier, space pilot, and so on. During this stage they progress to taking two complementary roles at a time. Thus, they may say things to themselves that their mothers have said to them, then reply in their own roles of children. If no playmates are around, they may enact the roles of both cop and robber in alternation.

Although Mead did not include toys in his analysis, toys in this stage may become important accessories. Children impute identities to their stuffed animals and dolls, who may become surrogate companions, sources of comfort and security, or targets of love, hostility, sympathy, and other sentiments. So, too, may toy racing cars, building blocks, doll houses, and costumes become devices for exploring feelings or self-images of power, age statuses, and sex roles. Toys, in these early years and later, facilitate the process by which children engage in imaginative behavior and prepare for subsequent roles and relationships.[26]

Returning now to Mead's own analysis, we find that, with further development the child enters the *game stage.* The importance of this lies in the fact that games involve an organization of roles, and the child participating has to take the role of everyone else. In Mead's famous example of the baseball game, the child

> must have the responses of each position involved in his own position. He must know what everyone else is going to do in order to carry out his own play. He has to take all of these roles. They do not all have to be present in consciousness at the same time, but at some moments he has to have three or four individuals present in his own attitude, such as the one who is going to throw the ball, the one who is going to catch it, and so on. These responses must be, in some degree, present in his own makeup. In the game, then, there is a set of responses of such others so organized that the attitude of one calls out the appropriate attitudes of the other.[27]

Then, as Mead puts it:

> This getting of the broad activities of any given social whole or organized society as such within the experiential field of any one of the individuals involved ... is ... the essential basis and prerequisite of the fullest development of that individual's self: only in so far as he takes the attitudes of the organized social group to which he belongs toward the organized, cooperative

social activity or set of such activities in which that group . . . is engaged, does he develop a complete self. . . . And on the other hand, the complex cooperative processes and activities and institutional functionings of organized human society are also possible only in so far as every individual involved in them . . . can take the general attitudes of all other such individuals with reference to these processes and activities and institutional functionings, and to the organized social whole of experiential relations and interactions thereby constituted—and can direct his own behavior accordingly.[28]

Mead's explanation of the development of the self, shaped by language and role taking, remains one of the basic building blocks in our understanding of how man functions in society. In certain respects it is unexcelled to this day, more than forty years after his death. But it contains some important omissions. For example, Mead does not distinguish among different kinds of utterance. His approach finds no significance in the difference between a parent's saying "Here's your ball" and "Don't do that!" The latter expression is important in ways that the former is not, even though both are statements made by the same role model and both help the child to categorize the world in linguistic terms. But the latter statement is made *authoritatively*. It is more than a simple categorization. It is a statement of a *rule*, and it carries with it the suggestion of a *sanction*.

Role models who can present themselves to the child with authority to state rules and to enforce them with positive and negative sanctions play a particularly decisive part in the development of the child's self. An admired uncle who pilots a plane may catch the child's imagination more than his or her own father who works at a nine-to-five desk job. But the father, as the model who wields the more effective authority over the child's life, is likely to have greater influence in shaping the child's social participation. He, along with the mother, makes the child aware of limits to acceptable behavior. In short, the child has impulses and attempts actions that are unacceptable to those who have effective authority to interpret his or her behavior in the light of norms and values and to offer rewards and impose penalties to encourage appropriate conduct. (Effective authority does not rest only with adults. When children play with their peers, they come under a system of norms and sanctions that define "playing fair" and "cheating.") The self is established, then, not only on the basis of taking the role of the other but also through the process of *internalizing the values and norms* that are effectively presented by authoritative role models. In one sense socialization can be summed up by saying that what was once outside the individual comes to be inside the individual. Society comes to exist within the individual as well as outside of him or her. This is the developmental change that makes all the difference.

But we must consider developmental change from another angle of vision as well.

SOCIALIZATION AND TIME

Socialization is an extended process. It takes time, obviously. Less obviously, it takes different kinds of time. To begin, let us make a basic distinction between *life-cycle time* and *social time,* after which we shall note some of their complexities.

By life-cycle time we mean a sequence of biological stages determined by maturation. Everywhere humans are born small and helpless. They then pass through a decade and a half or so of increasing strength. Sometime during the second decade puberty is reached and sexual maturity attained. For several decades thereafter, adult levels of energy are sustained, followed by a period of more or less precipitous decline. This sequence of stages is universal. The age at which changes occur varies according to many influences, but the sequence itself is not alterable.

Social time may be generally defined as the organization of events into socially meaningful units. As society changes, the organization of time is likely to change. For example, when people worked a six-day week, they had one day of rest called the Sabbath. With a five-day work week now standard, the nonwork unit is of two days' duration and is called the weekend, although it could conceivably have been called "double Sabbath." The weekend is not simply twice as long as the Sabbath but is very different in social meaning as well.

Every society, in organizing its social life, takes note of the biological states, a phenomenon known as *age grading.* Age grading is thus one type of social time. But every society does not make the same age distinctions, nor does every society consider them of equal importance. Furthermore, as a society changes, its age grading is also likely to change. Thus it may be said that the biological life cycle constitutes a substratum upon which society imposes its own distinctions as an overlay.

Social change is relevant to socialization. We discover from the work of Philippe Ariès, a sociologically minded historian, that the very notion of a distinctive period of life conceived of as childhood is of fairly recent origin. The many facts of childhood that seem so compellingly distinctive to us and lead us to differentiate the early years from those that follow did not have this impact in Western countries before about the sixteenth century. This was shown in many ways in earlier times. For example, once infants were out of swaddling clothes, they were dressed just like "the other men and women" of their social class; there was no distinctive dress for children in medieval society. After the age of three or four, children played the same games as adults, including card games and games of chance for money. Documents from the early seventeenth century reveal that adults did not refrain from gestures and jokes with children that would today be regarded as immoral or perverted. Ariès notes:

> In medieval society, the idea of childhood did not exist; this is not to suggest that children were neglected, forsaken or despised. The idea of childhood is not to be confused with affection for children; it corresponds to an awareness of the particular nature of childhood ... which distinguishes the child from the adult, even the young adult. In medieval society, this awareness was lacking....
>
> In the Middle Ages, at the beginning of modern times, and for a long time after that in the lower classes, children were mixed with adults as soon as they were considered capable of doing

without their mothers or nannies, not long after a tardy weaning (in other words about the age of seven). They immediately went straight into the great community of men, sharing in the work and play of their companions, old and young alike. The movement of collective life carried in a single torrent all ages and classes.[29]

The awareness of childhood as a distinct period of life is, then, a historical creation. Once this awareness developed, the nature of childhood and what should be done about it became a matter of ideological controversy, and it has remained so down to our time. At some periods and among some groups, the child has been regarded as basically tender and innocent. In opposition to this has been the notion that the child is wild and needs to be tamed. These two images continue to have their respective adherents.

Within any given society in a given historical period, the child passes through various kinds of sequences. Ariès describes how the school year has become a time unit for socialization:

Today the class, the constituent cell of the school structure, presents certain precise characteristics which are entirely familiar: it corresponds to a stage in the progressive acquisition of knowledge (to a curriculum), to an average age from which every attempt is made not to depart, to a physical spatial unit, for each age group and subject group has its special premises ... and to a period of time, an annual period at the end of which the class's complement changes.

The extremely close connection between the age of the pupils and the organic structure which gathers them together gives each year a personality of its own: the child has the same age as his class, and each class acquires from its curriculum, its classroom and its master a distinctive complexion. The result is a striking differentiation between age groups which are really quite close together. The child changes his age every year at the same time as he changes his class. In the past, the span of life and childhood was not cut up into such thin slices. The school class has thus become a determining factor in the process of differentiating the ages of childhood and early adolescence.[30]

Of course, while the child is passing through these school-determined age statuses, each with its own contribution to socialization, he or she is also passing through other gradations that are not institutionally determined or precisely delineated but which nevertheless mark significant steps. Such distinctions are numerous: for example, the progression from the play to the game stage in Mead's analysis. Or consider the progression from being a child who must come in when it gets dark to one who is allowed to stay out after dark with peers; or the farm child old enough to own a pony, the city child old enough for his or her first two-wheel bicycle. Language plays its part in these gradations as well; children are told they are too old to cry or too young to have some object they want. *In some situations their age status is negotiable:* They may persuade their parents that they are old enough to go to the movies alone or old enough to have a shotgun. The negotiation of age status as an interactive process between parents and children has not received much study.

All these progressions lead the child toward maturity, a concept that has relevance both biologically and sociologically. Indeed, one of the important considerations for an understanding of socialization is that biological maturation usually presents a challenge to society or its agents. The child who becomes able to walk wants to walk in places that are "off limits" (for example, on furniture or in mud puddles) and therefore evokes negative sanctions. In similar fashion, other aspects of biological maturation, from eating to sexuality, present a challenge to society and its agencies and a challenge also to the growing child's own self. With each new step in biological maturation, the child feels ready to do things that once were done for him or her or wants to do things that his or her role models do, whether or not they feel the child is ready. The child says "let me do it" when the adult would rather do it more quickly or judges that the action is one the child should not yet do at all, even slowly —as when a three-year-old wants to use a sharp knife or carry something too heavy. Thus, from one perspective, socialization can be regarded as the process through which an individual's biological potentialities are brought into relationship with society: they are developed and transformed through time and made social.

No writer has achieved a more comprehensive view of this process than Erik Erikson.[31] In a sweeping look at the whole life cycle, he has proposed that it can be divided into eight stages, each of which presents the person with a basic socialization issue or dilemma. The manner in which each issue is resolved will shape the child's social participation as well as his or her happiness.

1. The first issue facing the helpless newborn is that of *trust versus distrust.* The emotional attachment to the mother is crucial in determining how this issue is resolved. From this standpoint, the first social achievement of the infant is its ability to let the mother out of sight without becoming anxious or enraged. This is possible when the mother has become "an inner certainty as well as an outer predictability."

2. The second year of life is marked by rapid gains in muscular maturation, visual and auditory discrimination, and verbalization. All of these give children the possibility of greater control over their own actions, and they begin to experience a sense of autonomous will. At this time, during which children are often also expected to gain bowel control, they are subjected to closer scrutiny. The issue posed by this level of development, according to Erikson, is that of *autonomy versus shame and doubt.* If children are subjected to too much parental control, their sense of their smallness becomes overwhelming and they become vulnerable to shame or doubt about their ability to be self-directing.

3. In the next stage, about the third year of life, the child has mastered walking and is able to move about freely. His or her language capacity "becomes perfected to the point where he understands and can ask incessantly about innumerable things, often hearing just enough to misunderstand them thoroughly." Children's capacities for both language and locomotion enable them to imagine actions and roles that may frighten them. Thus is posed an issue of a *sense of*

initiative versus guilt. Children explore and get into things, both verbally and in action. Their sense of rivalry with others is heightened. They also become aware of sex differences. Successful passage through this stage enables children to feel that their own purposes have validity, that it is all right for them to move on their own toward things that seem interesting. If they are made to feel too frightened by their initiatives, they develop too stringent a conscience, dominated by a sense of guilt.

4. The next stage, extending over a period of several years, which Erikson calls the school age, is marked not so much by distinctive biological changes as by a more firmly modulated emotionality. (Schachtel's conventionalization of memory is proceeding at this time.) Children are ready to learn; they form attachments to teachers and parents of other children; they are interested in people practicing occupations that they can grasp—police officers, plumbers, garbage collectors, and pilots, for example. They are also capable of fuller cooperation with others (Mead's game stage). There is growing acquaintance with the objects and practices of the society's technology. The issue presented by this developmental stage is called by Erikson *industry versus inferiority.* Successful development through this stage gives children a sense of their ability to work at tasks, both individually and in cooperation with others. If things do not go well, children develop a sense of inferiority. This can come about in various ways:

> the child may still want his mommy more than knowledge; he may still prefer to be the baby at home rather than the big child in school; he still compares himself with his father, and the comparison arouses a sense of guilt as well as a sense of inferiority. Family life may not have prepared him for school life, or school life may fail to sustain the promises of earlier stages in that nothing that he has learned to do well so far seems to count with his fellows or his teacher. . . . It is at this point that wider society becomes significant to the child by admitting him to roles preparatory to the actuality of technology and economy. Where he finds out immediately, however, that the color of his skin or the background of his parents rather than his wish and

will to learn are the factors that decide his worth as a pupil or apprentice, the human propensity for feeling unworthy may be fatefully aggravated . . .[32]

5. The next period, adolescence, is the crucial period in Erikson's analysis of socialization. The period is initiated by puberty and is marked both by sexual maturation and by rapid growth in height and weight leading to the attainment of adult size. These changes set the basic task for developing adults: They must begin to find their own specific place in society. This is a period in which people must work out for themselves some integration of role models, values, norms, beliefs, emotional feelings. The issue of this period is that of *identity versus role diffusion.* Successful resolution of this issue produces individuals with a coherent sense of themselves and their relationship to society. Those who are not able to utilize this period—and adolescence becomes ever more extended in our society, although we may now be entering a period of contraction—to find and establish a coherent sense of identity, may be unable to find adult statuses and roles that are both personally satisfying and socially acceptable. They may be unable to settle upon an occupation and generally unable to find a worthwhile way of life. Such socialization failures may be induced by socialization agencies that do not give adequate scope to diversity: "Youth after youth, bewildered by the incapacity to assume a role forced on him by the inexorable standardization of American adolescence, runs away in one form or another, dropping out of school, leaving jobs, staying out all night, or withdrawing into bizarre and inaccessible moods."[33]

The remaining three stages of the life cycle in Erikson's scheme go beyond the major concerns of this book. For the sake of completeness, we mention them briefly.

6. As people emerge from their identity struggles, they face the issue of *intimacy versus isolation.* This involves the ability to enter into relationships that in some sense involve self-abandon within a framework of trust: love, friendship, erotic encounters, experiences of joint inspiration.

7. The biological capability for parenthood does not neces-

sarily lead to parenthood as a satisfying social role. The issue of this mature adult stage is *generativity versus stagnation,* generativity being "primarily the interest in establishing and guiding the next generation or whatever in a given case may become the absorbing object of a parental kind of responsibility."[34] Thus, Erikson does not mean that stagnation results from not being a parent in the literal sense. Rather, he means that the adult stagnates if he or she is not in *some* kind of role that involves fostering development, whether of a business or scientific research or a garden. (Indeed, sociologist Alice Rossi argues that parenthood in the literal sense —or at least motherhood—is an inappropriate role for many women and that American culture presses many women into maternity who are not very maternal and perhaps should not become mothers. Her view is gaining support.[35])

8. The process of aging confronts the person with the issue of what kind of life he or she has lived, the issue of *integrity versus despair.* Integrity in this sense means a sense of wholeness:

> an emotional integration faithful to the image-bearers of the past. . . . the acceptance of one's one and only life cycle and of the people who have become significant to it as something that had to be and that, by necessity, permitted of no substitutions. It thus means a new and different love of one's parents, free of the wish that they should have been different, and an acceptance of the fact that one's life is one's own responsibility. It is a sense of comradeship with men and women of distant times and of different pursuits who have created orders and objects and sayings conveying human dignity and love.[36]

Erikson is the only modern social science theorist who has attempted a unified analysis of socialization through the entire life cycle from birth to death. For this reason his analysis is helpful in thinking about some of the complexities of this topic. Two issues concerning time have come to be recognized as troublesome: First, to what extent, if at all, does early socialization affect adult social behavior? Erikson views socialization as a cumulative process in which the resolution of the central issue at one stage affects the resolution of the issues presented by succeeding stages. He does not make any simple claim that the mother's treatment of her infant in the first year of life determines what kind of social being her child will be when adult. Rather, he is saying that the child's socialization in any one stage generates certain expectations, which the child brings with him or her into new socialization settings. The socializing agents in the new settings have their own expectations, which they direct toward the child. These agents become new role models that the child adds to those he or she already has. The child, then, has the task of creating some internal order out of the expectations of the various socializing agents. The task is made easier, of course, when the expectations are similar, but as we pointed out early in this chapter, every child encounters some divergence of expectations.

The second question involves the relation of life-cycle time to historical time: How can parents (and other socializing agents) prepare their children to be adults in a society that will be very different when the children reach adulthood? The answer to this question is not simple—and is far from completely available. But certain things can be said. One is that social change is sometimes so great that socialization has in fact not fitted children for the changed conditions. Erikson, for example, describes the identity problems and social disorganization of Sioux Indians in North Dakota, who were still being socialized to the values, skills, and way of life relevant to hunting buffalo although all the buffalo had been wiped out decades earlier.[37]

Yet, clearly, in many situations adults do function in a society that makes available statuses and roles that did not exist when those adults were children. One explanation, offered by Albert J. Reiss, is that early values learned in the family setting are not internalized; the individual's behavior changes as he or she moves from setting to setting and encounters different values. To illustrate this, Reiss points out that the same individual was able to function successfully in Germany under the Weimar Republic, the Nazi regime, and the postwar democratic political system.[38] But although it is true that the same individual might have, under successive regimes, filled different roles for which there had been no specific preparation, the argument given by Reiss does not deal with the possibility that certain kinds of early socialization may prepare a child to function adequately under successive drastic changes. For example, if the prime value inculcated in the German child had been obedience to whatever authority held effective sway, he or she might in this way have been socialized to change roles in later life as the political institutions changed.

The relationship between socialization and social change is one of the most intricate, and it is not settled either by Reiss's argument or our objection to it. Perhaps Erikson again best captures the intricacy of the problem:

> each generation of youth must find an identity consonant with ideological promise in the perceptible historical process. But in youth the tables of childhood dependence begin slowly to turn: no longer is it merely for the old to teach the young the meaning of life. It is the young who, by their responses and actions, tell the old whether life as represented to them has some vital promise, and it is the young who carry in them the power to confirm those who confirm them, to renew and regenerate, to disavow what is rotten, to reform and rebel.[39]

Some of the various ways in which time and conceptions of time affect socialization are illustrated in the following chapter.

4 Socialization and Subcultural Patterns

 ny society that is large includes within it many different ways of life. To be sure, there are also important
elements shared in common. Thus, in North America, for
example, clothes, foods, tools, advertisements, kitchen appliances, drugstore displays, automobiles, popular sports, and
many other elements are widely shared. Indeed, these elements are shared not only across two North American societies—Canadian and American—but in varying degrees
across many others as well. But there are differences in the
emphasis that societies give even to these common elements.
For example, the United States has accepted—or embraced—
the automobile and given it far greater value than have other
industrial societies. This shows up in several ways. None of
the other societies that make extensive use of automobiles—
Canada, Britain, France, Germany, and so forth—has so thoroughly subordinated rail transportation to the automobile
as has the United States. (The United States has more than
half the world's motor vehicles but only 6 percent of the
world's population.[1]) Nor have these other societies been as
willing to tear down buildings and clear land in the down-
town areas of their cities for parking lots and garages. In
short, although the automobile is used and valued in many
societies, it has received greater emphasis in the United
States than elsewhere and has been more influential in
affecting various kinds of social and political decisions. As
concerns about the environment and about energy shortages
magnify, however, the age of "automobility," as some schol-

ars have called it, may well be coming to an end. One states that:

> Even the automobile manufacturers hope to diversify into "total transportation" companies by the turn into the twenty-first century. They anticipate that their main business by then will be selling modular transportation systems to the government. The automobile culture and the values that sustained it are no longer tenable.[2]

The above examples illustrate a concept of great importance for socialization, the concept of *culture.* This concept originates in anthropology but has proved extremely useful in all the social sciences. Like all such concepts that try to capture a complex reality, it has been variously defined and interpreted. But the following definition would receive wide acceptance among anthropologists and sociologists and is suitable for our purposes: *A culture is a way of life developed by a people in adaptation to the physical and social circumstances in which they find themselves. It tends to be passed on from generation to generation, but it changes as circumstances change. It includes some elements that are highly valued by the people themselves and other elements that are accepted as necessary or "realistic" adaptations but are not especially valued.*

A tricky problem is presented by the terms *a culture* and *a people.* The fact is, as Margaret Mead points out, that these terms are somewhat elastic and apply to units of different scope, depending upon what one is trying to understand:

> After deciding what larger unit we wish to refer to . . . then smaller observations are considered in terms of the regularities which have been identified for the whole. The term *cultural regularities* includes the way in which the versions of the culture found in different classes, regions, or occupations are systematically related to one another. So a member of the French bourgeoisie who is also a Protestant will manifest behavior which is French, which has certain peculiarities in common with the French bourgeois, and still others in common with his province, and others in common with his generation, etc. . . .

when we are making a cultural analysis, we are interested in identifying those characteristics—including, if not specifying, the possibilities of variation by class, region, religion, etc.—which can be attributed to sharing in the tradition of the larger group, whether that group be nation, tribe, province, or some even larger unit with a common tradition, such as the culture of an area like Southeast Asia.[3]

The question of what unit a culture refers to has assumed considerable importance in recent years for understanding differences in socialization. Does the child growing up in an isolated and poor rural hamlet in Kentucky have the same culture as a child growing up in the middle of New York, Chicago, or Houston? Does the child growing up in the slum have the same culture as the child growing up in the affluent suburb? The easiest answer to both questions is "No." The visible differences are so great that it has become common to insist that the children in these different settings are in fact being socialized into different cultures. Closer examination suggests, however, that some cultural similarities are simply less visible than the differences and that the differences are more likely to be necessary adaptations to circumstances than differences in values.[4] As an example, let us take the value of career success. There is no question that career success is a more dominant concern in some segments of society than in others. There are segments of American society, which we shall discuss shortly, in which men and women have no evident interest in career success, contrasted with others in which careers seem all important. It was fashionable at one time to regard the lack of interest in a career as evidence of a value difference. Closer examination has shown, however, that these people are not unmindful of the value society places on one's occupation. They have, however, for reasons that lie largely beyond their control, lost all possibility for success or even a job. They share in the value that others hold, but the value has lost meaning for their own day-to-day lives because there seems to be no way in which they can implement it.

This complex relationship of being both a part of a large society yet in some ways marked off from it, participating in a larger culture yet having a distinctive version of it, is expressed in the terms *subsociety* and *subculture.* Charles Valentine emphasizes both the distinctiveness of subcultures and their interplay with the larger culture:

> It is perhaps reasonable to assume that any subsociety may have a configuration of more or less distinguishable lifeways of its own. This configuration constitutes a subculture that is distinct from the total culture of the whole society in a ... special and limited sense. The wider sociocultural system has its own coherence to which subsocieties and subcultures contribute even with their distinctiveness.[5]

What is the importance of subcultures for socialization? First, children are socialized into a particular subculture, not into a culture as a whole. This means that initially children learn not the ways of their society but the ways of a particular segment of it. They develop outlooks and assumptions that are not necessarily shared by those outside that segment. If they spend their entire lifetimes associating only with those who share the same subculture, they may have difficulty understanding the thoughts, actions, and situations of those from other subcultures. The point may be illustrated with a hypothetical example. We might imagine a child in comfortable circumstances meeting a very poor child and asking him or her "How much allowance do you get?"—not realizing that in some parts of society children do not receive a weekly allowance. This is an example of a situation that affects all children in their early socialization but which most eventually leave behind as their experience widens: The things that are believed, valued, and done in one's own way of life lead to the implicit question "Doesn't everyone?"

A child's encounter with a different subculture can also take the reverse form. Instead of the revelation "I didn't know that everyone doesn't do what I do," the child may have an experience which takes the form "I didn't know other people do that." Thus, a young black woman whose mother cooked for a white family reports a childhood discovery:

> Sometimes Mama would bring us the white family's leftovers. It was the best food I had ever eaten. That was when I discovered white folks ate different from us. They had all kinds of different food with meat and all. We always had just beans and bread.[6]

A child's "emergence" from his or her own subculture into an awareness of diversity may come early or late in life, and for some living in isolated and homogeneous communities it may never come at all.

Of course, with increasing urbanization, mobility, education, and the widespread influence of television a smaller and smaller proportion of children grows up so completely insulated within a subculture as to be unacquainted with other ways of living in the same society. Even the very small towns come under the influence of urbanization and its divergent ways.[7] These changes mean that more and more children are learning at some point in the course of their socialization that the answer to the question "Doesn't everyone?" is "No, everyone doesn't." Everyone does not belong to a country club; everyone does not go to church every Sunday; everyone does not live in a neighborhood of crowded apartments; everyone does not believe that the most important thing is to get a good job that leads to advancement and a house in a nice suburb; everyone does not live in decaying wooden houses in muddy hollows.

The general implication of the fact that socialization starts within a particular subculture is that *every* child's socialization in some measure *limits his or her ability to function in the larger society.* The values, beliefs, assumptions, and ways of life that come to be "second nature" to children make it difficult for them to function effectively in some kinds of social situations involving persons who have been socialized in other subcultures. The limiting effects of socialization are currently receiving considerable attention in the United States and indeed have become a matter of political conflict. On the one hand it is stated that lower-class children are socialized in such a way that they do not know how to function in a middle-class society. More recently, on the other hand, the contrary is also asserted: Middle-class people are so "locked in" by their values and norms that they do not understand the different subculture of lower-class people. This issue finds its most intense expression between black people and white people; the long held belief on the part of many whites that blacks cannot acquire many necessary kinds of competence because of their inferior way of life finds its answer today in a growing insistence by blacks that the socialization of whites renders them incompetent to meet the needs of blacks and to serve as socializing agents for black children. These bitter problems are but the latest form of what early sociologist William Graham Sumner saw many years ago as a universal social characteristic, which he named *ethnocentrism:* "Each group thinks its own folkways the only right ones. . . . Ethnocentrism leads a people to exaggerate and intensify everything in their own folkways which is peculiar and which differentiates them from others."[8] As two more recent sociologists, Tamotsu Shibutani and Kian M. Kwan, have noted, ethnocentrism is one version of "trained incapacity"; it limits social competence.[9]

Although all cultures and subcultures necessarily generate some measure of ethnocentrism, some do so more than others. Isolation from other subcultures intensifies ethnocentrism, but so also do conflict and discrimination. Ethnocentrism is, in principle, modifiable, and many programs designed for its reduction are carried out by agencies concerned with human relations. Many social scientists go so far as to affirm that all socialization outcomes that limit social competence are modifiable by appropriate action programs.[10]

The importance of subcultures for socialization can be further appreciated by reference to concepts introduced earlier:

1. A person's *status* in society is partly determined by the subculture in which he or she participates.
2. A child's earliest *role models* are drawn from his or her own subculture, although by school age the child may already have encountered some role models from outside it.
3. Since a child's *self* is formed in large part by taking the role of others, and since the child's earliest significant

others tend to be from his or her own subculture, the child's self has an anchor in a particular subculture.

Subcultures are based on different types of social differentiation. In the remainder of this chapter, we shall consider three of particular importance—social class, ethnic group, and community of residence—and ask how each of these affects socialization. In Chapter 5 we shall consider the relationship between subcultures and the major agencies of socialization.

SOCIAL CLASS

Although social class is variously defined in social science literature, virtually all social scientists recognize the existence of socioeconomic strata in our society and acknowledge that different groups possess unequal amounts of wealth, influence, prestige, and "life chances." Such inequalities have consequences and ramifications that sociologists feel justified in interpreting as aspects of social class. Some North Americans play down or even deny the existence of social classes, because social classes involve rankings of categories of people and because of the belief that "every person is just as good as any other." But in practice even these people often make use of terms that differentially evaluate categories of people and their ways of life: terms such as "decent folks," "jet set," "red-necks," "silent majority," "lazy no-goods," "working people," "hard hats," and even "middle class" and "lower class."

Children can become aware of social class differences even at elementary school age if they have any opportunity to mingle with children of more than one social class. Thus, one investigator, in a study some years ago of a New England industrial town, reported that children between the fourth and sixth grades were able to distinguish such symbols of social class as evening dress and riding horseback clothed in a riding habit; and by the eighth grade, adult stereotypes of social class are quite generally known.[11] Another sociologist, studying children aged ten to twelve in "Jonesville," a city in the Midwest, found that children of the upper-middle class were generally judged by their classmates to be better looking and fairer playing than lower-class children, differences that were understandable only in terms of the social class positions of the children themselves.[12]

Social Class as a Way of Life

From the point of view of socialization, perhaps the most important aspect of social stratification is a group's "way of life" or subculture. There are many ways of life associated with social class, ranging from a very small "upper upper" class with its genealogy, mansions, servants, yachts, debutantes, and private school education down to the déclassé. For purposes of illustration and contrast, in this section we shall focus on socialization in two class groups—one, the so-called upper-middle class, the other generally designated the lower class.

Perhaps the readiest means of identifying a person's social class membership is by his or her occupation. The upper-middle class consists primarily of families whose breadwinners are relatively affluent (though not wealthy) professionals and business people. In the lower class the breadwinners are generally unskilled laborers who work irregularly. In these days, when unskilled labor is increasingly replaced by machines, it also includes men and women (and their families) who, having no skill, may be chronically unemployed. The lower class also includes families, often without a male in residence, whose income derives largely from public assistance. Thus, not the least important fact about the lower class is that it is poor, but the differences between it and the upper-middle class are not simply income and what it buys. Social classes are ways of life and therefore socialization environments for the children born into them. At the same time, as we have observed, the lines between particular subcultures are not always clearly drawn. This is particularly true with regard to values. There has been some controversy in recent years as to whether all social classes in a society are oriented to the same or different values. Considerable light on this controversy has been cast by Hyman Rodman, whose analysis of several research studies leads him to conclude that the lower class develops a "value stretch." As he puts it, "The lower class value stretch refers to the wider range of values and the lower degree of commitment to these values to be found within the lower class."[13] The implications of this will be discussed in this and the following chapters.

Upper-Middle-Class Subculture

Upper-middle-class men and, increasingly, upper-middle-class women, generally are greatly concerned with developing successful careers, whether as independent professionals or as salaried executives working in large organizations. This means that they are oriented to the future and look to expanding responsibilities, prestige, and income—at least until that time in life when they recognize that they have attained their maximum. One of the important distinguishing characteristics of middle-class as compared with lower-class occupations is that they require a greater degree of self-direction.[14] To carry on such an occupation with even a moderate amount of success requires a certain kind of self: a belief in one's ability to face and solve problems and to make judgments and decisions. Confidence that one's own actions make a difference in how things turn out is also required. Although there are uncertainties, anxieties, and disappointments in pursuing a career, and many people fall short of "making it" as they had hoped, numerous upper-middle-class lives are dominated by a concern with career and future. As they pursue these goals, upper-middle-class people are managing themselves and their situations.

The upper-middle-class woman is as likely as the man to think of herself as an effective, "doing" sort of person. She may or may not be employed, but in either case she manages a busy schedule of activities. Often she is involved in some kind of volunteer activity. The outspoken wife of one professional man compares herself with her husband in these terms: "We both handle people the same; we expect top work from employees. We have pretty high standards, but we're fair. It's all stated clearly, few words minced, and that's how it's going to be and we stay with it."[15] A woman with her own career told her husband, before they married: "I made the point—which he completely agreed with and obviously completely understood—that career was my way of life. And, that although I wanted a family also, I in no way considered this a matter of alternatives or substitutes, but a matter of both. And he completely agreed."[16]

The accomplishments of the upper-middle-class bread-winner generally provide an income that enables the family to live at a high level of material comfort. (In more and more such families, however, the standard of living depends upon two incomes—the husband's and the wife's.) The family residence is likely to be substantial, though not palatial, and it is well stocked with a wide range of consumer goods, some of which are likely to be rather costly. The dwelling usually is large enough for each child to have a separate room; when this is not the case, the family is likely to look forward to the time when its income will increase sufficiently for this standard to be attained. Privacy is a value, and it is felt that even children require privacy. Privacy in this form costs money, and the upper-middle-class family generally has enough money, sooner or later, to buy it.

The upper-middle-class way of life usually involves its members in a variety of institutions outside the family. The father's occupation, for example, may require him to be in contact with many organizations in addition to the one that employs him. If he is a businessman, he is involved in buying and selling relationships with people in other firms. If he is a professional, he is associated with hospitals or courts or universities or government agencies, where he meets other men with whom he collaborates or whom he helps, persuades, or teaches, as the case may be. He is, to use a somewhat quaint expression, "a man of affairs." (Sex roles have not yet changed sufficiently to allow us to speak of "a woman of affairs" in quite the same sense, but they have changed so greatly that mothers, too, are often involved in comparable organizational participation.)

In addition to occupational contacts with many organizations, the husband and wife are likely to have roles in numerous other formal organizations—associations of business or professional people (medical societies, law groups, chambers of commerce, and so on), church groups, country clubs or swimming clubs, and perhaps some civic betterment association. In addition to activities in these formal organizations, there is likely to be considerable entertaining at home, largely arranged by the wife, as well as such out-of-home entertainment as dining in good restaurants and attending the theater, concerts, and the like.

Children growing up in this class also begin early to have a diversified social participation, much of it sponsored and controlled by adults. They are likely to belong to one or more such organizations as the Boy Scouts, the Girl Scouts, athletic teams, church and synagogue groups, camera clubs, and community-center groups. The schools sponsor many extracurricular activities; in a study of an upper-middle-class suburb, one school principal reported that there were forty-two extracurricular organizations in his school.[17] In addition, children go away to summer camp and, during the school year, may take lessons in music, dancing, swimming, skiing, or tennis. It is part of the value system of this class, to quote one research report, that:

> Parents and adult leaders of children's associations expect the cooperation and gratitude of the child "for all that is being done for him." Such associations should, in adult eyes, satisfy all the child's recreational needs. Adult reaction to the child-centered, child-controlled associations which do develop outside the orbit of adult control is one of marked suspicion and some anger, the elders' direct response to a rejection of their well-meant efforts.[18]

Since the upper-middle class is increasingly concentrated in suburbs (although not all suburbs are upper-middle class or even middle class), children's social participation in these varied activities often involves their being driven from one location to another—not by an employed chauffeur but mostly by the mother, on weekends perhaps by the father, and sometimes by friends or neighbors through the medium of "car pools" which are formed by several parents whose children are engaged in similar activities. This is one device among many by which upper-middle-class parents guide and keep tabs on their children's way of life.

The upper-middle class is intently focused on its children's future and directs a great deal of effort to attempting to prepare children for it. At the same time, upper-middle-class people generally expect that their children's future will be quite different from their own current adulthood, although they do not know in what ways it will differ. Partly for this reason, self-direction receives great emphasis as a value in the upper-middle class. This emphasis derives not only from the anticipation of the future but also, as Melvin J. Kohn has shown, from the father's current position. Kohn analyzes the situation as follows: Values are products of life conditions. While many such conditions affect values, one that is particularly salient is the general structure of the man's work. Upper-middle-class occupations are distinguished from working-class occupations in that the former involve more self-direction and self-reliance, less close supervision, and—with certain exceptions—greater involvement with ideas than with things. The reverse is generally true for working-class occupations, although again there are exceptions.

Kohn finds that corresponding to this social class difference in occupations, is a difference in emphasis on values between these two classes. Middle-class people value both obedience and self-direction in their children but place greater emphasis on the latter. Working-class people, in contrast, place much greater emphasis on obedience and are less concerned with self-direction. This difference was found to hold not only in the United States but also in Turin, an industrial city in Italy, as well.[19] Related to this is a social class difference in disciplining children: Middle-class parents are more concerned with the intent of a child's acts, whereas working- and lower-class parents are more concerned with overt consequences of what children do. Middle-class parents are anxious that their children internalize standards; working-class parents are anxious that their children learn to behave respectably.[20] (Kohn's studies have dealt with the stable working class rather than with the lower class as defined above. We refer to his comparisons here because they help to clarify the value emphasis in the upper-middle class.)

Significant social class differences also exist in the use of language. As we pointed out in Chapter 3, language is one of the important ways—some sociologists believe the most important—in which social reality is organized. Insofar as social classes use language differently they are organizing their realities differently. Basil Bernstein suggests that one of the most significant relationships between social class and language is that in the upper-middle class language becomes the object of special attention and elaboration. The structure and syntax of middle-class speech are particularly complex and make possible a more subtle and complex grasp of reality than is the case in the lower class. Bernstein illustrates with a homely example, a middle-class mother saying to her child, "I'd rather you made less noise, dear." Middle-class children have learned to interpret "rather" and "less" as imperative cues for their response. Bernstein believes that lower-class children do not have available this kind of sentence structure and would have to translate the foregoing sentence into a form that they know from their own experience— "Shut up!"[21] Another study reports that middle-class mothers use many more words than do lower-class mothers in talking to their children, that more of the words are abstract, and that the sentences are longer and more complex.[22]

Bernstein's argument about language parallels Kohn's on values: both language styles and values arise as adaptations to class-based situations. Upper-middle-class values and language style both reflect the class's complex involvement in organizations and the requirements for self-reliance in making judgments about abstract matters.

The career and future orientation of the upper-middle class and the great emphasis on developing self-direction in its children have been interpreted to mean that the socialization of middle-class children, from infancy through college and graduate school, is characterized by their deferring basic gratifications in order to attain future goals. This deferred gratification pattern, as it was called, included such diverse aspects as the postponement of being employed and independent in order to attain a more elaborate education, saving money rather than spending it freely as the spirit moves, controlling aggressive impulses and staying out of fights, and avoiding sexual intercourse until one is married and "settled."[23] When the concept "deferred gratification pattern" was first introduced into the literature, few questioned its relevance.

Later efforts to gain fuller understanding of the working class and lower class, partly in order to understand what really differentiates them from the middle class, led to some challenge of the validity of the deferred gratification pattern. Thus, S. M. Miller and Frank Riessman asked:

> Is it really true today in the prosperous middle-class youth culture of the United States that most middle-class youth are deferring gratification when they go to college? More likely, many look upon it in anticipation and retrospect as coming closest in their total experiences to the realization of gratifications. Frequently, it seems that the working class is compared with an inner-directed, economically marginal middle class of yore than with an "acting-out," "other-directed," "affluent" middle class of today. The shifts in the middle class, murky as they are, make it especially difficult and dubious to use it as a yardstick for elucidating (and frequently evaluating) working class life.[24]

There was and is undoubtedly some justice in this challenge. To picture socialization of the middle-class child as being focused on austerity, asceticism, and self-restraint is to disregard the evidence that the American middle class allows more pleasure in the socialization of its children than was formerly true. However, it is doubtful that the earlier picture is now completely outdated. Miller and Riessman comment only on the college years, not on the childhood years of middle-class socialization. It seems likely that despite the greater indulgence of upper-middle-class children today as compared with the past, they nevertheless remain more closely supervised and more intensively guided toward adult roles than the children of the lower class or even the stable working class. In this same vein, though the college years may be gratifying, it remains nonetheless true that preparation for an upper-middle-class occupation requires sustained application and more or less rigorous self-discipline. Whether deferral of gratification is the most significant feature of this process may be questionable. But at the very least it would seem that the upper-middle-class child is more insistently reminded of the future and required to be more prudent in his or her actions. Although it is more than a quarter of a century since Allison Davis noted that the pressures on the upper-middle-class child generate an "adaptive" or "socialized anxiety," it is doubtful that Davis' observations have become altogether outdated by recent social changes.[25] Indeed, it seems evident that the *counterculture,* including the wide popularity of drug taking and the liberation of sexual expression among middle-class youth, is partly an effort to escape from the stringent pressures of upper-middle-class socialization (although these phenomena have other causes as well).

Lower-Class Subculture

The term *lower class* has two principal meanings. Its more neutral meaning denotes those in a society who have the least of the benefits a society distributes: income, influence, education, prestige, and the many additional benefits such as good housing and secure and possibly satisfying employment that follow from these. The term has additional connotations, particularly to many middle-class people: It is used to refer unfavorably to the way of life followed by people so situated. Thus, *lower class* implies ignorance; instability of employment and family life; "premature" initiation of heterosexual activity and subsequent promiscuity; "low standards" of personal grooming, housekeeping, and language usage—in short, a wide array of behavior that is unacceptable to middle-class people. These judgmental connotations make it difficult for middle-class people to consider lower-class life with detachment and therefore raise some questions about continued use of the label. We use the term of course in its first meaning.

Lower-class subculture is not strongly oriented toward the future—because lower-class people are intensively preoccupied with problems of survival in the present. Albert K. Cohen and Harold M. Hodges, in their study of lower-class life on the San Francisco Peninsula, identify four main aspects of the lower-class person's life situation.[26]

1. *Deprivation.* Lower-class people feel deprived. They have inadequate resources compared with their felt needs and levels of aspiration. Although it is possible to feel deprived at any level of life, lower-class people feel more chronically deprived of more things than do people at other class levels. These include not only income and what it can buy but also such valued goals as education, satisfying work, happy marriage, and enjoyment of life.

2. *Insecurity.* Lower-class life is especially unpredictable, entailing high vulnerability to sickness, injury, disability, death, and entanglements with the law. And when these misfortunes occur, there are fewer resources to deal with them. People have neither the funds nor the necessary skills, knowledge, and access to institutions that can help.

3. *Simplification of the experience world.* Lower-class people move in a more narrowly defined world, both geographically and socially, than do people of other classes. They have experienced a relatively limited range of objects and situations and have limited perspectives from which to define, classify, and evaluate their experiences.

4. *Powerlessness.* Lower-class adults have little "leverage" in society. Their relatively low level of skill makes them easily replaceable in employment; they have "the least access to and control over strategically important information." In general, they feel little ability to influence the course of their own lives. Not only have lower-class people experienced little previous success in shaping their own lives, they expect little in the future. Their pessimism is summarized by Cohen and Hodges:

"A body just can't take nothing for granted; you just have to live from day to day and hope the sun will shine tomorrow." No theme more consistently runs through the pattern of the LL's [lower-class person's] responses and distinguishes him from the others. In his view, nothing is certain; in all probability, however, things will turn out badly as they generally have in the past.[27]

Furthermore, lower-class people know that they are "at the bottom of the heap" and looked down upon by people more favorably situated in society. Thus, they face the problem of evolving a way of life that will, insofar as possible, reduce insecurity and serve as a defense against moral criticism. One way in which this is done is to maintain a network of relationships with people situated similarly to themselves, primarily neighbors and kin. In this way they are able to call upon others in time of need. Another aspect of this way of life is to place heavy reliance on fate, chance, or luck; belief in such factors as causes of their destiny helps to relieve the sense of failure. Yet these and other adaptations to a harsh reality do not always eliminate despair and a sense of ineffectiveness. Eleanor Pavenstedt describes what she saw in lower-class homes that she studied:

> The outstanding characteristic ... was that activities were impulse-determined; consistency was totally absent. The mother might stay in bed until noon while the children were kept in bed as well or ran around unsupervised. Another time she might decide to get them up and give them breakfast at 6, have them washed and dressed and the apartment picked up by 8:30. Or the children might get their breakfast from the neighbors ... These mothers always dressed their children.... None of the children owned anything; a recent gift might be taken away by another sibling without anyone's intervening. The parents often failed to discriminate between the children: a parent, incensed by the behavior of one child, was seen dealing a blow to another child who was close by. Communications by words hardly existed....[28]

This quotation emphasizes the disorganization of lower-class home life. Yet closer reading indicates some effort, even if only episodic, to live up to norms that are shared by the wider society—for example, washing and dressing the children, picking up the apartment. Inconsistency of behavior in the lower class, including inconsistency in socialization of its children, has been one of its most readily recognizable aspects since sociologists began studying differences in the ways of life of the different social classes. More recent observations and analyses have directed our attention to the fact that the lower-class subculture includes values and norms that are central to middle-class culture but which often cannot be sustained under the conditions of lower-class life. The lower-class person's actions oscillate between conformity to values and to countervailing circumstances.

Moreover, some of the characteristics that were often thought to be distinctive of lower-class culture are now more fully understood not simply as "their way" but as adaptations to deprivation. Thus, Cohen and Hodges, as have others, note that "toughness" is an important quality in lower-class life. This includes a "dog-eat-dog" ideology; pride in the ability to "take it"; and a general posture of assertiveness, a "don't-push-me-around" touchiness. But while toughness sometimes manifests itself as belligerence, other observers have emphasized another aspect, the capacity to endure hardship. One mother explains why she kept her children home from school:

> There was no food in the house and I didn't want them to have to go to school hungry and then come home hungry too. I felt that if I kept them home with me, at least when they cried and asked for a piece of bread, I would be with them to put my arms around them.[29]

The Lower-Middle Class and the Working Class

We have discussed upper-middle-class and lower-class subcultures because, on the one hand, they are two quite contrasting socialization environments within the same society, yet, on the other hand, there are some important similarities between them. Between the upper-middle and the lower classes in the urban world are other strata, conveniently designated "working class" and "lower-middle class." The former includes skilled workers in manufacturing, trades, and service occupations (such as barbers), who are generally employed steadily and whose way of life is seen as stable both by themselves and by others. Very often they belong to labor unions and thus have some sense of being able to influence decisions that affect their own lives. The lower-middle class includes many kinds of white-collar workers—owners of small neighborhood stores, supervisory employees in large organizations, many salesmen. Working-class people today generally have graduated from high school; lower-middle-class people have often had some college and many have graduated. The reader interested in learning more about these subcultures is referred to the appropriate literature.[30]

COMMUNITY OF RESIDENCE

Our discussion of social class subcultures has been based on work carried out primarily in metropolitan areas and in small towns. We were not concerned with community of residence as a basis for differentiating subcultures, although the residential community is increasingly linked to social class. Thus, upper-middle-class people increasingly live in suburbs (although, to repeat, not all suburbs are upper-middle class). Lower-class people live in slums in the "inner city" areas of large cities and in run-down areas in small towns. To an important extent, then, analyzing a subculture from the standpoint of social class and from the standpoint of community of residence are simply two different approaches to the same task. We believe that the social class approach contributes fuller understanding (although not all sociologists would agree). Nevertheless, a community's history, geography, and economy do contribute to subcultural variation and, therefore, to socialization, particularly if the community is relatively isolated. Let us present a brief sketch of one subculture in a relatively isolated area.

The Subculture of a Depressed Area

We shall describe some aspects of the subculture of the Cumberland Plateau, a mountainous area consisting of nineteen counties in eastern Kentucky, as it has been portrayed by Harry M. Caudill.[31]

The Cumberland Plateau is an area of steep ridges and narrow, winding valleys, part of the Appalachian Mountains. It is inhabited by about half a million people, most of whom are descendants of English, Welsh, Irish, and Scottish pioneers who first settled the area long before the Declaration of Independence. The people who live in the area today are part of that backwoods group derogatorily referred to in other parts of the country as "hillbillies."

Families and neighbors were divided by the Civil War. Cousins, brothers, and even fathers and sons often took opposing sides. When the occupants of a mountain cabin learned that a relative had died in the war, they took revenge against the nearest available family whose members were sympathetic to the opposite side. A tradition of hatred and violence was established, and it developed into the ferocious Kentucky mountain feuds that lasted unchecked until 1915. "Thus the mountaineer came to inherit the hatreds of his father along with his name.... The mountaineers' hatreds became so many-layered, so deeply ingrained and so tenaciously remembered that they were subconscious, and as such they have, to a remarkable degree, been transmitted to his present-day descendants."[32] The transmission of hatreds of ancient origin is one illustration of the way in which historic events can shape the socialization process.

Between 1875 and 1910 the mountaineers lost most of their land to big-city entrepreneurs from the North and East. Being isolated from the rest of the country, they were unaware of the growing industrialization and consequently of the value of the timber and coal on their lands. Also, being illiterate and unsophisticated, many had not adequately registered and secured title to the land, some of which had been given as a veterans' benefit at the close of the Revolutionary

War. Much of the land slipped from their hands either through acceptance of nominal payment or through court action.

Absentee-owned coal companies came to dominate the economy; the mountaineers were recruited to work in the newly developing mines. Since there were no towns in the region—the largest town was often the county seat with no more than 150 people—the companies built camps to house the miners. In many of them the housing was ramshackle, built of unseasoned lumber, so that in a few years the houses began to sag and sway. Miners were required to live in these company-owned houses, as a condition of employment, and to pay rent to their employer. Although the coal companies also built school buildings, the schools were inadequately financed because the companies were powerful enough to keep their taxes low. Since there was not enough money to pay qualified teachers, most left the area and were replaced by children of mountaineers; their training went no further than a semester or two at a state teachers college.

During the early years of the coal towns, some efforts were made by both companies and residents to keep them clean. This proved to be a losing battle as coal dust seeped into everything. The polluted atmosphere peeled paint from the walls and turned clothing yellowish gray. Despite best efforts, the communities turned "coal-camp gray." Caudill describes the effects on the women:

> Many women fought the dirt-and-grime battle through the best years of their lives and surrendered to it only in old age, long after the Big Boom and the Great Depression were history.... Realizing that the contest could not be won, they slowly capitulated to the unremitting clouds and allowed their homes to lose the sparkle and shine which had characterized the new towns. The spick-and-span gave way to the dull and disordered, and the women sat down on the front-porch swings and in chairs before the fireplaces and allowed the victorious enemy to run riot through the towns. There appeared the first symptoms of the vacuity, resignation and passivity which so marks the camp dwellers today, traits which could only deepen as the years brought new defeats and new tragedies.[33]

The boom period in coal mining ended in the late 1920s, and the economy of the area never really recovered, although there was a brief upsurge after World War II. One important factor was that coal mining became mechanized, so there were few jobs for men who knew no other skill but mining. By the end of 1957 more than half the people in some counties were regularly existing upon food supplied by government relief. Efforts of many men to find jobs in cities such as Cincinnati, Detroit, or Chicago were fruitless. Many younger people did succeed in leaving the area for jobs elsewhere, thus leaving the area depleted of energy and ability. The great unemployment and "the flight from the plateau of its hardier people" resulted, Caudill states, in "the growth of 'welfarism' on a scale unequaled elsewhere in North America and scarcely surpassed anywhere in the world."

One of the central features, if not indeed the dominant one, of this subculture at the present time is a sense of demoralization. Men over forty can find employment neither in the area nor elsewhere. Many of the homes are rotting and almost beyond repair. The area has one of the highest birth rates in the United States, and this, together with the extensive unemployment, leads to widespread, and often devious, efforts to become eligible for one or another program of public assistance. Children who manage to graduate from high school usually leave the area; by a year after graduation, no more than 4 or 5 percent of the graduates remain in their home counties. Some of the important consequences of this subculture for socialization are revealed in an interview with a fifty-six-year-old jobless miner:

> I hain't got no education much and jist barely can write my name. After I lost my job in 1950 I went all over the country a-lookin' fer work. I finally found a job in a factory in Ohio a-puttin' televisions inside wooden crates. Well I worked for three years and managed to make enough money to keep my young-uns in school. Then they put in a machine that could crate them televisions a whole lot better than us men could and in a lot less time. Hit jist stapled them up in big cardboard-boxes. I got laid off again and I jist ain't never been able to find nothing else to do.

But I kept my young'uns in school anyway. I come back home here to the mountains and raised me a big garden ever' year and worked at anything I could find to do. I sold my old car fer seventy-five dollars and I sold all the land my daddy left me and spent the money on my children. They didn't have much to eat or wear, but they at least didn't miss no school. Well, finally last spring my oldest boy finished up high school and got his diploma. I managed to get twenty-five dollars together and give it to him and he went off to git him a job. He had good grades in school and I figured he'd get him a job easy. He went out to California where he's got some kinfolks and went to a factory where they was hirin' men. The sign said all the work hands had to be under thirty-five years of age and be high-school graduates. Well, this company wouldn't recognize his diploma because it was from a Kentucky school. They said a high-school diploma from Kentucky, Arkansas, and Mississippi just showed a man had done about the same as ten years in school in any other state. But they agreed to give the boy a test to see how much he knowed and he failed it flatter than a flitter. They turned him down and he got a job workin' in a laundry. He jist barely makes enough money to pay his way but hit's better than settin' around back here.

I reckon they jist ain't no future fer people like us. Me and my wife ain't got nothin' and don't know nothin' hardly. We've spent everything we've got to try to learn our young-'uns something so they would have a better chance in the world, and now they don't know nothin' either![34]

This man's case is not atypical in the area. The interview suggests that the values in this subculture—at least with respect to preparing children for adult roles—are not very different from those of upper-middle-class subculture, although there are differences in many norms. The interview also indicates some of the ways in which even a relatively isolated subsociety is part of the larger society. And it brings out significant effects of economic conditions on a subculture and socialization into it. Stories of the relative success of some who have moved away and the view of the world offered by television provide some role models that are more diverse than those present locally and thus stimulate aspirations; but the resources actually operative in the subculture are insufficient to develop in the young more than a minimal competence to occupy adult roles in an industrial society. As Richard A. Ball points out in his analysis of Appalachian subculture, the young learn to expect defeat, and much of the culture can be understood as consisting of efforts to seek relief from insoluble problems.[35]

The effects of isolation on the socialization process are vividly brought out in a report from another part of Appalachia:

> Mountain people are indeed reared in a society of the "known," a rural environment providing little stimulation or opportunity, and thus acquire neither the attitude of mind nor the few skills needed for meeting new and different situations. There are few broadening experiences available to them—few simple experiences like sitting with people you don't know on a bus, asking for change from a busdriver, doing business with strangers in stores or supermarkets, meeting and playing with strange children in the park. . . . Because mountain children are surrounded by a culture that contains only what is known, they are often extremely reluctant and afraid to attempt any unfamiliar experience.
>
> For example, a group of men from our area were being housed in a YMCA in a city where the church was seeking to relocate them. One night a member of the group stopped in the lobby for a candy bar while the others went on up to their rooms. Following along afterwards, he entered the automatic elevator, which had always been operated by someone else in the group. Finding himself alone with the doors closed, he panicked. He yelled and screamed and beat on the sides of the elevator until someone on the outside punched the button, opening the doors for him. He was so shaken by this experience that the next day he boarded a bus for home. . . . Here was a young man in his early thirties who was so overwhelmed in this new situation that he could not handle his fear.[36]

Specialized Communities

Other communities also have distinctive characteristics that may cut through class, ethnic, and other subcultural divisions. Summer resorts in which the local residents distinguish between themselves and tourists (who may be viewed as "fair game") represent one example; Indian reservations in which the distinction between the resident Indian and the outside white underlies all interaction are another; relatively isolated mining towns in Canada in which residents look to the company or the government to serve their needs are still another.[37] The child in such communities grows up in a world of distinctions and social definitions that differ from those in other types of communities.

In recent years, another type of community setting—the *commune*—has received considerable attention. The term is used broadly to refer to a group of adults, not related by kinship, who have made a primary commitment to their group and who organize themselves into a "total institution," separate from conventional society. The members generally share their resources, their household, and their work. Communes vary considerably in several respects. For example, they may be rural or urban; economically, they may seek to be self-sufficient, specialize in one type of product, or live off the largesse of others; they may withdraw from the surrounding society or they may affirm a "mission" that requires interaction with others; they may be religious or secular, politically conservative or radical, authoritarian or anarchic. The variations are many.

The vast majority of communes are short-lived. For one reason or another, or more likely a combination, they have often collapsed within a few months of their establishment. Disruptive personality clashes, the lack of capital or skills to carry out their proposed projects, the complexity of the organizational problems all may play a part. Perhaps, above all, the commitment to the group or its ideology just wears thin.[38]

Communes have not ordinarily been established with the considerations of children in mind. Broad ideologies and utopias loomed large in earlier days. In more recent years, communes have represented an alternate life style in which the participants seek to "realize" themselves and obtain a more satisfying life. In those communes in which there are children, socialization is necessarily very different from that in conventional society. In the Israeli kibbutz—which besides being long-lasting is also distinctive in that it is part of a larger political system to which it makes a significant contribution—the kibbutz itself assumes responsibility for the physical and economic well-being and training of the child. Although there has recently been some change, the usual pattern is that, from birth, children sleep, eat, and later study in "children's houses," overseen by nurses, teachers, and other caretakers. But mothers and fathers still play an important role; they are recognized as parents and give their children nurture and affection, and the emotional bonds that develop are often quite strong. Psychoanalyst Bruno Bettelheim questions the depth of the personal relationships that can develop among children brought up in this type of arrangement, but others point to their independence and autonomy and to the stability of the community that has persisted through several generations.[39]

America's more informal "hippie" communes, which grew up in the 1960s and 1970s, present a very different picture. In theory, the child belongs to the commune rather than to the mother or the mother and father. The child has a variety of relationships with adults, and all the older members of the commune may serve as role models. Sex roles that are experienced are different from those in traditional families, since the mother and father roles are redefined with an emphasis on the sharing of child-care tasks. In a preliminary report of their research on the child-rearing practices of a number of such communes in California, Bennett Berger and his colleagues cite the pervasive ideology that children are "persons," equal in status to everyone else in the commune, but then note that in reality, age and status cannot help but make a difference.

One problem, they suggest, derives from a disparity between the ideology and the long-run obligations of parenthood. They quote one young mother, harried with caring for her two-year-old child: "What I wanted was a *baby;* but a *kid,* that's something else." Having babies was viewed as good, it was natural, organic, earthy, and beautiful, besides representing the potential of the human being free from all the corrupting influences of the repressive institutions in the larger society. The ideology provided few supports for the arduous tasks of child rearing, particularly in those situations in which interaction with the child was not immediately gratifying to adults.[40]

In these communes, as children get older they become less the responsibility of the mother and more the responsibility of the commune as a whole. Berger and his colleagues write:

> Infants and "knee babies" are almost universally in the charge of their mothers, who have primary responsibility for their care. . . .
>
> Children aged two to four or slightly older frequently "belong to the commune" in a stronger sense than infants and knee babies do because they are less dependent upon continuous supervision, although even with children of this age the conventional pattern of sharing their care is largely limited to the group of mothers-with-children. This is not to say that young children do not get a lot of fathering—they do; fathers hold the children often, feed them, cuddle them, and may be attentive in other respects. But this depends upon the personal predispositions of the men involved; there are not strong *norms* apparent which *require* the attentiveness of fathers.
>
> But for children older than 4 or 5, the responsibilities of either parents or the other adult communards may be much attenuated. All children are viewed as intrinsically worthy of love and respect *but not necessarily of attention.* As they grow out of primitive physical dependence upon the care of adults, they are treated and tend to behave as just another member of the extended family—including being offered (and taking) an occasional hit on a joint of marijuana as it is passed around the family circle.[41]

From the point of view of theory and research, communes serve as valuable experiments that may help us to understand better the complex processes of child rearing and socialization. We may wonder, for example, how commune-reared children will fare when they become adults in a society that is likely to remain highly individualistic and competitive. Will these children, when adult, continue a communal way of life? To take another point, adults in the communes Berger and his colleagues are studying appear to use a different notion of age-grading than does modern conventional society. In fact, it seems remarkably similar to the medieval conception that we have quoted from Ariès. In both, children are not a special focus of adult concern, and they mingle more freely with adults than is true in contemporary conventional society. Will this result in an easier, less conflicted socialization? It is too early to know, but the later outcomes of communal socialization will be awaited with great interest.

ETHNIC GROUPS

An ethnic group, in contemporary usage, is a distinctive minority segment of society. The members of such a group have *a shared identity* based on (1) *a common ancestry* and (2) *a common culture.* Each of these terms condenses several elements, which should be identified.

A *shared identity* can be based on the members' own beliefs and feelings, or on the beliefs and feelings of nonmembers who attribute such an identity to others, or on the beliefs and feelings of both members and nonmembers. Most ethnic groups include some people who have minimized or are in the process of minimizing their identity with the group. Nevertheless, nonmembers as well as members may still consider them part of the group, and this attributed identity may continue to have some impact on the socialization of the children. But the core of an ethnic group is usually made up of members who choose to identify themselves as members.

The concept of a *common ancestry,* although widespread in popular usage, is more complex than it seems. It seems to imply a common biological background, and there is partial truth to this. But few people, if any, can trace their biological ancestry more than seven or eight generations at most, at which point we lose track of who contributed to our genetic inheritance. People may say, "I'm mostly Irish, with a little

English and German mixed in," by which they mean that they know of some specific English and German contributors to their biological inheritance, know of many more Irish contributors, and assume that the ancestors far back beyond their knowledge were mostly Irish, in conformity with the recent majority they know of. The point here is that the notion of a common ancestry shared by members of an ethnic group rests on (a) their shared belief concerning their biological inheritance combined with (b) a sense of the group's having inhabited a given geographical area and, therefore, (c) their sharing in a distinctive group history.

A *common culture* here means a culture that is distinctive to the minority group in the midst of a dominant culture. Ethnic-group cultures usually involve one or more of the following cultural elements: (a) a language that is different from the dominant language in the society; (b) a religion; (c) a shared awareness of a historical background that is preserved in stories, legends, ceremonies, songs, costumes, holidays; (d) some values and norms that are distinguishable from those of the dominant majority.

These diverse components of what has come to be called "ethnicity" combine in different ways to result in different kinds of ethnic groups. Nationality groups, such as Italian, Polish, and Lithuanian, are distinguished by their origin in and ties to a particular political unit, a country of origin. There is in such nationality groups a sense of a common biological inheritance, but this is usually less prominent than the sense of coming from a politically designated geographic place where people spoke their own language and participated in a culture identified with that place. In contrast, a sense of biological distinctiveness is more prominent in what are thought of as racial minorities, such as blacks, Indians, and Inuit (Eskimo).[42] Other groups, such as Hutterites and Mennonites, have a shared identity based prominently on their distinctive religions, which serve them as bases for distinctive ways of life. Jews have had a shared identity based on a distinctive religion—in this respect they are like the religious minorities—but also based on a shared awareness of a distinctive historical background and language—in this respect they are like the nationality groups.

Except for the Indians and Inuit, who were already here, and the blacks, who first came as slaves, the population of North America derives from immigrants of many countries. First came the original colonizers, primarily from England, France, Spain, and Holland; then immigrants from northern and western Europe and from China; then immigrants from southern and eastern Europe. In the United States, free and open immigration was halted by legislation in the early 1920s, when it was replaced by a restrictive quota system based on national origins; some nationalities were preferred over others. In 1968 the national quota system was replaced by one giving priority to preferred occupational skills and to kinship ties. Recently, relatively more immigrants have come from Latin America, Asia, Africa, and the West Indies. In Canada, immigration has been relatively high for many years, with over 3 million persons—many from Italy, Portugal, Greece, India, Pakistan, and the West Indies—having come between 1946 and 1971.

Of course the largest ethnic group in the United States is not an immigrant group at all; blacks, who number some 25 million, have been in the country almost as long as whites. (In 1790, when the first census was taken, blacks made up 19.3 percent of the population.)[43] For generations, whites have regarded blacks as a distinctive minority group by virtue of their common African ancestry; increasingly, in recent years, blacks have also come to so regard themselves, accepting the definition the larger society has thrust upon them. Accompanying the new self-definition has come a change in feeling from one of derogation to one of racial consciousness and pride: "Black is Beautiful." The very same redefinition that focuses on an assumed common ancestry and on similarities rather than differences among individuals and subgroups has also been occurring among North American Indians who, generations past, saw themselves only as Iroquois, Creek, Dakota, Cree, Hopi, Crow, Ojibway, Arapaho, or whatever other particular tribal group they stemmed from. To indicate that they were the original inhabitants of the land, many Indians have also come to adopt the term "Native Americans."

From the perspective of socialization, the wide variation among ethnic groups and the rapidly changing social context make for a complex, confusing, and uncertain picture. The fourth- and fifth-generation children of Scandinavian and German immigrants may now see themselves only as American, hardly, if at all, aware of their ethnic origins. The third- and fourth-generation children of immigrants from southern and eastern Europe are more likely to be aware of their ethnic origins and, as we shall see, may or may not identify strongly with their ethnic groups. The children of more recent migrants from Mexico, Puerto Rico, Cuba, Vietnam, Hong Kong, and elsewhere cannot help but experience some dual-culture problems, akin in many respects to those experienced by earlier immigrant children.[44] Still another dimension is introduced for such groups as blacks, native Americans, and some Hispanics, who are part of active ethnic social and political movements fighting for increased recognition of their rights. It would be far too complex to discuss each generation or each type of ethnic group separately. Rather, through the analysis of the two key concepts of *identity* and *culture,* we shall seek to clarify some of the basic problems of ethnic socialization for the members of any ethnic group.

Identity

The ethnic identity of children, we have noted, derives from the "racial," religious, or national collectivity of which their parents are members. Children come to identify themselves as Hungarian, Jewish, Irish, Puerto Rican, Italian, or whatever. From the perspective of the social structure, these are positions or statuses; from the point of view of the individual, they are identities. They are self-designations that define an individual's position linking one to and setting one apart from others. Children can learn their ethnic statuses before school age. Compared with other children, says one reviewer, minority group children "show earlier and greater differentiation of their own group as well as more personal involvement in the group identification."[45] Studies among black and white children show that by the age of five, racial attitudes may already be quite complex. Using a doll-choice game technique, Judith Porter carried out an intensive study of 359 black and white children, ages three to five, attending nursery schools and kindergartens in the greater Boston area. She concludes:

> By five years of age, children of both races have clear knowledge of racial differences and their racial attitudes are already rather sophisticated; white children may realize that blatant and overt expressions of prejudice are somehow unacceptable, and the black child may be developing complex feelings toward both his own and the opposite race. But even at age four, children have internalized the affective connotations of color and begin to generalize these meanings to people. Although the three-year-old white child does not, on the whole, invest color with social meaning, the black child of this age does perceive vaguely that color differences are important and may be personally relevant.[46]

The ethnic self-definition may, depending on the particular context, encompass a broad or narrow range and may or may not correspond with the definitions of others. When do Chicanos in San Antonio consider themselves Mexican, Texan, or Mexican-American? Under what circumstances do Jews define themselves by the subidentity Orthodox, Conservative, or Reform; and when as American Jews, or just Jews, without national identification? When are Iroquois in upper New York State Indians, when American Indians, and when Iroquois of the same tribe as the Iroquois of Canada? When are Serbs, "Czechs," and Bulgarians "Slavs;" when are they not?[47] Identity is a concept that allows considerable flexibility; it varies among members of an ethnic group, it expands and contracts, it changes over time, it looms large or small depending on the particular context and possibly on the advantage to be gained from manipulating the ethnic label.[48] Children, in the course of growing up, learn their ethnic identities and subidentities and the uses of each.

A second major dimension of identity is affective. To know and recognize one's ethnicity is cognitive; to feel its sentiments and emotions is affective. The two, of course, are closely linked; yet the distinction between them is useful. Some ethnic-group activities are clearly cognitive. Children may be taught the language, history, and culture of their group and develop an information base that enables them to delineate those who do and do not share their common ancestry. Other activities are clearly affective, focusing on rituals, group singing or dancing, ceremonies, and other types of group participation that serve to develop a feeling of belonging and an emotional attachment to those one recognizes as sharing a common ancestry.

Closely associated with the affective identification with one's group is what Gordon Allport has called ego-extension, that identification with any object, persons, causes, and collectivities that are thought of as "mine."[49] Psychologically, the group and its symbols become part of one's self. In the same way that one's school, local football team, new bicycle, or home town may be an extension of one's self and arouse appropriate feelings, so too may one's ethnic group. The process is well known. The prominent activities of an ethnic-group member (for example, in hockey, Peter Mahavolich, of Croatian origin, or in tennis, Arthur Ashe, a black) are followed with particular attention by their respective ethnic-group members, who may experience their exploits with special excitement and gratification. Attacks on ethnic-group members may be considered personal insults. For example, the smearing of "Jew" on the poster of a Jewish candidate for political office may anger other Jews. Negative stereotypes, too, such as the identification of the Italian with the Mafia or the Irish with excessive drink may rouse a sense of outrage.

Ego-extension, in the process of socialization, can become even more than an emotional projection of one's self onto an ethnically associated symbol. It can lead to a particular way of viewing the world, suggesting what is important and how particular phenomena should be viewed. Blacks, for example, were for a long time aware of their inferior educational institutions, which they considered an important problem to be tackled. When considering lines of action, the leaders of the black community often stressed educational disparity more than other factors. In contrast, when the Jews, with their concern for ethnic survival, consider a strategy, they give more weight to the position of Israel in the Middle East. Thus the relevance and significance of issues depend on the orientation and concerns of the particular ethnic group. Children of different ethnic groups in this sense live in different worlds.

Children learn the symbols that tend to set their ethnic groups apart and that permit a differentiation between the outsider and the insider. One prominent symbol for many ethnic groups in the United States and Canada is language. It is also a relatively easily identifiable ethnic indicator. Names, pronunciations, accents, distinct vocabularies, and twists of the language may all at times, for example, serve to identify and set the Spanish-speaking apart from the English-speaking. A Mexican-born social scientist, in an autobiographical account, has described the socio-linguistic problems he had when his family migrated to Sacramento, California:

> The Americanization of Mexican me was no smooth matter. I had to fight one lout who made fun of my travels on the *diligencia,* and my barbaric translation of the word into "diligence." He doubled up with laughter over the word until I straightened him out with a kick. In class, I made points explaining that in Mexico roosters said "qui-qui-ri-qui" and not "cock-a-doodle-doo," but after school I had to put up with the taunts of a big Yugoslav who said Mexican roosters were crazy.[50]

On a broader socio-political level, language in Canada has become a symbol of the struggle of French Canadians to survive as an independent ethnic group. To the child who lives amid the struggle, the issue is more than simply the wider use of French; the French language becomes a symbol of a movement of increasing ethnic identity and solidarity.

Numerous other aspects of life may also become symbols of ethnic-group identification. Religion may loom important, for example, for the Greek Orthodox, the German Mennonites, or the Ukrainian Catholics; so too may dietary practices, special clothing, national folk traditions and ceremonies, or voluntary associations such as the Polish Boy Scouts.

For children, ethnic identity, with the group boundaries that are implied, has both functional and dysfunctional aspects. Perhaps the most obvious function of ethnic-group identification for children is that it may offer comfort and security in a mass society characterized by impersonality, and thus counteract influences toward a feeling of anomie. Ordinarily, within their own group, children will experience less social distance and will feel at greater ease. They may communicate more easily with insiders and enjoy participation in their activities and their causes.

Such group identification and the accompanying participation may also be a protection against the dangers of what has been termed self-hatred.[51] In a heterogeneous society in which ethnic groups are ranked on a scale of power, privilege, and prestige, members of the lower-ranked ethnic groups often come to adopt the perspective of the higher-level groups. Viewing themselves from the higher position, they rank their own ethnic group low and look down upon and perhaps even despise that which they themselves represent or are assumed to represent. Solidarity with an ethnic group can reinforce one's positive feeling of self worth and reduce the impact of the outsiders' negative definition.

This analysis was applied originally to Jews facing intense hatred during the 1930s and 1940s when Nazism stirred and amplified anti-Semitism in Germany. More recently the same argument has been made about blacks by psychiatrists who speak of the positive psychological value of social action and black consciousness.[52] That the solidarity-seeking social movement among blacks has had a positive effect is suggested in a recent study by Morris Rosenberg and Roberta G. Simmons in Baltimore, who found that black children, aged eight to eleven, ranked blacks higher than other racial-religious groups on the social scale. The authors suggest that children learn the valuation society places on ethnic groups, but pull their own group out of order, thus protecting their own feelings of self-esteem. By the time the black children are fifteen, however, they recognize that most Americans do not rank their group very high.[53]

For the children, ethnic identity may also have its dysfunctions, depending on one's values and goals. It may lead to a turning inward within the group. The child may live in an ethnically homogeneous neighborhood, attend a private ethnic or religious school, join ethnically exclusive clubs, and consume ethnic mass media, thus restricting his or her range of knowledge, contacts, and experience. The result may be a relatively comfortable and secure existence, but lead to a rejection of certain other opportunities and a limited development of latent potentialities. It may, for example, impede children from taking the psychological risk of venturing into new occupational spheres where they might develop untapped possibilities and conceivably achieve great personal success. This assumes, of course, that the ethnic child has a choice. It may well be, segregation and ethnic solidarity being what they are, that the child will have little choice. His or her very locale may place limitations that the child cannot possibly transcend.

Marginality refers to a situation in which a person has strong links to two or more divergent socio-cultural groups, but does not identify fully with either; he or she remains on the margins of both. In the context of majority-minority relationships, the child of the ethnic minority group has two statuses, an ethnic one and a status as a citizen or prospective citizen in the larger society (United States or Canada), which identifies the child as a prospective American or Canadian. As a person of Greek, Japanese, or any other background, the child may be proud of his or her national heritage and religion; as an American or Canadian, the child may be aware of the family's foreign-sounding name and his or her parents' strong accent. The child lives on the margins of two cultures, has loyalties to both, but does not fully and exclusively identify with either. As Shibutani and Kwan observe:

Many of the problems confronting such individuals arise from their having to perform for two different and incongruous reference groups. Since contradictory demands are made upon them by the two audiences, they experience inner conflicts. When a man lives in two social worlds, each of which is a moral order, he cannot live up to all of his obligations. Where standards are inconsistent, he will be wrong in the eyes of one of the groups no matter what he does. He may be plagued by a sense of guilt even when he has done his very best. Some persons sometimes have difficulty developing a consistent self-conception. As Cooley pointed out, a man comes to conceive of himself as a particular kind of human being in response to the manner in which others treat him. But what happens to a man who looks simultaneously into two mirrors and sees sharply different images of himself?[54]

Developing a consistent self-conception or identity is, as we noted earlier, a task for every child, but it is accentuated for the child who is marginal to two cultures. The comment of a Mexican-American girl, made more than a generation ago, is as applicable for some immigrant families today as it was then:

> My mother and dad got too many old-fashioned ideas. She's from another country. I'm from America, and I'm not like her. With Mexican girls they want you to sit like *moscas muertas,* dead flies, like that. If you tell them what the teachers say, they say the teachers don't know.... I remember when me and my sister told my mother we wanted to dress neat and American they beat us and said no.[55]

In such cases, it is generally the immigrant parents, unable to draw on the broader culture and social system to support their position, who make the major adaptation. In the terms of Erikson, in the quotation at the conclusion of Chapter 3, the children are not "confirming" their parents; the life that the parents hold out as correct does not represent a "vital promise" in the new environment, as the children see it. What is happening is that the children are changing their *reference groups,* those groups by whose standard one judges one's own behavior.[56] The parents and their ethnic group are no longer regarded as suitable reference points. The children increasingly judge themselves by the standards of their American age-mates or peers, because, of course, they are being judged by them on the street and in school.

Such ethnic marginality may be so easily handled by some individuals that it is hardly noticeable; on the other hand, it may involve a complex set of thoughts and feelings in which almost every ethnically associated situation becomes a dilemma of uncertainty and anxiety. On the positive side, marginal children have access to alternate ways of life and the opportunity thereby to enlarge their range of experience. Marginality may thus bring special insights into the problems of several groups, including those who are deeply committed to the preservation of their distinctive ethnic culture and those who feel caught in ethnic pressures and counter-pressures.

Culture

For any ethnic group the distinctive culture that makes up the content of socialization is not easily defined. For one thing, the culture varies among members within an ethnic group according to such factors as socio-economic status, age, occupation, and region of origin. Not all Poles or Mexicans, for example, uphold the same values or adopt the same life styles. Nor is any culture ever static; there are always drifts, trends, and counterbalancing forces, with inevitable differences between those in the vanguard and those in the rear guard of particular changes.

An ethnic culture, too, is likely to take on the features of its immediate geographic setting. Hylan Lewis describes the array of specialized institutions that make up the urban black ghetto to which many thousands of rural blacks migrated in recent decades:

> Carry-out shops, laundromats, and record shops have recently come to the ghetto in numbers. They join taverns, pool halls, liquor stores, corner groceries, rooming houses, second hand

stores, credit houses, pawn shops, industrial insurance companies, and store front churches as part of a distinctive complex of urban institutions that have undergone changes in adapting to the effective wants, limited choices, and mixed tastes of inner-city residents.[57]

And linguist Walt Wolfram writes of the Puerto Ricans:

> it seems safe to generalize that Puerto Ricans in Harlem and other centers of concentration in the city use both English and Spanish. . . . A Spanish domain is most completely approximated in the home, particularly (1) if the parents speak little English or are fairly new arrivals in the city, or (2) if there is frequent contact with new arrivals from the island. Children of preschool age apparently learn English from their siblings and companions on the street rather than from their parents, and many youngsters who are fluent in English speak Spanish to their parents and other relatives. In the neighborhood both English and Spanish are used, depending on the age and the Puerto Rican orientation of the speaker.[58]

Wolfram then goes on to discuss the English of Puerto Rican children, which varies depending on whether they have extensive or restricted contact with blacks.

Further, as we have observed, children do not passively accept all aspects of an ethnic culture. To a great degree they build their own reality, and the ambivalence and conflict that are part of the process of socialization may well include ethnic dimensions. As one aspect of a more general resistance to authority, children, perhaps with the support of peers and mass-media models, may reinterpret or reject the ways and expectations of their ethnic socializers, possibly perceiving them as cowardly, parochial, docile, or just old fashioned. Sometimes a child stumbles innocently into a conflict with authority, as happened to this Italian-American:

> Immigrants used "American" as a word of reproach to their children. For example, take another incident from my childhood: Every Wednesday afternoon, I left P. S. [Public School] 142 early and went to the local parish church for religious instruction under New York State's Released Time Program. Once I

asked one of my religious teachers, an Italian-born nun, a politely phrased but skeptical question about the existence of hell. She flew into a rage, slapped my face and called me a *piccolo Americano*, a "little American." Thus, the process of acculturation for second-generation children was an agonizing affair in which they not only had to "adjust" to two worlds, but to compromise between their irreconcilable demands. This was achieved by a sane path of least resistance.[59]

Recognizing such complexities in particular cases, what are the general features likely to be transmitted in ethnic socialization practices? Perhaps most obvious are the more visible aspects of a distinctive cultural heritage, such as traditional recipes, language, ceremonial and religious practices, certain gestures, particular interests and skills such as lace making or soccer, and a knowledge of the group's legends, myths, and heroes.

Less manifest, but equally recognizable, might be certain more subtle aspects of personal relationships, the distinctive conceptions of male (the *machismo* of Latin America) and female, the protective role of the older brother, the obligations of the godparents, the father's right to swear, the respect paid to the priest, the domesticity of the mother and perhaps her care in preparing a traditional holiday dish, and expected kinship patterns of hospitality and loyalty.

Also included may be a distinctive world view and codes of behavior that provide the raison d'etre for the behavior of the group. French-Canadian children in Quebec, for example, had long been taught that it was their sacred mission in the New World to maintain their distinctive language, religion, and traditional rural way of life. Currently, children of Estonians, Latvians, Lithuanians, and North American Indians are likely to be taught that they have been deprived of lands that are rightfully theirs.

Feelings and sentiments enter into all aspects of such transmission of cultural practices, ideas, and beliefs, including those that form part of daily routine and those that are part of heightened ceremonial occasions. Some groups have stringent rules governing diet, and their members feel revulsion in situations in which they might have to violate the rules: Hindus served beef or Moslems served pork, for example. Some solemn ceremonies call forth deep emotion, as when Ukrainian groups gather to honor the heroes and martyrs of the Ukrainian struggle for independence or when Jewish groups gather to commemorate the six million Jews annihilated in death camps by the Nazis in the 1930s and 1940s. Traditional deep-seated antipathies toward other ethnic groups may also be part of the heritage; for example, the antipathy of Irish Catholics to the English, and Greeks and Turks to each other. The origins of such feelings, passed on culturally from one generation to another, may lie in the remote past.

In the course of socialization, values become part of deeply ingrained personality characteristics. One classic study compared the reactions to physiological pain of old Americans, Jews from Eastern Europe, and Italians from southern Italy, all of whom were in a New York hospital. The three groups experienced pain differently, attaching different meanings to it and varying their reactions according to the setting. In general the old Americans sought to be "good" patients and to control their feelings; if pain was unbearable, they preferred to be alone. Both the Italians and Jews responded much more emotionally, but their attitudes differed. The Italian patients were concerned mainly with the immediacy of the experience; if drugs relieved them, for example, they would forget their suffering and manifest "a happy and joyful disposition." The Jewish patients, on the contrary, were more future-oriented and concerned with the significance of the pain for their health; often, for example, they were reluctant to accept the relief-giving drug, which they thought might be habit-forming.[60]

Other studies show that ethnic groups have varied considerably in their orientations toward achievement. In Canada, one study suggests that French-Canadian children have been less motivated to achieve than English-Canadian children,[61] and other investigators cite the low achievement motivation of Indian children in Canadian-controlled educational institutions.[62]

Some years ago Fred L. Strodtbeck compared Jews and

Italians in New Haven and reported that "Jews consistently have higher occupational status than the population at large, while, in contrast, Italians are consistently lower."[63] In a more extended analysis Bernard Rosen studied six ethnic groups in four northeastern states: Greeks, native-born white Protestants, southern Italians, East European Jews, French Canadians, and blacks. Four hundred and twenty-seven pairs of mothers and sons, the latter generally third generation or more, were interviewed. Rosen compared these groups in achievement motivations, relevant value-orientations, and aspiration levels, which together make up an "achievement syndrome." For each component of this syndrome, the white Protestants, Jews, and Greeks ranked higher than the French Canadians and Italians. The Protestants, Jews, and Greeks more often imposed standards of excellence, set high goals, and expected self-reliant behavior from their children; more often imparted values that implement achievement-motivated behavior, such as individual responsibility, future planning, and active striving for goals; and had higher educational and vocational aspirations. Blacks ranked high on all indicators but vocational aspiration.[64]

Running through all these elements that enter into an ethnic culture is the previously discussed concept, identity. In learning a language, participating in ceremonies, following family patterns, and the like, a child's identity with his or her ethnic group can be reinforced. Children are aware of and feel they belong to a collectivity that links them to some and sets them apart from others.

Except for the racially defined ethnic groups, the traditional image of immigrant adaptation in the United States was the melting pot—over a period of time, the various ethnic groups would lose their distinctiveness and become part of a common blend. Even as late as 1953, W. Lloyd Warner, one of America's most prominent sociologists of the time, wrote:

> The number, size, and importance of ethnic groups and sects in American life increased almost yearly. Many of them are disappearing, and others yield much of their cultural substance

to the influences of the other American world. All increasingly adjust to the later outlines of American society.... it seems likely that most, if not all of them, will ultimately disappear from American life.[65]

Certainly to some degree this prediction has been correct. Relatively few of the third- and fourth-generation descendants of immigrants to the United States and Canada speak the language of their forebears or follow the traditional customs and patterns of their family groups. They have attended standardized schools, mixed with children of all groups, and have been exposed to and participated in the same popular culture of television shows, advertising, movies, supermarkets, drug stores, popular music, and newspapers. Their professed core values too are the standard North American ones of individualism, materialism, egalitarianism, and the work ethic.

Yet, assimilation has not been complete. Intermarriage rates among members of ethnic groups are high but not random, it is reported; a high proportion still marries within their group or within closely associated groups. In large cities, ethnic-group members often live in the same areas, form clubs, and participate in various informal relationships.[66] More than in the past, we also now see the formation among ethnic groups of classes to learn language and ceremonies and specialized food centers. Many, it would seem, do feel a strong sense of identity with their fellow ethnic-group members.

Ethnicity, then, has changed its nature over the years. In the first edition of their book, *Beyond the Melting Pot,* published in 1963, Nathan Glazer and Daniel P. Moynihan argued that the national aspect of most ethnic groups rarely survives a third generation, although the religious aspect could still serve as a basis of subcommunity and subculture.[67] The second edition, published seven years later, reported a decline in the significance of religion but a renewed importance in ethnic identification, particularly as a basis for pursuing political goals. A book edited by the same authors and published in 1975 continues this line of analysis.[68] A comparable analysis has been presented for Canada by a sociologist who views ethnic groups as "forms of social life, rather than survivals from the past, as mobilizers of interests rather than bearers of cultures or traditions, and collectivities with which people choose to identify rather than as groups into which they are born and from which they struggle to escape."[69]

We may sum up the historical trend in these terms: A situation that began with the introduction of quite different ethnic cultures has evolved into a mosaic of loose ethnic groupings, all representing somewhat different versions of a larger culture. Currently these groupings do not seek to gain security by following traditional ways; rather they are forms of life in which members choose to participate.

The implications for the socialization of children are important. Children in an ethnic grouping may well come to learn and experience their ethnic identity, but they are not bound by it in their future behavior. They may choose, in all or part of their lives, to participate with members of their own or closely related ethnic groups; or they may live a life in which ethnicity plays little part.

The subcultures that provide the content of the child's socialization are brought to him or her by particular groups and institutions—agents of socialization, the topic to which we now turn.

5 Agencies of Socialization

Socialization occurs in many settings and in interaction with many people, organized into groupings of various kinds. Each grouping exerts particular kinds of effects on children and each has more or less distinctive functions in preparing children for social life. Each may therefore be called an agency of socialization.

Of course, while each agency has its own functions in socialization, functions that in certain respects may be contradictory, various agencies also reinforce each other's efforts, as was noted previously. Common cultural images of the child affect many agencies. Thus, when "getting along with others" was a dominant goal in socialization, as was true in the forties and fifties in the United States, family, school, church, voluntary associations, and even informal peer groups worked toward this end. David Riesman has given us an illuminating portrait of American society, especially middle-class society, in this period.[1] During the 1960s, socialization concerns changed in some degree; academic competence became a more important goal for many sections of both the middle and lower classes, particularly those parts of the latter made up of urban ethnic minorities. The middle class placed a somewhat greater emphasis on individuality and creativity as goals. These emphases were widely diffused, so that many socialization agencies reflected the changed values and goals. Thus, family and school tended to share the increased emphasis on academic achievement, although they may often have differed on implementation. Convergence and divergence of expectations coexisted side by side.

During the 1970s there has again been something of a shift in socialization emphasis. Although academic competence remains important in families, in schools, and elsewhere, it is not the focus of intense concentration that it was earlier. No other single concern has quite replaced it, yet the changes in society have yielded new emphases. One significant contender for the new dominant concern in socialization is that of revising or repealing old stereotypes, particularly sex-role stereotypes. Until recent years, socialization took place within a framework that led fairly clearly to different socialization paths for boys and for girls. Increasingly in the United States, more slowly in some other countries, these stereotypes are being revised. The telephone company publishes photographs of women climbing telephone poles to make repairs and of men working as telephone operators. Whereas each of these occupations was formerly restricted to the other sex, now both are open to both sexes.

This is but one illustration of a wide movement to change traditional expectations and therefore socialization experiences that had been sex-specific. This is not to say that everybody concerned with socialization is in agreement on the changes; the point is, rather, that the question of whether boys and girls should be confined to traditional sex-specific experiences is a question that is emerging near the center of attention for all persons who are in any way concerned with socialization. This question follows upon, and to some extent competes with, an earlier concern with revising minority-group stereotypes.

In sum, if we look back over the last thirty or forty years, we can recognize several shifts of attention and concern in socialization beliefs and practices. We can recognize a shift of emphasis from getting along with others to an emphasis on academic competence to a newer emphasis on revising sex-specific and minority-specific stereotypes. The earlier concerns are not discarded; they are edged away from the center of attention and worked into newer patterns as new concerns emerge.

Before proceeding to our discussion of particular agencies, it is important to make clear that some socialization outcomes are consciously sought by the agency of socialization, whereas others are unintended. Socialization always takes place in overlapping time frames. For example, when a parent tells a child to take his or her feet off the furniture, the parent is most likely concentrating on keeping the furniture clean and unscratched. The parent may or may not also be thinking at that moment about developing in the child "respect for property," "respect for authority," "self-restraint in disposing one's body," "neatness," and any number of other long-term objectives that might be considered socially desirable. But even though the parent may not have these latter objectives in mind, they may nonetheless be among the consequences of the interactions whose goal is simply to save the furniture. We are, then, alluding to an important distinction between *purpose* and *function*.[2] A purpose is a goal that a person or group wants to accomplish; it is an "end-in-view." A function is a consequence, or effect, of action and interaction. Purposes and functions may sometimes coincide; thus, knowledge of arithmetic is one of the goals, or purposes, that the elementary school endeavors to attain. It is also a function, that is, a consequence of teaching. If purposes and functions never coincided, socialization would probably be impossible. Nevertheless, it is important to bear in mind that socialization agencies have functions that are not necessarily among their purposes.

One reason functions and purposes do not entirely coincide is that although the family, school, and so on are agencies of the society, they also "have a life of their own." When we say that society—through law, custom, and public opinion—delegates certain socialization functions to specific agencies such as the family or the school, we are not describing a process that is the same as an army captain directing a subordinate to carry out an assigned task. Agencies of socialization necessarily have more leeway in how they achieve the goals assigned to them than does the captain's aide. Agencies of socialization are accountable to the society only within rather broad limits. A school that does not include arithmetic in its curriculum will be examined by a state agency or criticized by parents, and it will be required to meet at least a minimum standard. But a great deal of what goes on in schools, in families, or in other agencies of socialization is not scrutinized, not subject to sanction by society.

It is therefore not entirely useful—but useful up to a point —to think of agencies of socialization as carrying out society's mandates. Such agencies are not like machines processing a raw material into a predetermined product. Even in a society that attempts to predetermine with great exactness the outcomes of socialization, many things go awry. As sociologist Allen Kassof observes, the efforts of the Soviet Union to mold the attitudes of its young people through closely regulated youth programs do not, for various reasons, result in uniformly starry-eyed enthusiasts. "It is too much to expect that more than a small minority should emerge from the youth program with such unblemished views of a society where the noise of busy construction is interrupted only by the rhythm of happy dancing and skating ..."[3] The fact that socialization agencies develop purposes of their own and that persons being socialized also develop individualities of their own should keep us from thinking too literally of society as some kind of tightly integrated "system" and from developing what sociologist Dennis Wrong has called "the oversocialized conception of man in modern sociology."[4] Although all socialization occurs through some form of interaction, and although all interaction is patterned by values and norms of some kind, interaction also evolves in directions that are not necessarily specified in advance.

The concept of "agency of socialization" needs, then, to be understood in this somewhat complex way. Any such agency generates processes, purposes, and functions of varying import. Some are most relevant to society as a whole, some to a particular subculture, some only to the agency itself. In some respects, society's mandates are quite specific and agencies are expected to be diligent in carrying them out. (For example, all families are expected to carry out society's prohibitions of incest. All elementary schools are expected to teach children to read and write. All peer groups are expected to refrain from undue violence against authority.)

In other respects, society's mandates are general and even vague, leaving socialization agencies a great deal of leeway. For example, the family and the school are jointly expected to prepare children for gainful employment on reaching maturity. The school probably has more directly assigned responsibility for achieving this outcome, but the family is expected to cooperate with or at least not hamper the school in carrying out this mandate. But the mandate to the school is vague enough to be influenced by particular subcultures and by the educators in particular schools and school systems. Thus, the school may have the general obligation to help children develop their talents to the fullest extent possible so that, among other reasons, each may qualify for "the best job" of which he or she is capable. But in one subculture this may mean that the school should encourage and reward capacities for independent thought, whereas in another subculture the expression of such capacities might be regarded as evidence that the school is failing in its obligation to foster respect for authority, thereby disqualifying the children for jobs as well-appreciated participants in bureaucratic organizations.

With this understanding of the complex relationship between agencies of socialization and society, let us turn to an examination of some of the most important agencies in our society.

THE FAMILY

The family is the first unit with which children have continuous contact and the first context in which socialization patterns develop. It is a world with which they have nothing to compare and, as such, it is the most important socializing agency. True, the family is not as all-encompassing in our society as it once was, and its effects may be modified (some easily, some not so easily) by other agencies. Children now attend nursery school or summer camp at the age of three and watch television when even younger. Schools, hospitals, government agencies, and service industries have taken over many activities that were once conducted by parents or relatives such as grandparents, uncles, and aunts. Nevertheless, despite the greater exposure of the contemporary child to outside influences, the family remains crucially important for his or her socialization. This may be seen from several vantage points.

The Family in the Community

The family into which a child is born *places* the child in a community and in society. This means that newborns begin their social life by acquiring the status their families have, and they will retain this status certainly throughout the first few years of their lives, very probably until they reach adulthood, and only somewhat less probably as they move through adulthood.

To be born into a particular family, then, is to acquire a status (or set of statuses) in the community and in the society. The child's family-given status is an important determinant of the way others respond to him or her. The case of a boy named Johnny Rocco provides a pointed illustration:

> Johnny hadn't been running the streets long when the knowledge was borne in on him that being a Rocco made him "something special"; the reputation of the notorious Roccos, known to neighbors, schools, police, and welfare agencies as "chiselers, thieves, and trouble-makers" preceded him. The cop on the beat, Johnny says, always had some cynical smart crack to make.... Certain children were not permitted to play with him. Wherever he went—on the streets, in the neighborhood, settlement house, at the welfare agency's penny milk station, at school, where other Roccos had been before him—he recognized himself by a gesture, an oblique remark, a wrong laugh.[5]

Although the example reveals how family notoriety may be conferred on a child who has not brought notoriety on himself, the basic principle of status-conferral holds for other kinds of statuses as well. Most importantly, the family's position in the social class structure becomes the child's position. This affects not only how the child will be responded to during childhood but the child's adult status as well. In a large-scale study of the factors affecting occupational attainment, Peter Blau and O. D. Duncan found that "The family into which a man is born exerts a profound influence on his career, because his occupational life is conditioned by his education, and his education depends to a considerable extent on his family."[6]

The family's status in the community affects not only the way others respond to the child and the kind of formal education he is likely to receive; it also mediates for the child the culture available in the larger society. Any family participates directly in a limited number of subcultures and networks (one based on social-class position, one based on ethnic-group membership, possibly others based on kinship, occupations, or interests). These are the versions of the larger society that are made most directly available to the child through example, teaching, and taken-for-granted daily activity. At the same time, any family is likely to be aware of at least portions of other subcultures that may serve as subjects of emulation or derogatory comment. In these ways, the families into which children are born present them with selective versions of the larger society, with the result that children may become impressed early with the importance of religious devotion, or baseball, or school achievement, or making money, or sexual intercourse as a primary focus of attention, depending upon the emphasis of the subculture(s) in which their families participate.

In sum, the family is not simply a passive transmitter of a subculture to its children but plays an active part in screening in and screening out elements of available subcultures. This is accomplished (1) by means of activities—for example, going to church, inviting guests, visiting friends, going to football games—and (2) through comment and comparison—evaluating such activities and the people who do or do not participate in them and evaluating the groups and subcultures of which these activities are a part.[7]

The family's position in the community affects the age-grading of children. This is to say that what is expected of a child at given ages depends to some extent on the family's social position. Families thus differ in the rate at which they *pace* their children toward maturity. Generally, childhood is of longer duration in middle-class than in lower-class families. In the latter children take on serious responsibilities at an earlier age. For example, in a study of very poor black families living in a public housing project, David Schulz found that first-born daughters are given responsibility for caring for their younger siblings when they themselves are very young and, by the age of nine, may even be doing much of the grocery shopping and cooking in their households.[8] Although later-born girls are less likely to have such heavy responsibilities of caring for younger siblings, they are likely, as is their eldest sister, to begin having children of their own when in their early or middle teens. Child-care responsibilities thus begin at a much earlier age than is the case in the middle class, whether black or white. In a sociological sense, it can be said that childhood ends at an earlier age.

In Schulz's findings we see an illustration of the distinction between intended and unintended outcomes of socialization. The mothers intend that their first-born girls take care of younger siblings and also become competent in shopping and cooking. The mothers do not, however, wish to see their daughters begin giving birth to children of their own in their teens and, indeed, endeavor, however ineffectively, to prevent this from occurring. But since the mothers themselves began having children when they were adolescent, they provide models with which their daughters identify and which, therefore, weaken the impact of their strictures. Further, the subculture does not apply strong negative sanctions against early motherhood, in or out of wedlock. Most importantly, the pervasive discrimination practiced by whites against blacks, and especially against those who are poor, functions in various ways to prevent many young and poor black girls from developing effective goals for adulthood that would enable them to delay motherhood. Becoming a mother provides some feeling of self-esteem in a subculture with many deprivations and many norms shaped by discrimination.[9]

In sum, then, a child is born into a family, and the family locates the child in society. From the moment of birth, before he or she has had the opportunity to take any independent actions, the child is located in society—as middle class or working class, child of a teacher or truck driver, Christian or Jew, member of a dominant or a subordinate ethnic group, member of a family respected or scorned by neighbors. The family's—and therefore the child's—location in these social groupings affects the experiences the child will have as he or she matures. It will determine, to a significant degree, not only what form socialization opportunities will take, but also at what ages, in what order, and with whom. It will also play an important part, as Blau and Duncan note, in determining the child's later location in society when he or she has become an adult.

The Family as an Interaction Structure

Although one of the family's functions is to place children in the society and thereby directly or indirectly affect their experiences outside the home, this is not its only importance in socialization. The family has an organization of its own which has its own direct effects on children.[10]

From this perspective, perhaps the most important function of the family in socialization is that it introduces children to intimate and personal relationships. Since children's first social relationships are family relationships, it is in this group that they acquire their first experiences of being treated as persons in their own right. They receive care for their dependency and attention for their sociability. Because newborn children are both without experience and very needing of care and attention, their initial outlook is assumed to be, loosely, egocentric. The kind of care and attention they receive during their first and second years of life affects their resolution of the issues of trust versus distrust and autonomy versus shame and doubt—and therefore their capacity for establishing later ties with people outside the family.

At the outset newborns are unaware that they are separate and distinct persons. As time goes on, they become aware, first, that they and their mothers (or other care-taking persons) are separate and, then, that there are other members of the household—father and, possibly, siblings. Children learn that others have wishes, interests, and ways of their own and that it is advantageous to adapt to them. Others do not invariably appreciate children and their needs and wishes—indeed, the appreciation varies according to how responsive a child is. Living in a household shared with others, children learn that they must share the resources of the household— the space, the furnishings and other objects, the time and attention of parents and siblings. They learn the ways in which their cooperation is sought and welcomed and the ways in which they may compete for what they want when it conflicts with what other family members want. In interacting with children, parents may be more or less expressive of their feelings, more or less authoritative, more or less protective. The mother, in dressing a young child, may demand or plead for cooperation; the father, in disciplining the child, may be angry or businesslike. Siblings may be more or less jealous, more or less interested in accepting a child as a playmate and companion.

Through these various kinds of interaction with family members—such as being cared for, being disciplined, being accepted as a companion and playmate—the child develops initial capacities for establishing relationships with others. These capacities will find both later expression and further development in relationships with nonfamily playmates, coworkers, authority figures, friends, and, ultimately, a spouse and children.[11]

The family into which he or she is born is the child's first reference group, the first group whose values, norms, and practices one refers to in evaluating one's own behavior.

What this implies, as Talcott Parsons and Robert F. Bales have argued, is that the child identifies with the family as a group, so that its ways become part of his or her own self. These authors have thus amplified the concept of identification beyond the original meaning Freud gave it when he spoke of the child as identifying with the parent of the same sex.[12] This means, for example, that not only do the particular members of the family constitute models for the child's own behavior but *the pattern of interaction among the members* itself becomes a model. The child's socialization is affected not merely by having a hard-working or an alcoholic father, a loving or indifferent mother, a domineering or distant older sibling. It is affected also by whether the interaction in the family is characteristically relaxed and good-natured or tense and guarded, whether it emphasizes or minimizes the distance between parents and children or between males and females, whether it is typically cooperative or competitive.

One way of describing differences in family interaction patterns has been proposed by Herbert Gans, who suggests that there are three main types of family in North America. The *adult-centered* family is "run by adults for adults, . . . the role of the children is to behave as much as possible like miniature adults." In this type of family, children and their wishes are clearly subordinate to parents and theirs. Children are expected to conduct themselves in ways pleasing to adults and not make themselves intrusive. Parents in these families are not very self-conscious or purposive in their child rearing. They

> are not concerned with *developing* their children, that is, with raising them in accordance with a predetermined goal or target which they are expected to achieve. [They] have no clear image of the future social status, occupational level, or life-style that they want their children to reach. And even when they do, they do not know how to build it into the child-rearing process.[13]

In the *child-centered* family, parents are more attentive to the child. In this type of family, unlike the adult-centered, children are planned, and the parents' educational aspirations influence how many children they will have. In the child-centered type, family companionship is prominent; parents spend time playing with their children and give up some adult pleasures for them. They want their children to have a happier childhood than they had. The fathers assume that their children will be occupationally successful, at least matching and, they hope, surpassing the parental occupational achievement. In contrast, in the adult-centered family there is more concern about downward social mobility, with the parents seeking reassurance that the child's conduct is sufficiently satisfactory to prevent him or her from becoming a "bum."

The third type of family Gans calls *adult-directed*. Parents are generally college-educated and know what they want for their children much more clearly than do parents in the child-centered type. Emphasis is placed on individual growth. Children are taught to strive for self-development in accordance with their own individuality.

Gans finds that each of these three types of family is most characteristic of a particular social class. The adult-directed pattern is more common in the upper-middle class, the child-centered in the lower-middle class, and the adult-centered in the working class. Jack E. Weller concluded that the adult-centered type, which Gans found among working-class Italian-Americans in Boston, also typified the Anglo-Saxon mountain people in Appalachia.[14]

Although family interaction styles unquestionably tend to vary with social class, it also needs to be said that insufficient attention has been paid to variations *within* a social class or other social category. When such variation is the focus of research attention, the results suggest how family interaction patterns have effects on socialization that do not derive from social class. Norman Bell, for example, studied a group of working-class families, half of which had an emotionally disturbed child. He found that in the families with a disturbed child, relatives tended to be drawn into family conflicts in ways that exacerbated the conflicts, evidently with some impact on the child, whereas the families without a disturbed child were able to limit involvement of extended kin.[15]

One other aspect of family structure needs to be considered: the significance of persons in specific family statuses. The importance of the mother has been discussed in an earlier chapter. At this point we need only reiterate that the mother is ordinarily the first socializing agent. As such, she is the first representative of society to the child and, through the care she provides, initiates the development of the sentiments and symbols that give the child a human nature and enable the child to become a responsive participant in society.

The father's contribution to the child's socialization has received much less systematic attention. As Leonard Benson observes, "Mother is the primary parent. She is first by popular acclaim, in actual household practice, and in the minds of students of family life ... material on mother is much more extensive than that on fathers."[16] Nevertheless, certain ideas and findings about the father's importance have emerged.

One way in which the father is important, according to Talcott Parsons' analysis, is that his presence and participation in the family help the child to relinquish its dependency on the mother. At first the father tends to be regarded as "an intruder" into the close initial mother-child relationship. He is the main source of pressure for the child to modify an early love attachment to the mother, although she also works toward such modification. After a while the child identifies with the father; one result of this is that the child then works toward loosening the attachment to the mother. Further, since the father usually works and spends less time at home than the mother, he comes to be seen as a representative of the outside world and of "the higher demands" that the child is progressively required to meet. In this way the father is significant in turning the child's attention to the adult world outside the family and in expanding the child's horizon.[17]

Although the father's authority in the family is less absolute than it once was, Benson argues that the father still plays a decisive part in communicating to the child a sense of social order. In Benson's words:

> Father's influence on the social climate within which his children's many experiences occur is perhaps most important. It establishes the conditions for his basic value, or moral, function: to develop a generalized commitment to social order. His existence personifies for his children the inevitability of rules. . . . Of course the rules are implicit in the ordered behavior of almost everyone who enters the life of the growing child, but father commonly comes to "stand for" the absolute necessity of social order more than any other person. Even the social pattern the mother establishes is typically legitimized by the larger, more insistent parent lurking in the background.[18]

Not least important, the father provides a basic model of masculinity. For his sons, this model becomes a basis for developing their own male identity. For his daughters, the model provides a basis for developing images of male companions and perhaps a desirable husband. For children of both sexes, these images are influenced not only by the father's actual conduct but by the mother's evaluations of him as well. Further, there is evidence that the father's status in the outside world affects the way his children perceive him. One study of boys in the age bracket of nine to eleven found that middle-class boys tend to perceive their fathers as ambitious, competent, and successful; as interested in their performance in school and in other settings; and as responsive to requests for attention. Lower-class boys tended to see their fathers quite differently—as nervous, shy, and worried.[19]

In a variety of ways, then, the father is one of the child's most important links to the world that lies beyond the family.

Finally, in discussing the effects of family statuses on socialization, it should be pointed out that there is also some evidence that the size and composition of the sibling group affects socialization. James Bossard and Eleanor Boll compared one hundred families each with two children with one hundred families each of which had six or more children.

They found that there tended to be more "regimentation" and assigning of jobs in the large families than in the small and that in the small families "the children were often spared from all household chores in the interests of concentrating on their education, outside activities, and social life."[20] They also reported that siblings in the small families were more dependent upon their parents for security, whereas the children in the large families were more likely to find security "in the numbers of siblings who formed a cohesive group for defense, playing, confiding, teaching, even plotting against parents."

Bossard and Boll point to a greater probability that the small family will have children of all of one sex, and they cite census figures that report that 29 percent of American families have only girls, 30 percent only boys, and 41 percent, the minority, have children of both sexes.[21] Their emphasis on the fact that many children do not have the experience of growing up in a house with siblings of the opposite sex gains significance from the work of sociologist Orville Brim. Brim examined data collected by psychologist Helen Koch in a large study of personality traits of children in two-child families. Making use of George Herbert Mead's theory of social interaction, Brim reasoned that "taking the role of the other" should result in a greater frequency of typical cross-sex personality traits in children who have a sibling of the opposite sex than in children whose only sibling is of the same sex. When he examined Koch's data from this perspective, he found that his prediction was substantially correct. Thus, a girl with a brother was more likely to have "high masculinity traits" (such as ambition or competitiveness) than a girl whose sibling is another girl. Similarly, the boy whose sibling is a sister is somewhat more likely to show "high femininity traits" (such as affectionateness or obedience) than the boy whose sibling is a brother. These results suggest that the learning of sex roles is affected by the composition of the sibling group within the family. Brim cautions that the particular effects he found are limited to two-child families and that sibships of different composition would very likely result in different patterns. Nevertheless, Brim argues, sibling relations are important for sex-role learning. Although the parents are the major sources of sex-role learning, *variations* in this learning must be due in part to sibling differences (along with such other factors as the sex of neighborhood playmates), since most children have a mother and father to learn from.[22]

Variations in Interaction Patterns

The discussion of the family as an interaction structure has taken the nuclear family as the type case. The nuclear family, usually consisting of parents and their biological children, has for a long time been considered the "normal" (that is, preferred) and the typical (that is, most prevalent) unit for the primary socialization of children. In a trend that began during the 1960s, children increasingly are being socialized in other types of units, as alternative family forms come into being alongside the nuclear family. Demographer Paul C. Glick has analyzed figures from the 1970 United States census and has estimated that

> only 70 per cent of the children under 18 years of age in 1970 were living with their two natural parents who had been married only once. Among black children the figure was very low, 45 per cent, but that for white children was also low, 73 per cent. The proportion of *children of school age* living with both natural parents in their first marriage was even smaller than 70 per cent in 1970. Therefore, the remaining more than 30 per cent of school children were *not* living with a father and a mother who were in a continuous first marriage. This means that such children are no longer rare. Even though children of separated, divorced, or never-married parents still have many problems today, they at least have far less cause to feel unique or exceptionally deprived than similar children of yesterday.[23]

Those 30 percent of children under age eighteen who do not live in a nuclear family with their own parents are distributed in three main types of family-household groups. Also using 1970 census data, sociologists Betty E. Cogswell and Marvin B. Sussman estimated that 44 percent of the entire population (adults and children) live in a nuclear family; 15 percent live in a "reconstituted family" (that is, at least one partner is in a remarriage and there is at least one child from at least one partner's previous marriage); 13 percent live in a single-parent family; and 8 percent live in various kinds of experimental marriages and families.[24] Benjamin Schlesinger has estimated that approximately 8.9 percent of Canadian families can be classified as one-parent families, and that approximately two-thirds of these families have dependent children.[25]

As Sussman has pointed out, a child may live in several types of families before reaching adulthood. The child might be born into a three-generation household, then live in a nuclear family when his or her parents set up their own household, then live in a single-parent family after the parents divorce, and finally live in a reconstituted family when the parent he or she lives with remarries.[26]

Thus, although the nuclear family remains the most typical family unit in North America, and the great majority of children continue to grow up in households consisting of two parents and their biological children, an increasingly large minority have at least part of their socialization in other kinds of family or household units. The child in these other kinds of family or household units is likely to undergo distinctive socialization experiences. The child in a reconstituted family, for example, often has a "real parent" elsewhere as well as a stepparent in the house. The natural parent who no longer lives with the child is often reluctant to use visiting time as an occasion to impose discipline, according to one study.[27] Another study reports that social norms make it inappropriate for a stepparent to fully assume the role of a parent and that stepparents are reluctant, perhaps, to impose discipline.[28] Thus, it is conceivable that a child in a reconstituted family may have both a resident stepparent and a nonresident parent, neither of whom feels able or willing to function fully according to role expectations for a parent in an unbroken nuclear family. Such, at least, is the possibility suggested by fragmentary research now available. But, as one of the present authors has argued, it is a mistake to attempt to infer the quality of interaction in families by looking only at the formal membership composition. Every family, regardless of its membership composition, must construct its own patterns of interaction, including socialization.[29] The age of a child at the time of parents' divorce and at the time of entering into a reconstituted family is but one of the factors that affects the importance of a stepparent as a socializing agent.

The increase in variant family forms serves to call attention to one major issue concerning socialization in families. Many students of society have pointed out that in the nuclear family, in contrast to the extended family, the burden of socialization falls on a very small group. Two parents bear the responsibility of child care and provide the child with a restricted range of immediate role models. The growing interest in communes arises partly from efforts to counteract these alleged disadvantages. On the other hand, the single-parent family concentrates the responsibility and restricts the range of parental models even more than does the nuclear family. The reconstituted family increases the range of models, since a stepparent is added to the displaced natural parent, but may add to the parental burden as new relationships between the child and stepparent are being constructed.

While alternative family forms have become increasingly prevalent, the nuclear family has also been changing in significant ways. Most notable has been the increasing number of working mothers. Lois Wladis Hoffman and F. Ivan Nye, together with co-workers, have organized a great deal of information about this trend. In 1940, according to their estimate, only 8.6 percent of married women with children under age seventeen were in the labor force (that is, either working or actively looking for work). In 1972, 30 percent of women with children age five and under and 50 percent of women with children age six to seventeen but none younger were in the labor force.[30] This dramatic change means that the family interactions and consequently the socialization experiences of many children differ from the time when few mothers of young children worked outside the home. This change in labor force participation has led to considerable demand for an increase in the number of organized day-care facilities and an increase in government financial assistance to day care. Nevertheless, there remains considerable opposition: for reasons of cost, among other things, only 10 percent of the children age six and under of working mothers were in day-care centers in 1970.[31]

Hoffman has reviewed the available research on the effects of mothers' employment on their children. While this research is not yet comprehensive enough to yield definitive answers, certain general implications do seem to be emerging. There seems to be evidence that daughters of working mothers are more independent and have higher achievement aspirations than daughters of mothers who do not work.[32] But the explanation of this is not clear-cut:

> If the daughters of working mothers are found to be more independent or higher achievers than daughters of nonworking mothers, one cannot tell whether these attributes are products of the working mother as model, the fact that the father is more likely to have had an active part in the girl's upbringing, the fact that the father in working-mother families is more likely to approve of and encourage competence in females, or because the girls were more likely to have been encouraged by their mothers to achieve independence and assume responsibilities. All these intervening variables [possible links between mother's employment and daughter's characteristics] have been linked to female independence and achievement.[33]

The extent to which the employment of mothers has resulted in greater participation in child care by fathers has not yet been carefully studied. Also, the effects, if any, of mothers' employment on sons are not yet known.

One question that has concerned some observers of this growing trend toward the employment of mothers outside the home is whether children are thereby deprived of a stable relationship with an available nurturing figure. Available evidence indicates that middle-class mothers try to compensate for their employment by planning to be with their children at specific times and for specific activities. However, the question of whether their mothers' employment deprives infants and preschool children is unresolved at this time, for

> no data are available on whether maternal employment affects the amount of stimulation and person-to-person interaction available to the infant, whether the mother's absence interferes with her serving as the stable adult figure needed by the infant, or whether the attachment of the infant to the mother or the mother to the infant is jeopardized.[34]

In sum, although an increasing number of children are growing up in families that differ from the traditional nuclear family that has been (and continues to be) the prevalent type of family in North America, little is yet known with any assurance of the consequences of these changes for socialization. There are many questions, but only the beginnings of some answers.

THE SCHOOL

The importance of the school as an agency of socialization has already been suggested in several illustrations. Now we wish to treat this agency more systematically. For the sake of convenience, we shall divide our discussion into three subtopics: the school and society, the classroom, and the teacher. Although this division is somewhat artificial because each of these subtopics is fully understandable only in relation to the others, the distinctions will nevertheless be helpful in organizing our discussion.

School and Society

When children begin to go to school, they ordinarily come, for the first time, under the supervision of people who are not their kin. They thus move from a milieu dominated by personal ties to one that is more impersonal (although the degree of impersonality is theoretically less at the nursery school and kindergarten level than it becomes later). By involving children with teachers and classmates, the school plays an important part in lessening the emotional dependence on the family. Furthermore, the school is likely to be the first agency (in a literate society)—except perhaps for the church—that stimulates children to develop loyalties and sentiments that go beyond the family, that link children to a wider social order. The school is society's principal agency —at least its principal formally designated agency—for loosening children's ties to their parents and initiating children into social institutions that cut across kin and neighborhood groupings.

The school as an agency of socialization needs to be recognized, then, first as an organizer of social relationships and stimulator of sentiments. Some of the social relationships will be discussed in the following section on the classroom. As an example of its role in organizing sentiments we may observe how the school stimulates loyalty to the existing political and social order. One study of 12,000 children from second through eighth grades concludes that

> The school apparently plays the largest part in teaching attitudes, conceptions, and beliefs about the operation of the political system. While it may be argued that the family contributes much to the socialization that goes into basic loyalty to the country, the school gives content, information, and concepts which expand and elaborate these early feelings of attachment.[35]

This study also suggests that the school places greater emphasis on compliance with law, authority, and school regulations than on the rights and obligations of a citizen to participate in government. Neither does it promote the child's understanding of the efficacy of group action or other legitimate ways of influencing government.

Orienting children to and fostering their respect for the established social and political order is one of the ways in which the school functions as a conservative socializing agency. It seeks to pass on to children the knowledge, sentiments, skills, and values that have been built up over time and presumably thereby provide children with the resources they will need in their adult roles.

At the same time, there is growing recognition that the

pace of social change in contemporary industrialized societies is so rapid that transmitting a particular heritage of the past is not sufficient for socialization. A British professor states flatly that "in most countries of the world nearly all the education consciously given is already out of date. It is sometimes out of date at the time when education is taking place. It is more usually out of date in terms of the children's prospects."[36] A more complex picture is provided by an American sociologist who argues with reference to the United States that

> as a society we have decreed that the responsibility of our schools shall not end with the maintenance of the status quo nor even with the socialization of individuals who are able to adapt easily to a changing social and physical environment, but instead shall extend to the maximum encouragement of the creative abilities of new members of the society. Thus, paradoxically educational institutions have assumed a major role as agents of innovation and change along with their conservative role in assuring the cultural continuity of the society.[37]

He further argues that many of the issues in American education can be understood as debates over the relative weight that should be given to the school's conservative as opposed to its innovative function. Many observers have pointed out that socializing children for a society in such rapid change is a new task, one not encountered by any society before, and it is not surprising that no one is entirely sure how to do it. The problem is exacerbated by the fact that the school seems to change more slowly than other aspects of the society.[38] There are undoubtedly many reasons for this, among them being school responsiveness to conservative community pressure. Such pressure can in part be understood in terms of socialization, for socialization has the general effect of giving people a more definite picture of society as they *have* experienced it than as they *will* experience it in the future. Community pressures on the school system to socialize children for society as it has been known are therefore likely to be generally stronger than pressures to socialize for a society whose form is as yet unknown.

Although the British professor quoted above may be correct that almost all education is out of date by the time it is to be used, many observers note that the schools nevertheless seem to prepare some children better than others, whether preparation be defined in minimal terms as learning to "read, write, and reckon" or in more sophisticated terms such as learning how to cope with unforeseen problems. The reasons for this are multiple and complex, and a full exploration would take us far beyond the scope of this book. But the basic situation can be summed up as follows: *The effectiveness of the school as a socializing agency depends to a major degree upon the kinds of families its children come from.* Generally, the school tends to be less effective in educating children from families that are poor and of low status. Such children are often, though by no means invariably, from minority groups. Although there is wide agreement that schools are not as successful in socializing children from poor and low-status families as they are with those of higher income and status, there is wide disagreement concerning the causes of the discrepancy. Some observers attribute it to differences in what the schools give the children, whereas others attribute it to what the children bring to the school in the way of home-based socialization. There is evidence to support both viewpoints.

Considerable evidence has accumulated by now to indicate that the American school tends to reinforce the child's family-given status. This is brought about in a number of direct and indirect ways. Schools in neighborhoods where poor families predominate tend to receive smaller allocations of educational resources than those in higher income and status neighborhoods.[39] Schools that serve children of various status levels and that also have more than one classroom or section for each grade level tend to group the children in sections according to the status of their families, even though ability or achievement is the ostensible basis for grouping. In Britain, too, a study reports that

> although teachers genuinely intended to stream children according to their measured ability, they nonetheless allowed

these judgments to be influenced by the type of home the children came from.... Even where children *of the same level of ability* are considered, those from middle-class homes tended to be allocated to the upper streams and those from the manual working-class to the lower streams. Furthermore, children who were dirty or badly clothed or who came from large families also tended to be placed in lower streams, regardless of ability.[40]

Thus, children of lower social status tend to be perceived by school personnel as having less ability to benefit from education than children of higher status. In a recent study, sociologist Ray C. Rist reports:

Throughout the various levels of the St. Louis educational system we found commonly shared assumptions about "how things really are." The basic tenets may be summarized as follows: Middle-class students can learn, lower-class students cannot; white schools are "good," black schools are "bad": control is necessary, freedom is anarchy; violence works, persuasion does not; teachers can save a few, but will lose many; the school tries, the home will not; and finally, only the naive would dispute these beliefs, as the wise know. *The outcome of this set of attitudes, assumptions, and values is that the school as an institution sustains, in a myriad of ways, the inequalities with which children first come to school.* The school's response to issues of color, class, and control all mesh together to make two nets—one to catch winners and one to catch losers.[41]

Teachers in schools where pupils are predominantly lower status are more likely to be lower in morale and to seek transfer to "more desirable" schools than teachers in schools where pupils are predominantly middle class.[42] Teachers' dissatisfaction in these schools with lower-status pupils appears to be related to the fact that academic performance of pupils is lower in these schools. So we see what appears to be a circular and self-continuing process: Low-status children tend not to learn as much as those of higher status, thereby arousing discontent in their teachers, which impairs teachers' performance and which further depresses pupils' achievements.[43] Various studies thus strongly suggest that the school does not put forth its best efforts in educating pupils from poor and low-status families.

Other studies, not necessarily inconsistent with the above, suggest that such pupils tend to fare poorly in school partly because they begin school poorly prepared by their early socialization in the family. These children are seen as deprived of the kinds of experiences that would enable them to take advantage of what the school has to offer. Many studies point to the deprivation that derives from inadequate experience in using language, perhaps because the home is generally lacking in stimulation[44] or perhaps because the mother's language in interacting with her child provides the child with diminished opportunity for thinking and making choices.[45]

An interesting variant of this point of view is proposed by Fred L. Strodtbeck. He agrees that the financially poor home provides a language-deprived environment for children, as compared to the middle-class home, but he argues that the main reason is that the very poor family, especially one without a father, provides a much simpler role organization. The middle-class home provides a "hidden curriculum" that teaches children to use language with finesse in order to get what they want:

> the presence of both a father and a mother who are relatively equal in power provides a child with a motivation to attend closely to the state of normative integration. . . . The existence of two persons of power with small value differences yet parallel commitment to a core of common values, creates a situation in which careful use of language and recognition of subtle differences is required to attain personal goals.[46]

In sum, the school is organized in a way that assumes a certain kind of preschool socialization in the family. Children from poor and low-status families often seem not to have this preparation, but the school has only recently begun to change its organization (allocation of funds and personnel, methods of teaching, curriculum, and so on) in an effort to improve its performance in educating them. Also, the schools often exacerbate the problem by assuming that poor and low-status children are difficult to educate, even when this is not the case.

While the school generally functions to sustain children in the statuses to which they are born, it also functions to encourage upward mobility. Children who do well in school, whatever their family backgrounds, are likely to win awards and to be encouraged to go on to higher education. One study estimates that 5 percent of American university students during the 1950s came from lower-working-class families and 25 percent from upper-working-class families.[47] There is some evidence that communities vary in the extent to which they offer equality of educational opportunity, regardless of a child's family background.[48]

The Classroom and Socialization

For young children the school classroom constitutes a social situation without parallel. Ordinarily students spend about 1,000 hours per year in a classroom, and will spend approximately 7,000 hours in school between kindergarten and the end of the sixth grade.[49]

The structure of the classroom has both short-run and long-run implications for children. Since most of what children do in a classroom is done in the presence of others, they have to learn to cope with a more or less formalized multi-person situation. They have to learn to wait their turn, and this means not only waiting to satisfy one's wishes to speak or perform, but often abandoning those wishes if the activity moves on to something else. Also, children must learn to ignore and not be distracted by those around them. As one observer of classroom functioning notes:

> if students are to face the demands of classroom life with equanimity they must learn to be patient. This means that they must be able to disengage, at least temporarily, their feelings from their actions. It also means ... that they must be able to re-engage feelings and actions when conditions are appropriate. In other words, students must wait patiently for their turn to come, but when it does they must still be capable of zestful participation. They must accept the fact of not being called on during a group discussion, but they must continue to volunteer.... In most classrooms, powerful social sanctions are in

operation to force the student to maintain an attitude of patience. If he impulsively steps out of line, his classmates are likely to complain about his being selfish or "pushy." If he shifts over into a state of overt withdrawal, his teacher is apt to call him back to active participation.[50]

This is a good illustration of how children are induced to sustain responsive participation in society, which we discussed briefly in Chapter 3.

The time schedule that governs classroom activities has another effect on children: The beginning and ending of activities does not necessarily correspond to children's interest in them. Activities may begin before children are interested and may end before they have lost interest— sometimes "when it's just getting interesting."

These various aspects of adapting to the crowded classroom—learning to delay or suppress desires, to tolerate interruptions, and to turn aside from distractions—are part of what is referred to as the classroom's "hidden curriculum." This term is gaining favor as a way of calling attention to the informal and unofficial matters that are taught, matters generally unnoticed by those who have responsibility for teaching the official curriculum. While the pupils are learning skills (such as reading and handwriting) and subjects (such as arithmetic and geography), they are also interacting with fellow pupils and the teacher in ways that strengthen their membership in society.

Since pupils differ in the rate and quality of their learning and in the various kinds of social facility that are encouraged in the classroom (for example, promptness, cooperativeness, and cheerfulness), their progress toward desired goals is evaluated. Although the teacher is the main source of evaluation, children also evaluate themselves—they know when they can't spell a word or solve a problem. Also, the class as a whole may be asked to evaluate a student's work, "as when the teacher asks, 'Who can correct Billy?' or 'How many believe that Shirley read that poem with a lot of expression?' "[51] The classroom environment is one in which children are being evaluated in a variety of ways—by teacher comments, self-judgments, classmates' judgments, report cards, marks and comments (and perhaps gold stars, red stars, or blue stars) on exercises and papers, classroom displays of the "best" papers, requests that they stay after school or bring their parents in for a conference. Sometimes there is organized competition (as in spelling bees, which may pit boys against girls, thus emphasizing sex identity along with competitiveness and learning of the official curricular material), which adds to the evaluational process.

Evaluation begins in kindergarten. Rist followed a group of children, in a virtually all black school with an all black faculty and staff, from their registration for entry in kindergarten until about midway through the second grade. He found that the kindergarten teacher made permanent seating assignments on the eighth day of school. In seven days the teacher had sorted out the children.

> Within a few days, only a certain group of children were continually being called on to lead the class in the Pledge of Allegiance, read the weather calendar each day, come to the front for "show and tell" periods, take messages to the office, count the number of children present in the class, pass out materials for class projects, be in charge of equipment on the playground, and lead the class to the bathroom, library, or on a school tour. This one group of children, who were always physically close to the teacher and had a high degree of verbal interaction with her, she placed at Table 1.[52]

These children were all dressed in clean clothes that were relatively new and cared for. The children at Tables 2 and 3 were more poorly dressed, in some cases dirty. The children at Table 1 also displayed greater ease in interacting with the teacher, greater familiarity with standard American English, and also tended to come from families that were middle class. (The teacher had access to preregistration forms filled out by the parents and to a list of children from families receiving public welfare payments. Also, teachers exchange information about families, so that many children bring with them into kindergarten family reputations established by their older siblings. The case of Johnny Rocco is not unique.)

This ongoing and multifaceted process of evaluation contributes to socialization in two main ways. The first is that *the evaluations become processed into the child's developing self.* Children learn certain of society's values and norms, and in this way their selves are transformed: They learn to be neat, prompt, able to follow instructions, and so forth—or they learn that they are not very good at being neat or prompt or at following instructions. They learn to think of themselves as being good in math or not so good in math, good or not so good in reading, and so on. These evaluations of children's achievements in skills, subject matters, and social performances thus gradually accrue to their emerging selves. Children thus come to know themselves as particular kinds of social beings, ones who may aspire to certain kinds of future opportunities but not to others.

While their selves are thus evolving, children are also acquiring a certain kind of reputation among teachers and a "cumulative record" which is semipublic.[53] The quality of this record (and reputation) serves as a ticket of admission (or refusal) for later opportunities, and this is the second main way in which evaluation affects socialization. At any given point during the formation of this reputation and record, their quality at that point affects children's progression to the next step—for example, whether they will be put into a fast, slow, or average section, whether they are doing well enough in classwork to be allowed participation in school team sports, whether they have done well enough in lower grades to be admitted to college-preparatory curricula in high school, whether they have done well enough in high school to be admitted to a college (and, if so, to what kind of college, with how much encouragement in the way of scholarships, and the like). In short, the school classroom functions as a system of selection for sequences of interlocking opportunities leading to particular kinds of adult roles.[54]

It is evident that the classroom socialization that shapes children's evolving social participation includes several kinds of control over their conduct. In some schools, these methods include violence or the threat of violence. Rist reports observing in his study elementary school teachers threatening to throw children over the side if they did not stay close to the wall when descending stairs; a teacher telling first graders that she was not a mean animal and had never eaten a little child in her whole life, but they had to get her permission to go to the bathroom; a teacher pushing children down into their seats or to the floor; and teachers standing in the doorways of their rooms holding four- or five-foot long rattan switches while children passed through hallways in large numbers. In interviews, the teachers expressed the view that children lacked sufficient self-control and that the threat or use of violence was necessary to maintain order. He reports observing occasional use of the switches by the teachers.[55]

The Teacher's Functions

Many readers of this book will perhaps recall a particular elementary school teacher as especially influential or helpful; other readers will have no such recollections, all their teachers being dimly fused in one anonymous blur. How influential are teachers? Is there any evidence—apart from subjective recall—that teachers can be significant in the socialization of children? Some recent research suggests that they can be.

One study of particular interest examines and tests a basic sociological axiom formulated by W. I. Thomas: "If men define situations as real, they are real in their consequences." In a somewhat elaborated formulation, the process has been called "the self-fulfilling prophecy."[56] This means that one's beliefs lead one to act in such a way that the beliefs cannot help but be reaffirmed. A study by Robert Rosenthal and Lenore Jacobson explores "how one person's expectations for another person's behavior can quite unwittingly become a more accurate prediction simply for its having been made," and it asks specifically "whether a teacher's expectation for her pupils' intellectual competence can come to serve as an educational self-fulfilling prophecy."[57] To test the validity of this idea, the investigators conducted an experiment in a school whose pupils were mostly of lower-class background.

First, they administered to all the pupils an intelligence test, which they disguised with the highfalutin name "Harvard Test of Inflected Acquisition." They told the teachers that this test could predict academic "blooming" or "spurting," and they asked the teachers not to discuss the test with pupils or parents. Then, in a completely random way entirely unconnected with the test results, the names of about 20 percent of the students were selected and, at the beginning of the following school year, given to their teachers with the explanation that they might like to know which of their pupils were "about to bloom." Since the names of these pupils were drawn from a hat, in effect, "the difference between the children earmarked for intellectual growth and the undesignated control children was in the mind of the teacher."[58] Retesting showed that at the end of the school year the children with the "special" designation gained an average of more than twelve IQ points, whereas the others averaged a gain of about eight points. The differences were much greater than this at the first- and second-grade levels than at higher grades. Further, later retesting when the children had moved on to new teachers indicated that there was some persistence in the differential gain. Significantly, then, children who were expected by their teachers to "bloom" did so, much more than those for whom teachers did not have this expectation; and the younger the children, the greater was the effect of the teacher's expectation.

Exactly what went on between teacher and pupils to bring about these results is not clear, but the investigators suggest three possible explanations of the differences between age groups: (1) Since younger children are less fixed and more capable of change, they are more subject to the effects of "critical periods"; (2) younger children are less well known and have less firmly established reputations in a school, so that their teachers are more inclined to take somebody's word about a child's promise for blooming than are third- to fifth-grade teachers, who have confidence in reputations already established; (3) the effects of the teachers' expectancies may be greater on the younger children than the older ones, not because they really are more malleable, but because teachers *believe* that they are.

Although the precise reason for differential change at different age levels remains uncertain, the study not only provides evidence that teachers' expectations can have significant effects on socialization but also supports other work that indicates that a child's intelligence is not fixed at birth but is a complex product of his or her innate capacities and experience.[59]

If teachers' expectations can be so influential as strongly to influence a child's very intelligence score, and if the classroom is one of the important places in which children compete and are prepared for their adult statuses and roles, it is pertinent to ask whether children in one classroom have as good a chance as children in another to come under the influence of teachers who will have favorable expectations. Or, conversely, is there some social process at work that tends to make it more likely that certain kinds of children will come under the influence of teachers with less favorable expectations and that they will accordingly experience less "bloom-promoting" teacher-pupil interaction? We provided a partial answer to this question when we cited a study showing that teachers in schools with predominantly lower-class pupils are more likely to want transfers out. From this and other related studies we could infer that the children of these teachers tend to be evaluated more negatively than middle-class children. But can we go beyond inference and actually see teachers communicating different kinds of expectations to children, based on the children's status?

A study by anthropologist Eleanor Leacock examines this question.[60] She observed second- and fifth-grade classrooms and interviewed the teachers and pupils in four city schools, each located in a different kind of neighborhood. The predominant pupil background of the four schools was, respectively, lower-income black, lower-income white, middle-income black, middle-income white. Although she found certain similarities in the four schools—traceable to such factors as similar teacher training, similar educational philosophy, and the fact that the schools were all part of the same school system and therefore subject to similar administrative practices—certain differences were also significant.

The differences Leacock found among the teachers do *not* fall into any simple pattern; she did not find that all the "bad" aspects of teaching were in the lowest-status classrooms and the "good" aspects in the higher-status ones. For example, the second-grade teachers were somewhat more positive than fifth-grade teachers in evaluating pupil participation, and this was as true in the low-income black school as in any of the others. Teacher pleasantness or unpleasantness to pupils was unrelated to the status of the pupils in this study, as also was teacher competence. But one difference that did emerge was that teachers seemed to expect less of their pupils if they were from the low-income group. In the middle-income schools, the teachers were likely to work more actively with a child having difficulty with a problem, whereas those in the low-income schools would more quickly give up and turn to another child, making little effort to see that the first child understood. At the fifth-grade level the teacher in the low-income black school was observed to have difficulty explaining arithmetic, but made the pupils seem responsible for failure to understand. One general conclusion reached by the study goes counter to some currently fashionable interpretations of school life:

> What we observed in the [low-income black] classroom was not the attempt to "impose middle-class goals" on the children but rather a tacit assumption that these goals were not open to at least the vast majority of them. *The "middle-class values" being imposed on the low-income Negro children defined them as inadequate and their proper role as one of deference.* Despite the fact that some teachers in the low-income schools stated their felt responsibility to set "middle-class standards" for the children, their lowered expectations were expressed by a low emphasis on goal-setting statements altogether. In a three-hour period, clear-cut overt goal-setting statements numbered 12 and 13 for the low-income Negro school, 15 and 18 for the low-income white school, and 43 and 46 for the middle-income white school.[61]

Thus, the evidence of this and other studies converges to suggest that pupils from low-income and low-status families are more likely to be met by lower levels of expectation for accomplishment from their teachers. The likely result of these lower levels of expectation is a reduction in levels of aspiration, levels of accomplishment, and probably even levels of intelligence.

School and Society—a Second Look

A study by anthropologist John Ogbu adds some important new findings and ideas to the literature on the school as a socializing agent. In his investigation of "Burgherside," a low-income neighborhood of Stockton, California, in which 92 percent of the elementary school population consists of blacks and Mexican-Americans, he sought to understand why so many children from that neighborhood failed in school. Like Leacock in New York, Rist in St. Louis, and other observers elsewhere, he found that teachers expect low-income children to fail. He found that Burgherside parents have high educational aspirations for their children and that the children also have these aspirations. But he found, in addition, something that had not often before been reported as a central finding by an observer sympathetic to low-income children:

> Burgherside children lack a serious attitude toward their school work.... *Burghersiders do not fail in school because, although they try, they cannot do the work ... Rather, Burghersiders fail in school because they do not even try to do the work. They are not serious about their school work, and therefore make no serious effort to try to succeed in school.* [62]

In pursuing this, Ogbu found that the children were acquiring the belief that schooling was no use because it would not open up the opportunities that good school performance ought to.

> In general, Burgherside parents appear to be teaching their children two contradictory attitudes toward education. On the one hand, they emphasize the need for more education: *You are*

not going to grow up to be like me. Get your education. On the other hand, they teach their children both verbally and through their own lives that it is not easy for Burghersiders who have "made it" in school to "make it" in society. They believe that for one of them to get a good job he must be "twice as qualified" as a Taxpayer competing for the same job. A Burghersider who merely has the same qualifications as a Taxpayer has no chance of success in a competition with a Taxpayer. That is why, Burghersiders say, they become discouraged and give up, saying *Oh, I know I will never make it.*[63]

(Taxpayers are whites living in another neighborhood who not only pay taxes but are publicly acknowledged as and consider themselves to be Taxpayers. They consider themselves the bearers of mainstream culture and also the bearers of the costs of running the city. Although Burghersiders pay taxes, they are often publicly described and treated as Nontaxpayers.)

An important element in Ogbu's analysis is his distinction between subordinate minorities and immigrant minorities. Subordinate minorities are those that were incorporated into the United States against their will—American Indians, blacks, Mexicans of the Southwest incorporated by conquest after the Mexican War. The immigrant minorities are those that came to the country looking for religious, political, or economic betterment. He notes that "subordinate and immigrant minorities appear to differ in the way they perceive American society and in how they respond to the educational system."[64] He considers it essential to understand the historical relationship of the subordinate minority group to American society in order to understand their children's high rate of school failure. Reduced effort in school is a mode of adaptation to a longtime limited level of opportunity for social rewards.

The educational dilemma of subordinate minorities is that their children are expected to work as hard as whites in school for fewer ultimate rewards from society ... Faced with this educational dilemma, subordinate minorities apparently chose to stop working hard in school since they could neither expect more for their hard work nor force society to change its discriminatory practice. They thus have reduced their anxiety about having to work hard for little by adjusting their efforts downward to a level commensurate with what they think they will actually get for their education.[65]

Over time, the blacks and Mexican-Americans developed the belief that they couldn't "make it" in society; the whites developed the belief that these minorities were "inferior." Both sets of beliefs become the basis for behavior in the school. The black and Mexican-American children in Stockton maintain this pattern of school-failure adaptation by such practices as frequent absence from school and not taking schoolwork seriously. Taxpayers, including teachers, do their part in maintaining the pattern by adopting a patron-client relationship with Burghersiders.

> Teachers, as representatives of Taxpayers and of the dominant ethnic group, represent the power structure. Teachers decide when, where, why, and how they will interact with parents. Many regard themselves as service-oriented patrons and expect Burghersiders to reciprocate with manifest interest and cooperation if their "problems" are to be solved. Burghersiders do not accept the situation as defined by teachers; but, since they need what teachers have to offer, and since they have relatively little power to insist otherwise, they comply with teachers' expectations.[66]

The teachers often regard the Burgherside children's problems as psychological, while the parents more often see the problems as matters of instruction and educational guidance.

Under these circumstances, according to Ogbu's analysis, remedial programs that are entirely focused on the children in their school setting cannot succeed. Compensatory education programs in Stockton in the 1960s, he believes, were naive in trying to change attitudes and behavior patterns in eight months that had been developed and transmitted over several generations. Burgherside parents and schoolchildren perceive schooling in terms of its "payoff" in later employment opportunities. From this viewpoint, improved school performance by children of subordinate minorities depends upon enlarging the definition of equal educational opportunity to include not merely equal favorable learning conditions for all children but also "the equal enjoyment of the benefits or rewards of education by individuals and segments of the society according to their educational achievement."[67]

Thus, the school, the subordinate minorities, and the political and economic authorities in the society become involved in a mutually reinforcing set of self-fulfilling prophecies: (1) White employers believe black and Mexican-American workers are inferior and, for this reason, discriminate against them in employment even when they have requisite educational qualifications (Ogbu documented cases of such discrimination); (2) parents, knowing of such discrimination directly or indirectly, discourage their children from expecting occupational success; (3) children learn from their parents and others not to expect much economic reward even for good educational qualifications and so do not try to do well in school; (4) teachers see the poor performance of subordinate minority children, and this confirms their already existing belief in these children's inferiority, a belief they share with other "taxpayers," including prospective employers. Each category of person in this cycle has an expectation or "prophecy" about some other category of person and acts in such a way as to bring about the result that is anticipated.

THE PEER GROUP

While the family and the school are socializing agencies organized primarily by adults, the child also comes to be socialized into a world in which adults are peripheral. This world is generally designated by the term *peer group*. The term is a bit misleading, since it does not designate a single group in which a child participates but rather all those groups made up of children in which any particular child participates. Any given child is likely to belong to more than one peer group, although there may be overlapping membership. Thus, a peer group may consist of the children on one's block or in one's apartment building. Another may include one's playmates at school. A third may be the children in the same Boy Scout troop or those who go to the same summer camp or music school. Yet another may be made up of the cousins whom one may see as a group at periodic intervals. It would therefore be more accurate to speak of one's "peer world," since the child's actual peer groups might differ in significant ways and the child might have different roles within them. For example, adult values might be more prominent in a Boy Scout or Girl Scout troop than in the neighborhood backyard or back alley peer group. We shall use the conventional term, however, and the reader will be able to judge from the context when we are referring to a particular type of peer group and when we are more generally discussing the peer world.

The peer group as a socializing agency has certain distinctive characteristics: (1) By definition, it is made up of members who have about the same age status; (2) within the peer group the members have varying degrees of prestige and power; (3) the peer group is centered about its own concerns; whereas adult authority figures instruct the child in traditional norms and values with an awareness that the child must learn to function in adult society, the peer group has no such responsibility; (4) thus, any long-run socializing implications are largely unintentional. Children participating in peer groups do not do so with the aim of preparing themselves for adult society, though the peer group experiences do have such import.

The child's peer group participation may be said to begin in a very rudimentary way in the yard or the sandbox at about the age of two or so, although egocentricity, rather than any form of cooperation, is still the order of the day. This play may be followed by the formation of rudimentary pairs and later by a succession of peer groups. With increasing age, the peer groups gain in solidarity and complexity, and usually in size, while the activities and interests on which they focus change with the children's maturation and social development. For most children in the modern world, sports becomes one major vehicle for interaction and involvement in peer groups, with an accompanying exposure at different stages to new social norms and new roles.[68]

The Peer Culture

While children are absorbing the adult culture at home and in the school, they also sustain a subculture of their own, a subculture that is age-limited. The richness of this subculture is suggested by studies conducted in Britain by Iona and Peter Opie. One of these reports on some 2,500 games played by children ages six to twelve. While many of these are simply slight regional variants of basic games (none of which requires even such minimal equipment as a ball), children nonetheless sustain a great variety of games that can be roughly classified into eleven different types: chasing, catching, seeking, hunting, racing, duelling, exerting, daring, acting, guessing, and pretending. Excluded from the study were party games, scout games, team games, and any sport that required supervision.

This study, carried out over a ten-year period in many parts of Britain, discloses that certain kinds of rules appear repeatedly. There are, for example, rules for starting a game. Two or three children on a street or playground initiate the idea and then, to round up enough to play, they issue a traditional "summons" to others around. In one region, for example, children call out, "All in, all in, a bottle of gin; all out, all out, a bottle of stout."[69] While there is considerable local variation in the particular wording of the call, the practice of some such traditional way of starting a game is widespread.

Similarly, there are rules for avoidance of a disliked role. The investigators observed that

> the chief impediment to a swift start is the fact that in most games one player has to take a part that is different from the rest; and all children have, or affect to have, an insurmountable objection to being the first one to take this part. Tradition, if not inclination, demands that they do whatever they can to avoid being the chaser, or the seeker, or the one who . . . is "it."[70]

To avoid being first, children shout out some particular phrase or engage in some particular gesture. By general agreement, the last one to do so is first to be "it." And just as there are rules for choosing the first child who will be in a role that pits him or her against the others, so there are rules for changing roles. Thus, in chasing games, a touch results in a change of role.

It appears that games of this kind were once played by grown-ups and children together and that they did not become distinctively children's games until about the start of the eighteenth century.[71] Today they are virtually restricted to children and taught by children. The rules are sustained by children, as is the interest in them. The Opies note that games go through periods of rise and decline in popularity:

> it is no coincidence that the games whose decline is most pronounced are those which are best known to adults, and therefore the most often promoted by them; while the games and amusements that flourish are those that adults find most difficulty in encouraging (e.g., knife-throwing games and chases in the dark) ...[72]

In an earlier study the same investigators documented a vast amount of lore and language known mostly to children and evidently circulated largely by them. This takes such various forms as "petty verbal stratagems," riddles, parodies, "codes of oral legislation" (such as "finders keepers, losers weepers"), jeers and torments, secret languages, and many others.[73] The study turned up many parallels in the United States and some on the European continent, suggesting that at least certain aspects of the peer culture transcend ethnic and national boundaries.

On street and playground, children sustain a subculture. It consists of rules, traditions, language, interests and activities, and ways of making and breaking peer relationships that are somewhat apart from, and sometimes in opposition to, the subcultures the children are simultaneously absorbing from adult models and institutions.

Although our attention will soon focus on the distinctive

functions of the peer group considered as a world separate from that of adults, it should be remembered that some peer groups are organized around adult values and draw upon adult models. In our discussion of middle-class subculture we mentioned that children participate in many groups sponsored and controlled by adults. Working-class children also participate in such groups, often based in such institutions as churches, settlement houses, scout troops, and Little League baseball teams. Parental encouragement is often considerable. It should also be noted that parents sometimes intervene in child-organized peer groups, for example, by prohibiting their child to play with another child or to participate in a group that they consider undesirable, while encouraging the child to play with others they consider more suitable. Such parental intervention is often based on social class and ethnic evaluations, with the result that the child is led unwittingly to take on parental sentiments and attitudes toward other social classes and ethnic groups.

The link between the games of children's peer groups and the world of adults is probably nowhere as evident as in sports. In our culture, sports are not only a major form of leisure activity, they are held up for children as a means of achieving physical health; as a way of learning leadership skills, loyalty, and other desirable traits; and as valuable training in competitiveness and give-and-take relationships. The value, however, that stands out the most both in sports and in the surrounding world is achievement. As socializers of young children, adults are likely to stress the importance of self-development and fair play, but as children become older and more sophisticated, they themselves tend to give more weight to success and achievement. Harry Webb speaks of the professionalization of children's attitudes— "the substitution of 'skill' for 'fairness' as the paramount factor in play activity, and the increasing importance of victory."[74]

In a study of children in the public and parochial schools of Battle Creek, Michigan, Webb found that the higher the grade, the greater the importance placed on "beating one's opponent" and the less the importance placed on "doing one's best" or "playing the game fairly." He concludes by drawing a parallel with the business world, saying that to insist

> on play's contribution to the development of such "sweetheart" characteristics as steadfastness, honor, generosity, courage, tolerance, and the rest of the Horatio Alger contingent, is to ignore its structural and value similarities to the economic structure dominating our institutional network, and the substantial contribution that participation in the play arena thus makes to committed and effective participation in the wider system.[75]

In discussing the school, we noted that academic achievement may be an avenue of mobility, of achieving a higher socio-economic status than one's parents. Ability in sports is undoubtedly another such avenue, of which children soon become aware. The heroes of the sports world—especially in such television-publicized sports as football, basketball, and baseball—are honored and acclaimed in the child's as well as the adult's world. The pattern is not only North American. Speaking of soccer in Brazil, which she describes as "an all-consuming commitment bordering on fanaticism," Janet Lever writes:

> Soccer-playing begins very young in Brazil; one often sees four- and five-year-olds using small rubber balls to mimic their older brothers. By the time a boy is in his early teens, he is conscious that soccer might be his road to success, and many play as though they felt the eyes of the scouts boring into their backs.
> There are also, in Brazil, the equivalent of little leagues, where many middle-class boys spend hours on the soccer field perfecting their skills. But it is the poor boys, perhaps, who in the tradition of rags-to-riches American sports story, most desperately want to make it to the "juvenile teams" and then on to pro status. Too poor to afford soccer balls, these youths will practice the whole day through on beaches or empty lots with only tightly rolled stockings for a ball.[76]

In Brazil, Lever suggests, the mobility that comes from high athletic competence is generally short-lived, since it is not accompanied by the development of a higher education or any other occupational skills. In contrast, in the United

States, especially with its system of athletic scholarships, high competence—at least in some sports—may become a means of obtaining a college education, which in turn may become a basis for possible success in the business or professional world. For the socialization of the child, however, the basic point remains that in Brazil, North America, and elsewhere, outstanding athletic achievement is a significant ideal for lower-class boys (seldom for girls) who aspire to rise in social status.

Functions of the Peer Group

Philippe Ariès has stated that "The development of mass education is undoubtedly the most important social change that has ever taken place."[77] The reason he gives such emphasis to this development is that it has had the effect of setting children apart from adults, of making them a special group in society. True as this is, and significant as it is, this judgment overlooks the fact that the school is organized by adults and is specifically governed by the purpose of preparing children for adult life. So while the children are defined as a group apart, the school does not really keep them apart from adults and the adult world. The only social setting in which children are in fact separated from adults in any meaningful sense is in the peer group, governed as it is by the rules, rituals, interests, and logics of children. From this point of view, then, it would seem that one of the functions of the peer group is to keep children from being completely immersed in the process of socialization. But this conclusion must be qualified. Although it is probably true that the peer group retards socialization in the sense of keeping the child from being totally concerned by the rules, values, and norms of the adult world, there are other ways in which it contributes to socialization.

First, the peer group gives children experience in egalitarian types of relationships. In this group they engage in a process of give-and-take not ordinarily possible in their relationships with adults. In the family and in school children necessarily are subordinate to parents and teachers (however benign their subordination may be). In the peer group they gain their first substantial experience of equality. Children entering a peer group are interested in the companionship, attention, and good will of the group (particularly of the members of the group who are significant for them), and the group is in a position to satisfy this interest. For behaving in the appropriate or valued manner, the group rewards its members by bestowing attention, approval, or leadership or by giving permission to participate or to employ certain symbols. For behaving otherwise, the peer group punishes by disdain, ostracism, or other expressions of disapproval. Responding the same way as they do toward other socializing agencies, children come to view themselves as objects from the point of view of the group and in some measure to internalize its standards. While they are members, these standards are reinforced by the feelings of solidarity and support that children obtain from others.

The way in which games contribute to this process has been nicely described:

> the child disclose[s] his unsureness of his place in the world by welcoming games with set procedures, in which his relationships with his fellows are clearly established. In games, a child can exert himself without having to explain himself, he can be a good player without having to think whether he is a popular person, he can find himself being a useful partner to someone of whom he is ordinarily afraid. He can be confident, too, in particular games, that it is his place to issue commands, to inflict pain, to steal people's possessions, to pretend to be dead, to hurl a ball actually at someone, to pounce on someone, or to kiss someone he has caught. In ordinary life either he never knows these experiences or, by attempting them, he makes himself an outcast.[78]

A second function of the peer group stems from the fact that its characteristic equality actually holds only for some contexts but not for others. A game of tag or hide-and-go-seek may include children of both sexes and spanning an age range of about seven to twelve; all are equal, and they are likely to experience themselves as such. But when the group is practicing basketball or choosing sides for a baseball or hockey game, the differences in skill associated with age level are likely to become prominent. Age differences of a year or two become significant, and the older child who can skate faster or catch a ball more reliably becomes a role model for the younger one. Thus, in some contexts, the age differences within the peer group (and associated skill differences) become more significant than the basic age similarity. The younger children see in the older ones a model of what they might become *soon* (while still children), while the older children become aware that they can be a model to younger ones.

A third function of the peer group is that it provides the setting within which children develop close relationships of their own choosing. Within the larger peer group of equals, children begin about the age of eight and a half to establish special friendships, to find chums.[79] The child begins to construct relationships based on discriminated affinities with others, rather than on simple availability.

The development of friendships within the peer group includes friendships across sex lines. Recent evidence suggests that the once sharply segregated male and female peer groups of preadolescence are gradually giving way. In one study of elementary school children in a small southern city, Carlfred B. Broderick and S. E. Fowler found that about 20 percent of fifth graders chose someone of the opposite sex as their best friend and more than 50 percent of them chose someone of the opposite sex as one of their four best friends. The authors report that, compared with earlier data, this pattern represents a definite change.[80] They see this as part of a larger pattern of convergence of sex-role expectations and more sharing of values, leading to reduced antagonism between boys and girls, which had been traditional at this age level.

The importance of the peer group in sex education is suggested by further data. For example, in the study just mentioned 65 percent of the fifth graders of both sexes reported having been kissed. Other work cited by Broderick indicates that there is evidently variation from community to community in the rapidity of development of heterosexual activity; he cites some data from a middle-class midwestern city, predominantly Protestant and middle class, in which 50 percent of a sample of 291 boys had engaged in heterosexual play by age eleven, and about 60 percent had done so by age thirteen. More than 20 percent had attempted sexual intercourse by age thirteen.[81] There is evidence to support the view that heterosexual knowledge and activity occur even earlier among lower-class segments of the black community and that the peer group provides the opportunities as well as normative support.[82] However, it must also be said that there has actually been less intensive investigation of peer group sexual practices among white children, both middle class and lower class, than among black lower-class children, so that there is some possibility that apparent differences may be due to the fact that more complete data are available for the latter group.

The subculture of the peer group not only provides a world of standards that is *apart from* that of adults, but it also provides one that is *in opposition to* that of adults. Adults couldn't care less about the proper way to avoid being "it" in a game; they leave that to the children, if they have any awareness of such "problems" at all. But adults often do care about such things as modesty, respect for elders, and other "proprieties," and children often develop corresponding "improprieties." These include ways of talking about subjects that adults frown on and various acts that adults would disapprove of if they knew about them.

Through this distinctive peer culture of childhood and through the new kinds of relationships that children establish in the peer group, they become more independent of parents and other adult authorities. In the peer group children develop new emotional ties and identify with new models. They seek the attention, acceptance, and good will of peer group members and view themselves according to the group's standards. Success in sports, dancing ability, sexual exploits, audacity in provoking adult authority—matters that may be quite unimportant to one's family—now become primary considerations in the child's self-image. And as the peer group defines the culture heroes of its time—the ath-

letes, the movie stars, the pop singers, the TV performers—
children establish a solidarity with their generation. When
they reach adulthood and see their children and *their* peer
culture, they become aware that their own childhoods were
passed in a particular time and under historically limited
circumstances that make them members of a particular generation.

THE MEDIA OF MASS COMMUNICATION

The media of mass communication comprise newspapers,
magazines, comic books, radio, television, movies, and other
means of communication that reach large heterogeneous audiences and in which there is an impersonal medium between the sender and receiver.[83] Unlike the other agencies,
the mass media do not directly involve interpersonal interaction. Nevertheless, as Donald Horton and R. Richard
Wohl point out:

> One of the striking characteristics of the new mass media—
> radio, television, and the movies—is that they give the illusion
> of face-to-face relationship with the performer. The conditions
> of response to the performer are analogous to those in a primary
> group. The most remote and illustrious men are met *as if* they
> were in the circle of one's peers; the same is true of a character
> in a story who comes to life in these media in an especially vivid
> and arresting way. We propose to call this seeming face-to-face
> relationship between spectator and performer a para-social rela-
> tionship.
>
> In television, especially, the image which is presented makes
> available nuances of appearance and gesture to which ordinary
> social perception is attentive and to which interaction is
> cued.... The audience ... is ... subtly insinuated into the pro-
> gram's action and internal social relationships.... This simula-
> crum of conversational give and take may be called para-social
> interaction.[84]

Since the media include a wide range of materials, they
should not be viewed from a single perspective. In content,
The New York Times, a comedy television show, a soap

opera, and a science fiction comic book do not have much in common. Nor can the mass media be considered in isolation. They are ordinarily seen or heard in group settings, and the family and peer group have a considerable influence in guiding exposure to, and generally defining, their content.

Themes and Implications of Mass Media Content

The mass media, by their content alone, teach many of the ways of the society. This is evident in the behavior we take for granted—the duties of the detective, waitress, or sheriff; the functions of the hospital, advertising agency, and police court; behavior in hotel or airplane; the language of the prison, army, or courtroom; the relationship between nurses and doctors or secretaries and their bosses. Such settings and relationships are portrayed time and again in films, television shows, and comic strips; and all "teach"—however misleadingly[85]—norms, status positions, and institutional functions. They provide the child with images of what it might be like to be in such situations and relationships. Until he or she encounters these situations in actuality, and unless the images are discounted by the child's significant others, the images serve as effective "knowledge" of them.

The recurrent themes and story types present values and ideals associated with particular statuses. The Western story form, for example, generally assumes that a law enforcement officer fights for justice and that people who dishonestly seek wealth are evil; the romantic musical implies that love, rather than wealth, makes one happy, and that the world of show business is exciting and glamorous.

The mass media also present models of behavior—of heroes, villains, and comics; of occupational, ethnic, and personality types. The models presented by the media wax and wane with the changing times, but certain of their qualities persist through their change of dress. Tarzan faded, but his agility and courage lived on in such successors as Batman, whose mode of levitation was more appropriate to the start of the space age. Although the Western hero still survives as a model of good judgment and self-reliance, he gradually gives way to the detective, the store-front lawyer, and other urban types who take up the twin causes of good character and social order.

Socializing Influence of the Mass Media

The nineteenth-century crusader against vice, Anthony Comstock, began his comprehensive survey of Satan's schemes for victimizing children, *Traps for the Young,* with two chapters on "Household Traps." Among the most sinister of these, in his judgment, was the daily newspaper. An example of how the newspapers do their dirty work of corrupting the young is provided in this account:

> The daily papers are turned out by the hundreds of thousands each day, and while ink isn't yet dry the United States mails, the express and railroad companies catch them up, and with almost lightning rapidity scatter them from Maine to California. Into every city, and from every city, this daily stream of printed matter pours, reaching every village, town, hamlet, and almost every home in the land. These publications are mighty educators, either for good or evil. Sold at a cheap price, from one to five cents each, they are within the reach of all classes. More: they enter the homes—often files of them are preserved—and are especially within the reach of the children, to be read and re-read by them. The father looks over his paper in the morning to ascertain the state of the market, to inform himself as to the news of the day. His attention is attracted by the heavy headlines designed to call especial attention to some disgusting detail of crime. A glance discloses its true character. He turns away in disgust, and thoughtlessly throws down in his library or parlor, within reach of his children, this hateful debauching article, and goes off to business little thinking that what he thus turns from, his child will read with avidity.[86]

Comstock does not tell us whether the home newspaper files were kept by the father in spite of his disgust or whether they were preserved by children who scavenged debauching articles in the parlor after they had been thrown down by the father.

Today, there are commentators who still consider the parlor a scene of debauchery, though the name of the room has been changed to "family room" or "den" and the debaucher is now television instead of the newspaper. According to one study in San Francisco, conducted in the 1950s, 82 percent of children watched TV by the age of five, but none read the newspaper, and only 9 percent had parts of the paper read to them.[87] Furthermore, young readers were introduced to newspapers by their pictorial content rather than by their headlines, and among readers age ten to fifteen, comics were by far the most read items in the paper, followed by news pictures and public affairs cartoons.[88] Such patterns, presumably, persist.

While television may have replaced the newspaper in the minds of critics as a corrupter of the young, the newer and the older view both assume that these media of mass communication can affect children and in ways that are considered to impede their preparation for productive membership in adult society. If Comstock's view seems ridiculous today, are his modern-day successors more justified in their concern about the effects of television or comic books?[89]

Before attempting to answer this question, it should be noted that children are exposed to a wide variety of media: TV, movies, radio, comic books, magazines, and newspapers. Since children begin watching television before they can read and before they go to school, and because children spend many hours watching, even after they have begun school, this medium has been felt to be far more significant in its impact than the other media. It has, accordingly, in recent years attracted the most attention both from critics and social scientists. We shall therefore focus our own attention primarily on television.

Children's Use of Television

Children spend a good deal of time watching television. Practically all American and Canadian homes have access to a TV set. In the United States the proportion of homes (of those wired for electricity) with at least one TV set is 99.9 percent,[90] and in Canada the proportion of the population reached is over 97 percent.[91] This nearly universal availability makes possible near-universal viewing. Although there are no national studies that actually measure the prevalence of children's television viewing, it is highly probable that virtually all children in North America watch at some time or another. Smaller-scale studies certainly support such a conclusion. For example, a study in 1970 by Jack Lyle and Heidi R. Hoffman of 158 children, age three to six, in a town near Los Angeles, found that 98 percent of these children said they like to watch television.[92] Other studies—of school-age children—also turn up few if any nonviewers.

The amount of television viewing among children, however, varies greatly; and for any one child, the amount varies from day to day, from season to season, and from situation to situation. One report, for example, carried out in the late 1950s, indicated that in winter television viewing was greater in an isolated Rocky Mountain town than in a city with a milder climate, such as San Francisco.[93] These diverse sources of variation have led some researchers to conclude:

> Exact estimates of the number of hours per week are difficult to make because of the unreliability of different methods of assessment, and seasonal and situational variation in viewing. Furthermore, there is such wide variation among individuals that an average figure is meaningless. In a sample of 100 children, mothers reported that their children watched from 5 to 88 hours of television per week. [Another study found that] on a given day, about one-fourth of their sixth graders reported no viewing; at the other extreme, about a fourth reported over 5 hours of viewing.[94]

Although it is true that an average figure for all children or even all children of a certain age would be somewhat misleading, studies do show certain trends by age categories and by ethnic and social-class groups. Lyle and Hoffman studied 274 first-graders, 800 sixth-graders, and 500 tenth-graders in the same California town in which they conducted their preschool study. They conducted individual interviews with the first-graders and their mothers (rather than with the mothers alone, as earlier studies had done) and also obtained from each of them a one-day viewing record. They obtained five-day viewing records from each of the sixth-graders and tenth-graders. (The necessity of using somewhat different research procedures with children of different ages points up one of the difficulties in carrying out studies that compare different age groups.) The results are suggestive. Lyle and Hoffman estimate that first-graders in this town spend between twenty-two and twenty-four hours per week watching television, sixth-graders spend thirty to thirty-one hours, and tenth-graders spend twenty-seven to twenty-eight hours.[95]

Lyle and Hoffman compared their 1970 results with those obtained in a seven-city study in 1959[96] and found that children at all three grade levels were watching more television in 1970 than in 1959, as much as an hour more on weekdays and (depending on grade level) from fifteen minutes to two and one-half hours more on Sunday.

The authors also report ethnic and social-class differences. The research site is predominantly a working-class community with a sizeable Mexican-American minority. There is some tendency for sixth-grade Mexican-American girls in this community to spend more hours per week viewing television than do the "Anglo" girls, but this difference is not found among sixth-grade boys.[97] In a direct comparison of social-class levels, they find that for sixth-graders and tenth-graders, in both the 1959 and 1970 studies, "blue-collar children tended to watch more television than white-collar children."[98]

Bradley S. Greenberg and Brenda Dervin, in a study in East Cleveland, Ohio, in 1969, also were interested in ethnic and class differences. Their sample of 392 fourth-graders and fifth-graders included both black and white children. They were primarily interested in studying viewing among the poor, but there was enough range in income for them to be able to compare the poor with a group they call high income. Their high-income group would, in a national context, more appropriately be regarded as middle income. They concluded that "Low-income children watched longer than high-income children. Black children from low-income families averaged almost 7 hours of viewing on a given weekday in comparison to 4 hours for white youngsters from high-income families."[99]

Although children undoubtedly watch a substantial number of hours of television per week, the significance of the number of hours is not clear-cut, for it seems that, much of the time, children do not give full attention to what they are watching. For example, 81 percent of the first-graders in the Lyle-Hoffman study report that they do one or more of the following things while watching: eat, talk, play, draw, study, read. Not quite half of the sixth-graders report that they sometimes or usually study while watching.[100]

Another complication derives from the possible connection between television viewing and interpersonal relationships. Lyle and Hoffman, in the comparison of the 1959 and 1970 studies, noted some important changes over the decade: "In 1959, heavy use of television among white-collar children was found to be related to high conflict with parents. The 1970 situation was far less clearcut, perhaps due to the generally higher levels of viewing among all the groups."[101] Thus, to analyze the significance of the number of hours spent in front of a TV set is obviously a complex matter.

The television programs children prefer, as might be expected, also vary by age. During preschool years, children's favorite programs tend to be those with animals, cartoon characters, or puppets. During the early school years, children's program interests broaden to include child-oriented adventures, family situation comedies, and what some researchers have called "hip adventure programs."[102] Some differences are also reported in program preferences between boys and girls as early as the first grade; boys show greater preference than do girls for action programs that feature a strong male character, while girls show greater preference for family situation comedies in which a woman either dominates or is at least coequal with the male lead character.[103]

Socializing Influences of Television

We know, then, that children spend much time watching TV, and we know that they view a variety of kinds of programs, beginning with those that have high animation and proceeding to programs with more talk and people. What effect does watching have on children and how does the effect come about? Is it the content of the programs? the amount of time spent watching? Does television subvert parental influence? school influence? Does it lead them to be antisocial? Does television affect children at all? The questions seem momentous, and the contemporary counterparts of Anthony Comstock have no doubt that television is not merely influential in the lives of children but fundamentally destructive. An assessment of such evidence as is available leads to a somewhat more complex judgment concerning the significance of TV for socialization.

Suppose we begin with the question of whether or not TV subverts parental influence. One survey of the attitudes of 2,500 adults revealed that parents with children under the age of fifteen—both mothers and fathers—were more likely than married people without young children or than single people to believe that children are better off with than without television and that TV's virtues outweigh its drawbacks.[104]

Parents do have objections to TV. They object to certain aspects of the program content—most strongly to the depictions and enactments of violence—but even more strongly they object to the intensity of children's involvement with the medium. Parents complain that it is difficult to get children to do simple things they should do, such as eating meals, helping with housework, or doing school homework.

Yet fewer than half the parents with children under age fifteen have definite regulations about when and what children may watch. And parents who are fundamentally opposed to television are scarcely more likely to claim regulation of children's viewing than are those who believe children are basically better off with TV.

Despite objections, parents also believe that children learn valuable lessons from TV. Further, parents often admit to using TV as a way of keeping children occupied and thus not doing what parents don't want them to do.

The complexity of parental attitude has been nicely summarized:

> So all in all, so far as adult judgments are concerned, television helps to educate the child, but watching it interferes with his education. It helps keep him busy and out of mischief, but it also keeps him too busy to do his chores. It keeps the kids in when you want them, which is good, except for some of the bad things they see. And it keeps them in when you want them out—which is bad even if they see good things. Ideally, then, TV should provide interesting, educational programs that intrigue children when parents don't want to be bothered with them—but not when they ought to be outside doing something else.[105]

If parents are not entirely enchanted with television's effects on their children, believing that watching it deflects children from the proper paths of socialization, they nevertheless find that at times it eases the burdens of their parental responsibilities. Further, parents believe that children learn something from television.

In fact, just about everybody who has anything to say about the matter believes that children learn from television, but the effect of what they learn on their overall socialization is still subject to some uncertainty. To examine this question, we might oversimplify and argue that what children learn from television is (1) good for them and for society, or (2) bad for them and for society, or (3) probably not too significant one way or the other.

Supporting the first view is the argument that television is broadening, that it enlarges children's knowledge of the world. Studies done at a time when television was not yet available in all communities allowed various comparisons between children with and without access to television. The results seem to indicate that children who watch TV begin school with larger vocabularies and greater general knowledge than those who do not, but that this advantage does not last very long once schooling has started.[106] Seventy percent of the elementary-school children studied in San Francisco thought television helped them in their schoolwork, particu-larly in studying current events. Some felt it helped in science. Summarizing a detailed array of research findings, Wilbur Schramm and his co-workers reached these main conclusions: (1) Children probably learn most from televi-sion before they learn to read well; (2) both the brightest and the dullest children seem to derive greater learning benefits than do children of average intelligence; (3) most of chil-dren's learning from television derives from entertainment programs rather than those that are avowedly informational; (4) although television seems to help children get off to "a faster start" in school learning than when TV is not avail-able, the performance gain is only temporary, a result that had also been obtained in an English study.[107]

Since television has become nearly universal in North America, research attention and thinking have moved on. One more recent development that has aroused interest is the effect on young children of programs that are explicitly intended to teach them concepts and attitudes that are con-sidered worthwhile—"prosocial content," as it is called (in contrast to antisocial content). One experimental study of ninety-seven preschool children (age three years ten months to five and a half) sought to compare the impact of programs considered to have violent content (Batman and Superman cartoons) with the impact of *Mister Rogers' Neighborhood,* a program that emphasizes themes of "cooperation, sharing, sympathy, affection and friendship, understanding the feel-ings of others, verbalizing one's own feelings, delay of grati-fication, persistence and competence at tasks, learning to accept rules, control of aggression, adaptive coping with frus-tration."[108] The children were assigned randomly to the "ag-gressive program condition" or to the "prosocial program condition," or to a "neutral film condition," that is, viewing films that were neither obviously aggressive nor prosocial. The research investigators found that

The clearest main effects of the television programs appeared on the self-controlling behaviors. Children exposed to the prosocial television programs showed higher levels of rule obedience, tolerance of delay, and persistence than children exposed to the aggressive programs. Those in the neutral condition generally fell between the two television groups. The differences among conditions were greatest for high IQ children.[109]

The concern with academic competence during the 1960s that we mentioned at the beginning of this chapter led to the development and production of *Sesame Street,* an educational TV program that was intended to stimulate the intellectual development of preschool children. The program went on the air in late 1969, and has been continuing for several years thereafter, and it was estimated to be reaching almost 9 million children between ages two and five by 1972.[110] The production of *Sesame Street* entailed many social innovations, but we must confine the present discussion to the effort that was made to find out what children were learning from the program.

The goals of the program included having children learn such things as the names and functions of body parts, several skills with letters of the alphabet and with numbers, and skills in classifying items according to several criteria. Several different studies produced similar results: The more frequently a child viewed the program, the more the child learned the information the program was trying to teach.[111] However, as Gerald Lesser, an educational psychologist who long served as advisor to the Children's Television Workshop, producers of the program, points out:

> Television is not an isolated experience in a child's life. Each child uses it in his own way. What a child learns from television is only one element in a complex balancing act of simultaneous influences—peers, siblings, parents and people in his neighborhood as well as television. One example ...: Among the disadvantaged children who watched at home, those who gained most had mothers who often watched *Sesame Street* with them and talked with them about it.[112]

An interesting conclusion drawn by the producers is that "television programs by themselves will not have continuing long-range effects," and for this reason, as well as for financial reasons, the Workshop is creating toys, games and books based on *Sesame Street* and on *The Electric Company,* a program that was added for elementary-school-age children.[113]

The second view of television—that it is bad for children and society—is based most heavily on the belief that the principal effect of television on children is that it stimulates them to violence. Journalists and psychiatrists have often expressed alarm that this is the case.[114] Psychologist Urie Bronfenbrenner reviewed the research available up until about 1970 and concluded:

> The implications of these research findings for the impact of television on its viewers are obvious. Given the salience of violence in commercial television, including cartoons especially intended for children, there is every reason to believe that this mass medium is playing a significant role in generating and maintaining a high level of violence in American society, including the nation's children and youth.[115]

The implications are not as unmistakable as this statement declares; and it would be more correct to say that although there is *some* reason to believe this (rather than "every reason"), there is also some reason to doubt it. To explain this more restrained conclusion, we must turn to a widely discussed effort to explore the question.

In 1969, a United States Senator from Rhode Island, John O. Pastore, asked the Secretary of Health, Education and Welfare to direct the Surgeon General to appoint a committee to "devise techniques and to conduct a study ... which will establish scientifically insofar as possible what harmful effects, if any, these programs have on children."[116] As a result, the Surgeon General's Advisory Committee on Television and Social Behavior was appointed on June 3, 1969; the committee included sociologists, psychologists, psychiatrists, an anthropologist, and a political scientist. Ten of the twelve members were academic people, while the other two were social scientists in charge of research at two of the TV networks. With a budget of one and a half million dollars, the committee hired a staff that commissioned twenty-three research projects (sixty research reports in all, since some projects produced more than one study) dealing with various facets of the question.[117] The committee reviewed this large amount of material and produced an integrated summary of findings that has come to be known as "The Surgeon General's Report."[118]

As is characteristic of much research, findings from the separate studies do not always fit neatly into a clear explanation of what happens when children watch TV. With sixty new research reports to consider, together with earlier studies that had been available, committee members had to work very hard to achieve an agreed-upon report. We shall mention some of the problems shortly. First, we briefly state the committee's conclusions. On the basis of the evidence available, the committee stated that the findings of various studies

> converge in three respects: a preliminary and tentative indication of a causal relation between viewing violence on television and aggressive behavior; an indication that any such causal relation operates only on some children (who are predisposed to be aggressive); and an indication that it operates only in some environmental contexts. Such tentative and limited conclusions are not very satisfying. They represent substantially more knowledge than we had two years ago, but they leave many questions unanswered.[119]

Senator Pastore wanted a clear-cut answer to his question, one that would make it possible to decide what the government should do about TV programs that children see. The committee felt able to provide only a qualified answer. Why? Space permits us to do no more than indicate briefly what the problems are; we list them and discuss each in a few words.

1. How should violence be defined? Can gun-shooting in westerns and detective stories be added to the newsclips of street riots, civil wars around the globe, and plane crashes, and further added to the goings-on in children's cartoons to produce a figure that can be called "the total amount of violence on television"? Urie Bronfenbrenner, quoted above,

cites the violent cartoons aimed at children as an important contributor to violence in this society. But what are we to make of a study that reports, " 'Monster' or 'horror' cartoons were found to be less violent than the seemingly more benign 'Bugs Bunny' or 'Tom and Jerry' cartoons"?[120] Is it possible that the element of playfulness in a Bugs Bunny cartoon in effect communicates some other message than a message of violence, at least to children of some ages? Violent program content is presented in different styles or modalities—fantasy, cartoon, ominous drama, news report, and others. There is, as yet, no firm basis for judging that the content is more important than the modality, no firm basis for assuming that the violent contents can be taken out of their contexts to provide a single cumulative category that can be called "amount of violence in TV programs."

2. What causes the harmful effects? The unsettled issue here is whether "amount of exposure" or "gratification" is the serious consideration. Is it the number of hours a child watches TV or watches violent programs that is harmful or is it a question of whether violent programs are the child's favorite programs? If the latter, then a child might watch many hours of all kinds of programs, but if violent ones are not his or her favorites, then the young viewer would be less damaged than a child whose favorite programs are the violent ones (however violence is defined).

3. What is the best way to study the effects of TV on the child? The issue here is the relative advantages and disadvantages of controlled experiments as compared to field studies. Controlled experiments place children in a laboratory; some are shown a brief segment of violent programming, while a matched group is shown something benign. Then the children are given the opportunity (some critics of this type of work say they are given an encouragement) to express violence in some way, for example by hitting a doll. Field studies are usually interview studies with children or their parents or both, to find out which programs children actually watch, how many hours they watch, and so on.

4. What effects should be taken as evidence? Should the

number of fights on the street and in the playground be the concern? Should it be rather the rates of juvenile violent crime and adult crime? Efforts have been made to correlate the amount of violence in TV programs with crime rates during the same year and in the next year (on the assumption that seeing violent programs in one year might lead to criminal activity in later years); these investigations yield no evidence of a correlation.

The Surgeon General's report has given rise to considerable debate and discussion. The various studies carried out for that report, together with earlier and later ones, have been further studied and analyzed by several social scientists. Psychologists Robert M. Liebert, John M. Neale, and Emily S. Davidson have reviewed the literature on the subject and have concluded:

> While some quibble, violence continues to become a way of life. The quibbling is unwarranted. On the basis of evaluation of many lines of converging evidence, involving more than 50 studies which have included more than 10,000 normal children and adolescents from every conceivable background, the weight of the evidence is clear: The demonstrated teaching and instigating effects of aggressive television fare upon youth are of sufficient importance to warrant immediate remedial action.[121]

These authors believe a stronger relationship between TV viewing and violent activity has been demonstrated than does the Surgeon General's Advisory Committee. Among other things, they point out that two members of the committee were consultants to the TV networks and one was a former network executive; these three, plus the two network officials mentioned previously, all of whom had some direct financial association with the television industry, constituted a large minority (five out of twelve) of the committee.[122] Furthermore, the Secretary of Health, Education and Welfare had given the industry a veto power over prospective members of the committee, with the result that seven well-known social scientists were excluded as possible committee members.[123] The overall result of the selection procedure, in the view of Liebert, Neale, and Davidson, was a report that quibbled, hedged, and perhaps even misrepresented some of the research on which it was based.[124]

Some of the sharpest criticism of the Liebert-Neale-Davidson interpretation has come from British psychologists at the Mass Communication Research Centre of the University of Leicester. Dennis Howitt and Guy Cumberbatch review much of the same American research as do the Liebert group and come to a very different conclusion:

> In summary, there is no reliable evidence that television exposure, whether general or violent, has any causal relationship with relevant dependent variables such as aggression or delinquency. A number of studies which at face value indicate a relationship can be seen to be flawed in that controls for essential variables such as sex are neglected. This failure confounds a relationship which becomes insignificant when appropriate controls are made.[125]

According to their examination of the evidence, "the mass media—as far as it is possible to tell using social scientific methodologies—do not serve to amplify the level of violence in society."[126]

Grant Noble, a psychologist formerly at Leicester and now at Trinity College, Dublin, Ireland, has examined this issue from another perspective. He argues against the idea that television viewing "injects" violence into the viewer. Like Howitt and Cumberbatch, he judges that the research fails to make a convincing case that viewing increases aggression or violence. More importantly, he considers that the significant question to ask is "what people do with the mass media, rather than what the mass media does to people."[127] He argues that children use television both to retreat from society and also to take part in it at the same time. They retreat from the stresses of everyday socialization by watching, yet simultaneously they are interacting with the characters depicted on the TV screen and thus learning about and experimenting with a variety of role relationships. (He conceives of television viewing not as a matter simply of being influenced but as a situation of parasocial interaction, the Horton and Wohl concept which we cited on p. 160.)

From his own studies as well as other work, Noble has concluded that it is necessary to distinguish among various kinds of aggressive content in TV programs. Some kinds may make children anxious rather than inclined to violence themselves (this is a point on which some other researchers on this topic agree); other kinds that are "stylized," such as the violence in Westerns, may induce creative play; and some may stimulate aggressiveness in the child viewer.[128]

Noble's conclusions are not decisively established, and there are aspects of his theory that are not well worked out. But his focus on viewers as active users of TV presents a perspective that needs to be considered alongside the one that considers them simply as absorbers of what is presented.

We have some reservations of our own concerning the Bronfenbrenner thesis, as well as the more recent Liebert-Neale-Davidson statement of a similar theme. Even assuming the validity of the evidence that aggressive programs stimulate children to aggressive feelings and actions, to claim a cause-effect relationship between TV violence and "the high level of violence in American society" entails a great analytical leap. An analysis of the causes of violence in society cannot be based only on a particular set of childhood experiences but must include consideration of institutions, social strains, and the question of which groups of people are especially prone to what kinds of violence under what kinds of circumstances.

A second reason for doubting a direct connection between the violence on television programs seen by children and the level of violence in American society is that it is by no means clear that the latter is greater than it was in previous periods or than it is in countries where television does not exist or does not feature violent programs. Although it is not certain that there has been an increase in violence in American society, it does seem likely that there has been an increase in the number and articulateness of people who believe that violence can and should be reduced, and this increase may lead to the belief that the amount of violence has increased.

Historian Richard Maxwell Brown writes that

violence, and nonviolence as well, has been a major aspect of our nation's past. . . . Why, then, have we had such a violent past, and why, today, are we such a violent people? . . . The answer . . . is that repeated episodes of violence, going far back into our colonial past, have imprinted upon our citizenry a propensity to violence. Our history has produced and reinforced a strain of violence, which has strongly tinctured our national experience.

The historical process of imprinting began in the early American period, with the insurgencies, riots, and slave rebellions and conspiracies of the colonial period, with the violent resistance to the mother country in the revolutionary period, with the rise of vigilantism and lynch law on the frontiers of South Carolina and Virginia, and with the emergence of the revolutionary-era concept of popular sovereignty as a powerful philosophical rationale for civil violence.[129]

A third reason for skepticism is that much of the research demonstrating that children are stimulated to aggressive feelings and actions by watching aggressive programs is restricted to that issue. Such research has not sought to investigate other possible effects, although television undoubtedly teaches many lessons, of which violence is but one. To illustrate our meaning, we may consider the cartoon programs that are popular among young children. These programs often show one animal (or human) intent upon harming another. Commonly these attempts fail, as the intended victim repeatedly outwits the would-be assailant. The latter repeatedly devises new stratagems to attain his goal. Now this type of program might teach children to feel aggressive and to behave aggressively after viewing it. But conceivably it might also teach children to maintain their courage or "cool" under attack (by identifying with the clever intended victim) or to maintain determination in the face of repeated frustration (by identifying with the often disappointed would-be assailant). Yet research has not been carried out (or at any rate, has not been published) that investigates, much less weighs, these alternative possibilities. The thematic content of such programs at least suggests the possibility that the main lesson children may learn from them is that resourcefulness *can* prevail over brute force. (Similarly, rather than teaching the satisfactions of violence, Westerns may be teaching that law and order must prevail.) Psychologist Eleanor Maccoby, summarizing some of the literature on the effects of the mass media, notes that it is not yet clear what kinds of behavior are most easily transmitted through observation of characters on a screen, and she concedes the possibility that observing evildoers punished may contribute to the moral education of children.[130]

Although concern with instigation of aggression has been the major basis for considering that what children learn from television is bad for them and society, there have been some others. Lotte Bailyn found that children who spend more time with the mass media (movies and comics as well as television) are more prone to stereotyped thinking.[131] Reviewing this study and others, Maccoby notes inconsistent results among them.[132]

This brings us to the third possibility mentioned above: Perhaps the effects of television are neither as harmful nor as helpful as some have claimed.

Some students of television audiences have noted that children's "involvement with commercials is as deep and intense as it is with programs,"[133] and another notes, "It may be that the commerical message is the most influential aspect of TV."[134] Although few published studies have investigated this aspect of children's involvement with TV, mothers who receive repeated requests from their young children that one advertised item after another be purchased would surely conclude that the most obvious socializing impact of TV is to induct children into the role of consumer in the marketplace. While this may not be the most significant socializing consequence of TV, at this writing it appears the least open to question. Yet even on this point we should note a study cited by George A. Comstock, who served as senior research coordinator on the Surgeon General's Advisory Committee: "By the second grade, children begin to express distrust of commericals, and by the sixth grade 'global' distrust is said to exist."[135]

Somewhat surprisingly, the Liebert group agrees with this

finding. After stating that they will show "how the content of American children's television has become a continuous chain of often questionable, sometimes dangerous advertisements,"[136] Liebert, Neale, and Davidson conclude their discussion of children and TV advertising by saying:

> In sum, by age 11 children have become cynical about the purpose and credibility of commercials, feeling that they have been lied to in an attempt to get them to buy products which are not as desirable as the adman's copy would have it. It is not surprising, then, that children do not pay full attention to the ads and that as they grow older they less often try to influence parental purchases.[137]

Liebert and his co-workers do not attempt to explain how children develop the ability to become skeptical of commercials. Nor do they attempt to explain why children can become critical of commercial content but not become critical of violent content. There may be a valid explanation—assuming that there is a real difference that needs to be explained—but Liebert and the others do not attempt to provide it. None of the research studies carried out for the Surgeon General's report seems to have interviewed children to find out what *they* think about the many varieties of violence.[138] They *were* interviewed about commercials, and an important finding is that children learn after a time not to be so heavily influenced by them. Perhaps interviews would disclose that they learn to be critical of some kinds of violent content as well.

Clearly, establishing the socializing impact of television is not so easy as it seems. We have to remain dissatisfied with research results (or the interpretation of them) that tell us that watching violence on TV stimulates children to imitate the aggression, but that watching commercials stimulates them to be cynical about commercials. On the basis of such results, we might expect that television is more powerful in stimulating children to be aggressive than it is in stimulating them to buy advertised products. One need not be happy with the general run of television programs or commercials to conclude that the research has brought us to an unlikely situation. To emerge with the finding that television teaches children both to feel and to act aggressively but that it also teaches them to resist being influenced by the commercials must leave us with the judgment that the theory explaining how television influences children remains insufficiently developed.

Cynicism is a complex human sentiment; perhaps aggression is an even more complex sentiment than all the researchers have assumed. Sociologist Herbert Hyman has suggested that studies of this area have been deficient in not making use of a concept of human sentiment, and deficient also in not investigating whether television does not, at least under some circumstances, contribute to the development of sympathy in children.[139]

We cannot leave the topic of television without mentioning that the entire issue of whether violent content in TV programs instigates violent behavior is embedded in a clash of values. Perhaps the main disagreement relevant to socialization is between those who say that violent TV content should be greatly reduced in quantity because it is harmful to children and to society and those who, in contrast, say that violence is part of life and therefore children should learn about it.

An important corollary issue is whether a small number of cases of violent behavior instigated by viewing television violence is sufficient justification for firmer government regulation of what is shown on television, and how far such regulation should go. Should the violent scenes of the Vietnam War have been kept out of the TV news programs? To answer yes is to say that such censorship is justified because the sights of war would damage children. To answer no, on the ground that such censorship of news is a bad precedent, leaves open the question: Why allow war scenes to be shown on news programs while insisting that the violence be removed from Bugs Bunny cartoons?

It should be noted that Howitt and Cumberbatch take a stand against the showing of brutality just for the sake of providing "kicks."[140] Noble says that where possible I would try to prevent my young child from watching news violence and violence seen in the neo-realistic police and detective programs. These latter types of violence, I fear, do show that violence is normal and accepted in everyday life and possibly define the targets at whom aggression can be directed. The sight of children in the news throwing stones at soldiers is for me the worst offender. Such violence takes place in streets similar to those in which our children live, the soldiers are recognizably different and thus a uniform target and overall such sights show your child how his counterparts in the wider society do conspicuously behave. There is danger that by mere exposure we legitimate such acts of violence. I would have no fear, though, about children, whether aggressive or not, watching *Tom and Jerry,* since the violence therein is stylistic, removed from life and even, dare I say it, imaginative.[141]

Noble is writing from Dublin, near a fierce civil war in Northern Ireland. Those same news scenes of boys throwing rocks at soldiers would very likely have very different meaning when seen by American or Canadian children on their news programs. The difference in meaning derives from the difference in social context.

Personal and social values are inextricably intertwined with judgments about the effects of television content on children's behavior. This can be seen clearly if we compare in outline form the views of the Liebert group with those of Noble:

LIEBERT-NEALE-DAVIDSON	NOBLE
1. Children should be protected from violent television content that damages them.	1. Children should be protected from violent television content that damages them.
2. Violence in cartoons, private-eye and detective shows, and most other kinds of entertainment programs damages them.	2. Violence in news and in police-detective programs, but not in cartoons or other stylized programs, damages them.

| 3. Increased government regulation is necessary to protect children.[142] | 3. Parents should regulate what their children see on television to protect them.[143] |

And we may conclude this discussion by citing the value position of Howitt and Cumberbatch, which differs from that of both the Liebert group and Noble:

> There is little doubt that mass media portrayals of violence can cause distress and anxiety in the audience. However, whether this is a good or bad thing is uncertain. It is difficult to conceive that one would wish to protect the public forever from the horrors of war, armed conflict, aggression and the like, but it is also true that one would not wish the audience to be assaulted simply "for kicks." The question must be one of balance involving various incompletely specifiable factors related to the justifiability of different sorts of events ...[144]

Other Agencies of Socialization

We have discussed the major agencies of socialization; others, too, may be of great significance, depending upon the child and the particular conditions of his or her life. The church, for example, although less important in modern America than in rural French Canada or early Puritan New England, may still be instrumental in teaching a child to distinguish the sacred from the profane and in instilling feelings of group solidarity. Community agencies, such as YMCAs and YWCAs, may have a marked influence, especially insofar as they help widen the outlook of ethnic and lower-class children. Of special importance for many children are athletic teams—some formally organized by adults, such as school teams and the "little leagues" of baseball and hockey, and some informally organized by the children themselves—which may well play an important part in developing values, aspirations, and peer relationships. The summer camp, particularly for middle-class children who attend every year from age three through adolescence, may be important for relationships with both peers and authority figures. Nursery schools and day-care centers are growing in number, but the research on their implications for socialization remains inconclusive.[145]

Although specific effects of these agencies remain somewhat elusive, they all function to weaken the child's ties with the family, give the child new statuses, teach different perspectives, and broaden his or her range of experience.

6 Sex and Socialization

$\mathbb{T}$he first statement anyone is likely to make about a healthy newborn baby is either "It's a boy" or "It's a girl." Newborns vary in several visible characteristics. Some are born with hair, some without. Some are very wrinkled, others less so. They vary in weight and in length. But among these differences, only the identification of the external genitalia, attesting to maleness or femaleness, results in the newborn being assigned to one of the most fundamental categories in society, the category of sex. This assignment sets in motion an ongoing series of beliefs, values, expectations, and conduct on the part of others with respect to the newborn, a series that will be highly consequential for the life that newborn baby will live in society. One of the great public issues of our time is whether the genital difference that separates newborns into males and females ought to be as widely significant in a person's life as it has been up to this point in human history.

The importance of external genitalia at birth lies in the fact that they signify biological differences that are not visible at birth. Male and female bodies will later differ considerably in appearance and functioning, and it is the social awareness of these later changes that gives importance to the initial visible differences.

Biologically, the infant genitalia forecast different roles in reproduction for males and females when the newborns reach sexual maturity. For women, the fact that they can bear and nurse children has, throughout history, been taken to be the most decisive fact about them. It has usually led to a belief and expectation, shared by men and women alike, that women *ought* to bear children. And since it was assumed that women *would* bear children, their social roles have, in one way or another, been shaped by their presumed and expected childbearing activities. The maintaining of a domestic household has most often been assigned to women because child care has been regarded as a "natural" sequel to childbearing, and homemaking a "natural" extension of the fact that women's childbearing and child caring restricted their freedom to move around. Their early socialization has, throughout history, generally been carried out with this later role in mind. In contrast, men have been freer to fight or to do work that takes them away from the household, at least since the time when they engaged in hunting and warfare and could use their greater speed and strength to advantage.

In important ways, then, women and men have always had different fates within any particular society (although there have also always been individual men and women whose lives were not typical for their own society). In our own time, however, being asked with new urgency are the questions: To what extent is the difference between male and female lives due to biological differences, to what extent due to society's *interpretations* of those differences? Is it inevitable that women be primarily responsible for child care and for maintaining a household? Why have military activities almost universally been organized and carried out by men? Is it because males are biologically more aggressive than females or is it because adult men and women have socialized their young sons but not their young daughters to be prepared for military activity? In short, *How compelling is human biology for human social life?*

The question is more easily asked than answered. Only in the last few years has the question of sexual biology's relative importance for social organization received concentrated attention, and no conclusive answer is yet available. But the question itself has become enormously controversial under the impact of the women's movement. It has also become apparent that, under the conditions of a modern industrial society, the preferred social expectations for males and females are not comfortable for all persons of the sex to which they are presumed to apply, a fact that implies that sex-role expectations are not necessarily "natural," in the sense of being entirely based on biology. The fact that societies differ among themselves in what they expect from males and from females also suggests that human sexual biology cannot be absolutely decisive in determining the place that women and men have in society. But set over against these facts are others that point to certain general patterns that distinguish men from women and boys from girls. These different facts, if they are facts, have given rise to controversy, and we shall discuss these issues in this chapter. First, we must turn to a matter of terminology.

One indication that the social significance of sex for socialization is increasingly controversial is the effort made by some writers to change the terminology for discussing the subject matter of this chapter. Sociologists have long recognized that all societies have different expectations for males and for females, and they have referred to the different clusters of expectations as "sex roles." The term was considered appropriate because it captured a prevailing outlook in almost every society: Men and women are different in anatomy, physiology, contribution to reproduction, and in other ways, and they should accordingly have different patterns of participation in society. In modern society, some critics consider social assignment on the basis of sex to be inappropriate, except and only for the period when people are actually engaged in producing children. All social assignment on the basis of sex beyond this seems to them arbitrary and inappropriate. Some have therefore proposed restricting the term "sex role" to only those aspects of behavior that involve the genitals, while behavior and expectations attributed to persons of a particular sex, but not describing genital activity, should be designated by the term "gender," a word imported from grammar into sociology. So we now sometimes hear of gender roles and of sex roles, where once the latter sufficed. But this new usage has not increased clarity, as sociologists Jean Lipman-Blumen and Ann Tickameyer have noted.[1] Some writers in fact use the terms "sex" and "gender" in quite opposite senses. Thus, the fact that girls are expected to become housewives and boys to become economic providers would be described by some writers as their gender roles assigned because of their sex and by other writers as their sex roles assigned because of their gender. We find the dual terminology confusing.

The fundamental fact we are dealing with is that the person's sexual anatomy and prospective generative role in sexual reproduction form the basis for the much wider-in-scope social-role assignment. Babies with male sex organs at birth are foreseen as potential fathers; they are judged male, and they are socialized toward certain attitudes, self-concepts, and performances in behavior and conduct that are considered masculine—that is, appropriate for a male in his particular society. Babies with female organs at birth are foreseen as potential mothers; they are judged female, and they are socialized toward certain feminine attitudes, self-concepts, and performances that in noticeable ways are different from those toward which the male is socialized. The concept of gender cannot be used in a sensible way unless it is connected with sex, and once it is connected with sex it becomes unnecessary. We shall therefore use the term "sex role" to refer to the attitudes and conduct expected of a person of given sex in a particular society. It is important to emphasize that adopting this term in no way implies approval or disapproval of any society's sex roles. The term simply denotes the fact that societies tend to develop social expectations linked to sex.

Sex-role socialization, like all socialization, involves many processes. Since these processes involve the impact of social organization upon babies and children defined by their biological sex, it will be helpful to discuss both biology and social organization to provide a background for discussing socialization to sex roles. We shall begin with biology.

SEX AND BIOLOGY

If any phenomenon in the human world can be considered an incontrovertible fact, it would be this: A human being can *either* beget a child *or* bear a child. No human being can do both. This difference in body functioning between males and females in reproduction is universal; it occurs in all human societies, and there is not a single known exception. Although there are cases of individual hermaphroditism—being born with genital organs that are not unambiguously male or female—there are no known cases in which that hermaphroditism enabled the person both to beget and to bear a child. In reproductive function, the two sexes are absolutely and unambiguously distinct. This much seems certain, and it has probably seemed certain to all of humanity since the beginning of human history. It may well be the basis for the elaboration in society of so many other expectations based on sex.

Not so long ago, to have called attention to sex differences in reproductive function would have been belaboring the obvious. This is no longer the case. Now it is necessary to gain increased precision and clarity concerning what is fixed and what is variable, because many of the characteristics of males and females that once seemed to be as thoroughly dichotomous and biological as their distinctive contributions to procreation are today less certainly so. The occurrence of cases of hermaphroditism has, in fact, prompted ever more careful study of just how a person's biological sex is formed. John Money and Anke Ehrhardt, medical psychologists in a clinic of the Johns Hopkins Hospital that treats congenital abnormalities of the sex organs, have considered the implications of the 150-or-so cases of diverse abnormalities that have been seen at the clinic over a period of many years. Their work has obliged them to think carefully about the stages by which sexual differentiation comes about. In order to understand various abnormalities, it is necessary to have a clear view of the normal process, and they have provided a useful summary. The discussion of biological development that follows is based largely on their account.[2]

Money and Ehrhardt contribute to the terminological confusion by referring to "sexual dimorphism" [the fact that the two sexes differ in body form], but then to "gender role" and "gender identity," and further by using the expression "psychosexual (or gender-identity) differentiation."[3] We shall disregard these unexplained shifts in terminology, particularly since Money and Ehrhardt consistently refer to sex rather than gender when they are discussing the purely biological aspects of their topic.

A person's biological sex is established through a series of four main processes or stages, each of which contributes a component to biological sex. These four components are: (1) chromosomal sex; (2) gonadal sex; (3) hormonal sex; (4) morphologic sex.

Chromosomal Sex

Conception occurs when the father's sperm unites with the mother's egg, or ovum. Each parent contributes twenty-three chromosomes—strands of genes that control biological development—to the fertilized egg which is the first phase in the development of a new individual. Twenty-two of the chromosomes determine the person's physical characteristics—eye color, hair color, shape of head, height, and many others—except sex. The twenty-third chromosome is known as the sex chromosome, and it occurs in two forms, known as X and Y. The mother's egg always contains an X chromosome; the father's sperm may contain either an X or a Y. When a sperm with an X chromosome fertilizes the egg, a female child is conceived; its chromosomal sex is XX. When a sperm with a Y chromosome does so, a male child is conceived, and its chromosomal sex is XY.

Gonadal Sex

Chromosomal sex by itself does not result in a male or female body. Rather, the chromosomes contain "coded information" or "directions" for the next step in sexual development. For the first six weeks after conception, the original fertilized egg, a single cell, divides into an increasingly complex, but still sexless, embryo. One embryonic organ is the gonad, a gland that will become either an ovary or a testis. When the embryo is chromosomal XY, the gonads begin to differentiate into a pair of testes, starting at the sixth week after conception. When the embryo is chromosomal XX, the gonads begin to differentiate into a pair of ovaries, starting at the twelfth week after conception. "The normal rule in embryonic development is that the primordial gonad begins its differentiation as a testis, if that is to be its fate, after the sixth week of gestation, and about six weeks ahead of the timing of ovarian differentiation."[4] Money and Ehrhardt do not comment directly on whether the earlier development of the male gonads has any significance. They do note that the way in which X and Y chromosomes regulate gonadal differentiation is not yet understood.

Hormonal Sex

The testes or ovaries, once formed in the embryo or fetus, begin to produce chemical substances known as sex hormones. These hormones are important in three main ways. First, male sex hormones and female sex hormones are produced in both male and female gonads. Males produce far larger quantities of male hormones (androgens) than do females, and females produce far larger quantities of female sex hormones (estrogens) than do males. The quantitative differences are significant, but so also is the fact of overlap. Second, the fetal sex hormones control the development of the internal and external sexual anatomy. Evidence indicates that if no hormones were present in the fetus, it would develop as a female. Testicular hormones are necessary for the fetus to develop as a male. Third, the sex hormones apparently influence brain organization. Since male and female sex organs are different, the pattern of nerve endings is different, both in the sex organs and in the way these nerves are linked to the central nervous system.[5] There is also some evidence that hormones act directly on the brain during critical periods of fetal development. Another specialist states:

> It would appear that following exposure of the brain during these periods to certain kinds of hormonal influences, a powerful imprinting process occurs on cells involved in complex regulatory circuits so that both behavior and endocrine functions may be profoundly modified in the adult animal.... It should be emphasized that "critical periods" will differ for different species. The bulk of the information in the literature is based on experimental procedures using the rat—a species in which the state of cerebral development at birth resembles that of man during the early part of pregnancy.[6]

This same author also cautions, however, "that information concerning the effects of hormones on the CNS [central nervous system] is limited, scattered, and for the greater part indirect."[7]

Still another biologist working in the field of hormones states: "For those mammalian species (guinea pig ... rat ... rhesus monkey ... and human being ...) in which social experience also contributes to the development of sexual and sex-related behaviors, I propose the hypothesis that early hormonal influences predispose the individual to the acquisition of specific patterns of behavior."[8] (Sex-related behaviors refer not to sexual activity but to activities such as rough-and-tumble play, chasing behavior, threatening behavior, which, among rhesus monkeys, are much more frequent in males than in females, but present in both sexes.)

Morphologic Sex

The sex of a newborn baby is identified not by its chromosomes or its hormones but by the form of its external genitalia; this is its morphologic sex, and this is the criterion that society uses in assigning sex roles. Some adult males are never able to produce sperm that can fertilize an egg. Despite this gonadal insufficiency, they are judged male because their morphological sex is male. Some women are unable to bear children. They are nonetheless judged female because their morphological sex is female.

The very existence of the Johns Hopkins clinic, among others, which treats cases of hermaphroditism, suggests that in modern society, at least, there is social pressure toward certainty of morphologic sex. There is no way of knowing, of course, how many parents who have hermaphroditic children do nothing to resolve the ambiguity. But neither is there any known sentiment specifically in favor of letting hermaphroditic children remain morphologically ambiguous throughout their lives. Sex roles change from period to period in our history; they vary from one society to another; and there are important changes both advocated and under way in our own society at the present time. Morphological sex appears to represent, however, an ultimate limit in the social acceptance of variation. Ambiguous sexual morphology is regarded in our society as something to be "corrected," brought into conformity (by surgery or hormone treatments) with one of the two acceptable morphologic sexes.[9]

SEX AND SOCIAL ORGANIZATION

A baby's morphological sex at birth affects the way that baby will be socialized in its society. Since societies differ in their norms, values, beliefs, and institutions, it would be reasonable to expect that socialization to sex roles would be as variable as these other aspects of society. Although sex-role socialization does indeed vary among societies, there also appear to be certain characteristic ways in which sex enters into social organization, and these characteristics constrain sex-role socialization within narrower limits than might otherwise be expected. We shall consider three such characteristics that seem to hold true of societies in general—authority, division of labor, and social status.

Sex and Authority

Anthropologists M. Kay Martin and Barbara Voorhies note that "A survey of human societies shows that positions of authority are almost always occupied by males. Technically speaking, there is no evidence for matriarchy, or rule by women, Amazonian or otherwise."[10] They go on to observe that (1) authority is not the same as power; and (2) women may exercise power in certain societies even if they do not exercise authority: "Power refers to the ability to coerce others toward desired ends, whereas authority refers to legitimate or legal power."[11] The survey of societies thus seems to indicate that authority is "almost always" exercised by men (the authors do not actually cite any exceptions) but that power is sometimes wielded by men, sometimes by women. This situation brings us to a crossroads where two research questions compete and perhaps collide.

Martin and Voorhies ask the question: How does it happen that women, even though they do not have authority, are able sometimes to exercise power? The general principle they consider to have operated in the past is that "power attaches itself to those who control the distribution of food or wealth, irrespective of sex."[12] In some societies, women have controlled the distribution of food or wealth, and this has been adaptive for the particular society. For the future, however, these authors, applying a functional perspective, foresee that differences of power based on sex will become less important.

> The major trend for men and women in the future as we see it, is that gender roles will become increasingly unimportant. History teaches us that gender roles have been ubiquitous, occurring in every known society extant today, and in those of the reconstructed prehistoric past. But history does not teach us that these roles are fixed or inevitable.... Gender roles seem to be increasingly dysfunctional in complex societies. The division of persons into two groups is becoming increasingly opposed to the requirements of social segmentation required in industrialized, urban environments. The plethora of different occupational specializations required in these societies are most efficiently met by training people for their occupational roles on the basis of talent and aptitude rather than on the anatomy of their reproductive systems.... societies have perpetuated sex categories to facilitate socioeconomic interdependence and cooperation

among group members. In industrial societies this interdependence is now insured by other, more complex and more appropriate forms of integration. Gender categories thus have much less adaptive significance in modern societies than in ancient ones.[13]

Sociologist Steven Goldberg recognizes that women sometimes exert power, but his attention is drawn to the universality of male authority. In his view, this is the important fact requiring explanation. Thus he asks a somewhat different question: Why is it that authority in all known societies has been placed in the hands of males? The views and conclusions of Martin and Voorhies and of Goldberg have different implications for socialization.

Martin and Voorhies concluded that future society can and ought to deemphasize sex-role socialization. Goldberg, on the other hand, concludes that there are strict limits to the extent of possible deemphasis because the universality of male authority suggests "the inevitability of patriarchy," and, in addition, the inevitability of "male dominance." Patriarchy he defines as "any system of organization (political, economic, religious, or social) that associates authority and leadership primarily with males and in which males fill the vast majority of authority and leadership positions."[14] Patriarchy thus refers to male authority in the wider society. Male dominance he defines as "the *feeling* acknowledged by the emotions of both men and women that the woman's will is somehow subordinate to the male's and that general authority in dyadic and familial relationships, in whatever terms a particular society defines authority, ultimately resides in the male."[15]

In presenting his theory, Goldberg reviews the evidence from both anthropology and sex hormone research. Regarding the former, he concludes that the universality of patriarchy "in a world of thousands of (formerly) isolated, unconnected societies that demonstrate nearly every conceivably possible configuration of religious, economic, and familial systems at nearly every conceivably possible stage of development" points toward some general explanation.

Regarding sex hormone research, he concludes that the available evidence concerning differences between males and females points to a greater likelihood of males striving for attainment in hierarchies and for dominance in dyadic and familial relationships. "The male hormonal system" according to Goldberg, "gives men a head start (in terms of probabilities) that enables them to better deal with those elements of the societal environment for which aggression leads to success."[16] (Goldberg later substituted the term "dominance assertion" as preferable to "aggression.")[17] Goldberg sees the actual exercise of patriarchy and dominance stemming from socialization as well as from hormonally based predispositions, so that the ways in which patriarchy and dominance are manifested differ from one society to another.

In Goldberg's analysis, the fact that societies tend to socialize boys and girls differently is based on societal members' perceptions that boys and girls do show a different likelihood of asserting dominance. Socialization, in this view, conforms to a recognition of a biological reality, but it also tends to exaggerate the reality. (By exaggeration he means that the socialization process amplifies the initial biological tendencies and also that conformity to stereotyped sex roles is imposed on individual girls and boys who are not well-suited for the stereotyped versions of the roles.)

> My point is not that the boy is not socialized differently from the girl or that such differential socialization does not run very deep. I do not doubt those environmentalists who claim that by the time an infant is three months old the nature of the socialization it receives from its parents will be determined by its sex; shortly after their births we dress male infants in blue and female infants in pink. While it is doubtful that this makes much difference to newborn infants, it does show that differential socialization by the parents begins at birth. But this simply indicates the strength and importance of sexual hormonal reality and the necessity of any society's socialization conforming to that reality. For the environmentalist to demonstrate that biological reality does not underlie the directions in which societies socialize the young he must demonstrate not that socialization

runs deep but that it would be possible to socialize boys away from, and girls toward, aggressive activities. No society has ever done this. Nor could any society ever do this.

This is the environmentalist's dilemma: he faces the insuperable task of explaining, without referring to either masculine aggression or feminine propensity, how the men of every society without exception manage to turn the women into people the feminists find so distasteful while themselves attaining nearly all the positions of power and authority and why no society fails to socialize young girls away from aggressive areas. *He must find a universal cultural-environmental factor comparable to the biological factor proposed here.* This is the point that is always forgotten by those who would deny the biological factor or who would claim that this factor is no longer relevant and that the institutions that cater to it are no longer necessary. The biological factor explains universality where no other explanation can.[18]

In a recent nontechnical presentation, John Money and Patricia Tucker have summarized the evidence concerning the effects of prenatal sex hormones. Their statement seems supportive of Goldberg's theory:

> The prenatal sex hormone mix apparently does not create any new brain pathways or eliminate any that would otherwise be there. The wiring for all the affected behavior is present in both sexes. What your prenatal mix did was to lower the threshold so that it takes less of a push to switch you on to some behavior and to raise the threshold so that it takes more of a push to switch you on to other kinds. More androgen prenatally means that it takes *less* stimulus to evoke your response as far as strenuous physical activity or challenging your peers is concerned, and *more* stimulus to evoke your response to the helpless young, than would otherwise be the case. *How* you respond once you're over the threshold depends on many things—your age, health, strength, physical development, cultural heritage, gender schemas, environment, training, and experience—but not simply on your prenatal sex hormone exposure.
>
> Prenatally determined differences in sensitivity to stimuli help to explain why dominance behavior and activities involving a high expenditure of physical energy are more characteristic of boys' play than of girls', and why parental behavior is more characteristic of girls' play than of boys'. When nativists of the

"anatomy is destiny" school and sex chauvinists cite this difference as evidence that men are predestined to be active and dominant, women to be passive and nurturant, however, they ignore the fact that all these behaviors are characteristic of both sexes, and they discount the heavy cultural reinforcement that maximizes the original slight difference in the thresholds.

... The nativists and sex chauvinists are right to the extent that if cultural influences were neutralized, one would still expect to find more men than women among those striving for dominance and those who prefer activities that demand a high expenditure of physical energy, and more women than men among those who prefer child care to other kinds of work. The prenatal sex hormone mix would still influence preferences. The point is that society need no longer insist that for a man to be a man he must be active and dominant, or for a woman to be a woman she must be passive and nurturant, no matter what capabilities and potential the interaction of nature and nurture may have given them.[19]

Goldberg is aware that women often have power, which he believes they obtain in any one of three ways: (1) they assume power in situations or activities in which men are not interested and therefore do not compete for; (2) power is specifically delegated to them by men; (3) perhaps most importantly, women have "feminine ways" of "getting around" men. All three of these roads to power for women, as a group, involve implicit—and sometimes explicit—recognition that men have the final authority.

Goldberg presents his theory in terms of statistical probability. Most males in a society are likely to be more dominance-assertive than most females in that society. But some women will be more dominance-assertive than some men. The great unanswered question posed by this theory is how much change in women's assertiveness and access to positions of authority could be accomplished by changes in institutions and by socialization. At the present time, according to his estimate, the percentage of women in positions of top authority ranges from zero in some societies to a maximum of 7 percent in others. Although the theory clearly states that female dominance is impossible in any society and that socialization will reflect this, it is not clear how high a percentage of female participation in positions of high authority may result from social change. Somewhere between his estimated present upper limit of 7 percent and the 51 percent that would give women dominant authority lies an indeterminate area for possible change that is compatible even with Goldberg's theory.

We should note here a study by sociologist Elina Haavio-Mannila in Finland that contradicts Goldberg's figures; her study shows that the percentage of members of Parliament who are women increased from 9.5 percent in the 1907–1954 period to 14.7 percent in the period 1958–1966.[20] This finding, as well as others from her study that could be cited, suggests that no upper limit can be set with assurance. The figures, when compared with Goldberg's, also suggest that there are problems that need to be worked out in defining "high authority."[21]

Goldberg has attempted to state his theory in a form that would enable it to be proved wrong, and he has also stated what facts would lead him to change his theory:

> I would have serious doubts about the crucial importance of male physiology to male attainment of position if women attained twenty percent of the highest positions (say, equivalent to election to the Senate), thirty percent of a somewhat lower position (election to the House of Representatives), or thirty percent of the higher state legislative positions. It is worth remembering that presently women constitute zero percent of the Senate, three percent of the House, and about five percent of the membership of state legislatures.[22]

As the socialization of both men and women changes in the direction of greater equality, the percentage of high offices held by women is likely to increase. In the middle 1970s, for the first time in the history of the United States, two women were elected state governors on their own merits, without first following a husband into the office. This trend is likely to continue, although it is not clear whether the trend will reach an upper limit short of full equality in the sharing of authority.

The present period is perhaps the first in all human history in which the viewpoint represented in Goldberg's theory is being directly challenged by an organized social movement that is setting out to prove it wrong. We do not venture to predict the outcome; our purpose is to make the issue clear. But it is evident that even a biologically based theory of male dominance leaves room for increased female participation in high authority, although less room than the theory's critics think possible.

Sex and the Division of Labor

Most societies make some distinction between work that is appropriate for women and work that is appropriate for men. Anthropologist Roy D'Andrade, using data from 224 societies first compared by George Murdock, analyzes how these societies assign twenty-two subsistence activities and twenty manufacturing activities to the two sexes. For example, of 179 societies that hunt for their food, men always do the hunting in 166 societies and usually do it in the other thirteen. In contrast, of the 201 societies for which information is available on who does the cooking, it is always done by women in 158 societies, usually by women in twenty-eight, usually by men in one, always by men in five, and by either men or women in nine. The study reports that in 121 societies weapons are always made by men and never by women, and in no society studied is this type of work open equally to men and women. In contrast, in twenty-nine societies, leather products are always made by men, while in another thirty-two, they are always made by women. D'Andrade suggests that:

> One possible explanation for the sex differences found in the manufacture of objects is that the objects being made are intended for use in activities that are directly related to physical differences. Thus weapon making is anticipatory to activities that do involve physically strenuous and mobile behavior.... The thesis here ... is that the division of labor by sex comes about as a result of generalization from activities directly related to physical sex differences to activities only indirectly related to these differences ... [23]

Clearly, this process of generalization proceeds differently from one society to another, since an occupation such as making leather products can be decisively assigned either to men or to women. Any link with biological sex in such an occupation seems tenuous indeed, but the connection is clearer in other occupations.

Although there are some difficult technical problems in studying the division of labor by sex in a large industrial society, certain general characteristics do emerge. In a comparison of women's work in the United States at two time periods, sociologist Valerie Oppenheimer found that of seventeen occupations that were 70 percent or more female in 1900, fourteen were still 70 percent or more female in 1960, including nursing, teaching, clerical work, private household work, operator's work in the clothing and textile industries, practical nursing, hospital attendants, and waiting on tables in restaurants.[24] Occupations that are judged to be more appropriate for one sex may continue to be so regarded for a long time. Although few occupations in modern society are restricted 100 percent to males or females, the concentration of one sex in an occupation leads to its being widely regarded as "men's work" or "women's work." An occupation that has been regarded as more suitable for one sex can become redefined as more suitable for the other. When the label change is from "men's" to "women's," as in the case of bank tellers, the occupation may then be considered of less importance.[25]

These labels and associated beliefs, together with the social visibility of men and women in their jobs, affect children's perceptions and expectations. A journalist who writes about parent-child relations reports that, despite his and his wife's best efforts, their four-year-old daughter is

> already blanketed in stereotypes. She's had a woman pediatrician, but insists all doctors are men ... her favorite activity is "dress-up"—second only to playing house—and practically the only garment she willingly wears is a dress. And lately, when furious, she has given up threatening personal retaliation. Instead she informs us that the boy up the street, a macho 4-year-old, a preschool protector and enforcer, will break our necks. All

this would be even more disturbing, of course, if we felt alone in it. But we don't. Whenever we bring up the subject, someone else has a similar story.[26]

A study of sixty-three middle-class suburban children between the ages of three and six conducted by sociologist Ann Beuf in 1973 revealed that over 70 percent of both the boys and girls chose sex-stereotypic jobs when asked what they wanted to be when they grow up. An interesting aspect of her study was that she also asked the children what they would want to do if they were of the other sex. The girls had relatively little difficulty responding to the question; the boys, however, not only had not thought about the matter before, they also did not want to think about it in the interview. Several boys told her, "That's a weird question," and one answered, "Oh, if I were a girl I'd have to grow up to be nothing."[27]

Socialization in childhood tends to conform to the existing distribution of occupations by sex. Later in this chapter we shall describe how boys and girls tend to be socialized in different occupational directions. At this point, it is relevant to note that widespread beliefs about the particular aptitudes of men and women affect the assignment of occupations to one or the other sex. Women are believed to be more nurturing than men; the occupations that require nurturing, such as nursing, nursery school teaching, and social work, are held out to girls as the types of occupations they should seek to enter. Men are believed to be more direct and aggressive, and in line with this belief, occupations such as the military, firefighter, and corporation executive, among others, are held up as more suitable for boys to look ahead to. Socialization practices usually encourage movement toward occupations that are considered congruent with what are believed to be sex-linked temperamental characteristics and sex-linked abilities.

Sex and Social Status

In modern discussions of sex roles and socialization, few topics have received as much attention as the status of women. The implications of much of this discussion are pointed up in the very title of an article published in 1951 that gave the topic new prominence—"Women as a Minority Group." In this article, sociologist Helen Mayer Hacker pointed out that women are discriminated against on the basis of physical and cultural characteristics, just as are members of ethnic minorities.[28] Whatever the validity of Goldberg's position that males are biologically more prepared for high-status attainment, discrimination has clearly played an important part in the differential status of men and women.

No one questions that males as a group have higher status than females as a group. Lipman-Blumen and Tickameyer state: "Perhaps one of the most theoretically interesting (and existentially frustrating) aspects of sex differentiation is its constancy and its invariant rank ordering: the male role is always more highly valued than the female role."[29] The discrepancy in value may be large or small and may take different forms. In rural Greece, "the word 'child' is synonymous with 'boy.' When asked how many children they have, parents answer 'I have two children and two girls,' meaning that they have two boys and two girls."[30] In Sweden, in contrast, the ideal of equality of treatment of boys and girls has been an explicit goal of the public schools since 1962; girls with interests in technology and science should be encouraged to develop them and "conventional attitudes toward these matters should be opposed."[31] In rural Greece, the negative attitude toward the female changes as soon as she becomes a mother: "From that moment she assumes a role that is idealized and considered 'holy.' Despised and suspected as a woman, she is revered, trusted, respected, and obeyed as a mother."[32]

Status differences between men and women do not remain fixed. As a rough generalization, it may be stated that as industrialization increasingly pervades society in all parts of the globe, societies will tend to abandon the type of pattern of which rural Greece is an example and will tend to move toward the pattern exemplified by the goal expressed in the Swedish school doctrine. Each country's circumstances are different, and there will therefore be national differences in the ways change takes place and in its speed.[33] At any given time, until status differences completely disappear, they will be visible in many ways. Authority and status tend to go together; as long as males have more authority, they will tend to have higher status. Currently, women tend to be concentrated in lower-paid occupations and in lower-paid ranks of high-paid occupations. Women are also still in the process of gaining all of the legal rights that men have had in the United States[34] and Canada.[35]

The status differences between men and women are built into interpersonal behavior as well as into social institutions. Writing on the ways that nonverbal behaviors contribute to maintaining traditional sex roles, psychologists Irene Hanson Frieze and Sheila J. Ramsey cite research that shows that men do more touching than do women and that women are touched more by both sexes. In speaking of the uninvited touch, they conclude that "The higher status individual has the social right to breech the spatial boundaries of the lower ranked."[36] They add that:

> One of the major indicators of women's low status is their lack of territory. This symptom is itself a perpetuating factor since having space allows one privacy and the freedom to control what information about oneself will be made available to others as well as who or what will enter one's space. . . . From another point of view, nonverbal behaviors which communicate low status and submission are precisely those crucial to attributions of femininity. Traditional role behavior dictates that women take up the smallest amount of space, speak softly and politely, refrain from initiating prolonged eye contact, and present an affable exterior. A woman who rejects these low status behaviors is often accused of being too assertive or aggressive.[37]

SOCIALIZATION AGENTS AND PROCESSES

Boys and girls are born with different reproductive potential. The adults who receive them into society and who guide their participation in it, both initially and later, anticipate that boys and girls will come to have different patterns of participation when they are adults, patterns that are sex-appropriate and that are termed sex roles. The newborn baby does not, of course, have any awareness of himself or herself as a person of a particular sex. In the course of time he or she will develop such an awareness and a pervasive sense of self as a member of one sex or the other. This is the person's *sexual identity,* which may be defined as

> the image of self as a male or a female and convictions about what membership in that group implies. Sexual identity, the individual's basic, sex-typed self image, is built up gradually from early infancy. It is the result of learned conceptions about the self, as a male or as a female. It includes beliefs about how one *ought* to think, act, and feel by virtue of having been born male or female. It includes learned ideals of masculine and feminine behavior and the proper authority relationships between the sexes.[38]

A person's sexual identity may be viewed as a part of a larger identity which is

> the total conception that people have of who they are. It includes all the beliefs that make up the individual's conception of self. It also includes the beliefs that people have about their worth as human beings—beliefs that determine self confidence and self esteem.... Identity is the product of the roles individuals have played and the definitions of self contained in these roles.[39]

The persons who socialize children attempt to lead boys and girls to develop sex-appropriate identities, according to whatever standards of appropriateness are current in the society and in the groups to which they belong or refer. For their part, children make their own observations of the social life that takes place around them and contribute to their own sexual identity by fitting their own feelings and behavior to the varieties of male and female behavior that are part of their observed world and world of interaction. The development of sexual identity and the development of sex roles are parts of the same complex process. In this section, we shall present some of the main aspects of this process as now understood, with particular attention to the United States and Canada.

Family Interaction

We have discussed the discrepancies between men and women in authority, work accomplishment, and status, and two of the main theories proposed to account for them—one based on biological predisposition and one based on men's discrimination against women. These two theories can be regarded as opposed to each other, but they can also be regarded as complementary; that is, the theory of male hormonal advantage in expressing dominance can help to explain why males always succeed in discriminating against females and why there are no societies in which women have gained the authority that would enable them to discriminate against men.

A third theory, based mainly on the work of psychologists, can also be introduced here. It may be regarded as an alternative to the two just cited, or equally well as a third component joining them to result in a more inclusive theory. This third theory (or component) seeks to explain why women fail to achieve to a degree that is in keeping with their intelligence. Lois W. Hoffman states: "The failure of women to fulfill their intellectual potential has been adequately documented. . . . the precursors of the underachieving woman can be seen in the female child." She presents her theory as follows:

> It is our theory that the female child is given inadequate parental encouragement in early independence strivings. Furthermore, the separation of the self from the mother is more delayed or incomplete for the girl because she is the same sex with the same sex role expectations, and because girls have fewer conflicts with their parents. As a result, she does not develop confidence in her ability to cope independently with the environment. She retains her infantile fears of abandonment; safety and effectiveness lie in her affective ties.[40]

Hoffman draws on Erik Erikson's theory of development that emphasizes the ages between one and four as critical for the development of independence and competence. "By critical, we mean a period when independence and competence orientations are more efficiently learned than at other times. There is a rapid building up of notions about the self and about the world."[41] Hoffman summarizes and interprets the available research bearing on her theory, recognizing that it remains incomplete. We shall draw upon her review, supplementing it with the references to some additional studies.

Boys and girls seem to differ from birth, with boys being somewhat more active than girls and girls being more sensitive to touch and to pain. The sex differences in sensitivity to touch and to pain are found in infants less than four days old and still in the hospital nursery.

It is not clear from the available research, however, in what ways, if any, mothers treat infant girls and infant boys differently. Hoffman cites one study showing that mothers handle and stimulate males more than females, and another study that suggests that such maternal attentiveness stimulates exploratory behavior. But sociologist Lenore J. Weitzman, in another summary, cites a study reporting that mothers handle and talk to infant girls more often, noting specifically that girls at age six months were more frequently touched. This study also showed that infants, both boys and girls, who were touched most often at age six months sought the most contact with their mothers at age thirteen months.[42] The inconsistency among the studies indicates that the facts concerning maternal interaction with infants are not easy to establish. The topic will require much careful research.[43]

Studies of the preschool years give some support to Hoffman's theory that parents encourage the independence strivings of boys more than they do of girls. According to one study, when mothers are asked at what age they would first allow their children to use sharp scissors without adult supervision and at what age they would allow their children to begin playing away from home for long periods without telling where they will be, mothers of boys give earlier ages than do mothers of girls.[44] Several other studies have indicated that dependency is discouraged in preschool boys but is more acceptable on the part of girls. Generally, mothers seem to consider girls more vulnerable and fragile than boys and thus in greater need of protection. A Canadian study reports that both French-Canadian and English-Canadian mothers and fathers, when hearing a child's demand for comfort for a minor injury, would more likely withhold such comfort from a boy than from a girl.[45] Boys also are more often punished by spanking, which prompts a kind of reactive independence, while girls are more often punished with threats of loss of love, which prompts continuing obedience and dependence on the parent who uses this power.[46]

Complementing the encouragement given to boys toward earlier independence is their greater tendency to come into conflict with parental authority. They are therefore disciplined more often, and these experiences facilitate separation of the self from the parent. Hoffman then suggests:

> One implication of this is that girls need a little maternal rejection if they are to become independently competent and self-confident. And indeed a generalization that occurs in most recent reviews is that high achieving females had hostile mothers while high achieving males had warm ones. . . . Our interpretation of these findings then is that many girls experience too much maternal rapport and protection during their early years. Because of this they find themselves as adults unwilling (or unable) to face stress and with inadequate motivation for autonomous achievement. . . . The theoretical view presented in this paper is speculative but it appears to be consistent with the data.[47]

In assessing the differences between girls and boys that appear to result from different patterns of family interaction, Hoffman notes that several studies show that girls tend to underestimate their ability and to avoid difficult tasks, whereas boys are more self-confident and challenged by difficult tasks. Boys, she suggests, may even be pushed prematurely into independence. Ruth Hartley, in support, points out that the socialization of boys is often harsh and demanding. Boys are told to be "manly" much earlier than girls are told to be "ladylike." But the greater difficulty for boys is the fact that they are subject to demands to be manly, not a sissy, not feminine, and yet they are under the supervision of women most of the time during their early years.[48]

Toys and the Media

Although the differences in parental handling of infant girls and boys are still to be adequately described, it nonetheless seems clear that those differences begin fairly early. By the time children are two or three years old, parents are applying fairly distinct conceptions of femininity and masculinity. Girls are considered to be feminine when they show interest in pretty clothes, domestic activities, and babies, and when they display social awareness and behave coquettishly. Boys are considered masculine when they show interest in objects or ideas, not persons, and in getting things to work.[49] Parents express their ideas, in part, by the toys they give to children. These conceptions also tend to be supported in picture books for children and in TV programs.

In recent years, some research attention has turned to children's toys. One research finding, the explanation for which is not clear, is that children of thirteen months show different toy preferences by sex.[50] A study of four-year-old nursery school children found that boys spent more time in that part of the playroom where blocks, wheel toys, and carpenter's tools were located, while girls spent more time in the area having the doll houses, cooking equipment, and dress-up clothes.[51] These preferences in nursery school activity may well result from earlier experiences in the home.

Sociologist Janet Saltzman Chafetz reports a research study, carried out by her students, of the Christmas toy catalogs of Sears, Roebuck and of Montgomery Ward, the two largest mail-order companies in the United States. The catalogs were each divided into a boys' section and a girls' section; the latter was full of dolls, household goods (dishes, appliances), and beauty aids; the former featured athletic items, technological toys such as tractors and building materials, toy soldiers, guns, cars, as well as some male dolls of football player Joe Namath, G.I. Joe, and an astronaut. One illustration showed boys being served tea by girls. The catalog illustrations showed a total of thirteen boys and one girl riding a toy; twenty-nine boys and no girls operating a model vehicle (train, car, tractor); and twenty-nine boys and two girls operating construction toys.[52] Presumably, adults' toy purchases tended to follow these conceptions of sex-appropriateness.

Another study has explored several aspects of the sex-typing of children's toys; the study combined analysis of toy catalogs, observation in toy stores, interviews with toy store executives, and questionnaires directed to adult and child attitudes toward toys. Christmas toy catalogs of nine department stores showed 102 categories of items illustrated only with pictures of boys, compared with seventy-three illustrated only with girls. Observation revealed that adults spent more time choosing toys for boys than in choosing toys for girls. (Total number of hours of observation is not reported; however, in one thirty-hour period of observation before Christmas, not a single scientific toy was bought for a girl.) Three out of four chemistry sets picture only boys on the box top; the remainaing 25 percent pictured both boys and girls.

> A doctor kit marketed for boys had "stethoscope with amplifying diaphragm ... miniature microscope ... blood pressure tester ... prescription blanks, and more." The nurse kit, on the other hand, came equipped with "nurse apron, cap, plastic silverware, plate, sick tray with play food." ... "Masculine" toys are more varied and expensive, and are viewed as relatively complex, active, and social.... "Feminine" toys are seen as most simple, passive and solitary.[53]

These differences appear in toys bought for children over age two; for children younger than that, adults seem to buy similar, non-sex-differentiated toys.

Studies of television commercials presented during children's programs also report distinctive sex roles as well as a greater emphasis on boys. Charles Winick and his associates examined 236 commercials representing forty-two advertisers of 127 (mostly food, beverage, and snack) products. They found that "Real-life or animated puppet human children are found in almost two-thirds of the commercials." They report that about 58 percent of these commercials had boy characters, while about 35 percent had girls.[54] Chafetz had her students study 100 TV commercials during children's programs in February 1971. Although it is not clear whether her categories refer to children, adults, or both, she too reports distinctive patterns of portrayal of males and females. Thus, she reports that seventy-nine of eighty-three narrators were male; seventeen females were shown engaged in domestic activities as compared to five males; eight males but no females were shown doing something mechanical; forty males and four females were shown as physically active; twenty-two males and two females were shown in provider roles; sixteen females and no males were shown as economically dependent; fifteen females and three males were shown as responding to social pressure.[55] Summarizing both her TV commercial and toy catalog studies, she concludes:

> One recurring finding in these studies of children's media is that many more males were portrayed than females. This could be a reflection of the fact that both males and females in our society find males much more interesting characters, capable of doing a wider variety of things and doing them well. An alternative explanation ... is also possible.... little boys need to piece together their concept of masculinity from a variety of sources, where young girls need only imitate a model readily available to achieve femininity.[56]

Two studies of the prize-winning Caldecott Medal picture books for preschool children report results substantially similar to those of toy catalogs and TV commercials. The Caldecott Medal is awarded by the Children's Service Committee of the American Library Association for the most distinguished picture book of the year. The winning books are ordered by most children's librarians throughout the country; parents look on library shelves for the gold seal that designates the winner; and sales may reach as high as 60,000 copies.[57] One of the studies, by Alleen Pace Nilsen, examined the winning and runner-up books for a twenty-year period from 1951 to 1970, eighty books in all. Among the findings are: (1) fourteen of the titles include a male's name, while four include a female's; (2) the illustrations depicted a total of 579 males and 368 females; (3) in one book entitled *A Tree Is Nice,* the illustrations show eleven boys and three girls in the branches of trees, with all the girls in the lowest branches; "The other girls are pictured in such poses as waving to a boy who is high in a tree, dragging a little boy through the leaves, helping another little boy into a tree, standing with a sprinkling can, and standing dejectedly alone while the boys climb a magnificent tree."[58] Nilsen finds, further, that the percentage of girls in the illustrations declined from 46 percent in the 1951–1955 period to 26 percent in the 1966–1970 period.[59]

Weitzman and co-authors focused on the Caldecott winners for the 1966–1970 period and they report 261 pictures of males and twenty-three pictures of females, a ratio of 11 to 1 or about 9 percent females. The apparent discrepancy between 9 percent and 26 percent in the two studies of the same set of books is possibly due to the fact that Nilsen was counting only children while the Weitzman group was counting all "males and females," including adults. The Weitzman group also made a separate count of animals, which was even more heavily weighted in favor of males, while Nilsen includes animal characters in her overall count of males and females although she refers explicitly to "boys" and "girls" in giving her percentages. In sum, both studies agree that women, girls, and females are pictured less often than men, boys, and males. We note, however, how different procedures for counting and reporting figures can affect the presentation of a problem. In this instance, the differences did not happen to affect the basic results.

Both studies essentially agree also on the way the books present males and females:

> In the world of picture books, boys are active and girls are passive. Not only are boys presented in more exciting and adventuresome roles, but they engage in more varied pursuits and demand more independence. The more riotous activity is re-

served for the boys.... In contrast, most of the girls in the picture books are passive and immobile.... the girls are more often found indoors.... Even the youngest girls in the stories play traditional feminine roles, directed toward pleasing and helping their brothers and fathers.... While girls serve, boys lead.[60]

The School

Schools contribute to the differential socialization of boys and girls. But in appraising the impact of schools, it is useful to keep in mind the comment of educational sociologist Sarah Lawrence Lightfoot:

> Teachers are not totally responsible for the socialization that occurs in classrooms. Children also socialize teachers into certain behaviors. Much of the sex-role patterning of boys and girls has been deeply rooted by the time the children enter school at five years of age. Without making her first move, the teacher sees boys building boats in the block corner and girls playing house in the doll corner. If the teacher wants to expand the behaviors and attitudes of her children, she must engage in countersocialization by introducing compelling alternatives.[61]

Even in nursery school, boys and girls act differently in some respects and are responded to differently by teachers. One study, which focused on fifteen female teachers of pupils age three to five, with twelve to seventeen pupils per class, found that boys ignore teachers more often and are more often aggressive, while girls more often stay within arm's reach of the teacher. There were no differences between the sexes in crying or in asking for help. Boys received more loud reprimands for disruptive behavior than did girls, but the boys also received more praise when they did what they were supposed to do.[62]

Educational psychologist Betty Levy has examined the school's role in sex-role stereotyping of girls. She acknowledges that hers is a feminist review of the literature. However, many of the studies she reviews were not conducted from a feminist perspective; some were conducted by men, and the overall import is not essentially different from the general trends that have emerged thus far in our analysis. She finds the following:

1. Traditional sex roles are reinforced through the authority structure of the elementary school. Eighty-five percent of all elementary school teachers are women; 78 percent of all elementary school principals are men.[63]

2. Teachers often separate boys and girls for seating, lining up, hanging up coats, and other activities, thus calling attention to sex distinctions.[64]

3. "Elementary schools reinforce girls' training for obedience, social and emotional dependence, and docility. That girls on the whole like school better than boys and perform better in most respects may be due in part to the consistency of the sex role demands of home and school."[65]

4. "The schools' emphasis on neatness, order, punctuality, and performance of often meaningless and monotonous tasks is an important part of the 'domesticating' function of schools, particularly in the case of girls."[66]

The high ratio of males to females that we reported for preschool picture books has also been found in a study of 134 elementary school readers put out by fourteen publishing companies and used in three suburban New Jersey towns. The study further reports that in sixty-seven stories, "one sex demeaned the other, sixty-five of these were directed against girls, only two against boys."[67]

Not all research on schoolbooks supports a conclusion that boys are emphasized. At least one study which focuses on changes over the years points to an increasing emphasis on girls. In a study of introductory reading textbooks in the United States from colonial days through 1966, educational researcher Sara Goodman Zimet found that "From a character count, it was noted that textbook authors began to increase the number of female characters in the stories as formal education was opened to girls (between 1776 and 1835). This trend continued so that by 1898 and up through

1966, girl characters actually outnumbered boy characters in the texts."[68] She also finds, in keeping with an earlier study, that first-grade readers avoid aggressive themes and that dependency "was particularly frequent in the books ... from 1921 to 1966, and was rewarded overwhelmingly for both sexes and all age levels. ... Interestingly enough, the dependency model for the male was even more striking in frequency than for the female."[69] Zimet's study is confined to primers, the books children are presented in their first school-organized formal reading instruction. Many other studies sample from a larger (or at least a more varied) range of elementary school reading materials.[70]

Although most kinds of elementary school reading materials beyond the primers may emphasize males, this does not seem to make boys better readers than girls. Various studies show that from the second grade through the sixth, girls are better readers than boys. Caution is required, however, in any effort to find universal generalizations. A cross-cultural study of four countries where English is spoken revealed that in the elementary grades girls are better readers than boys in the United States and in English-speaking sections of Canada, while boys are the better readers in England and Nigeria. The explanation given is that:

> Teachers in our culture expect girls to excel in reading as compared to boys, and they do. ... Reading ability of boys is more highly valued in England and Nigeria than it is in North America. In Nigeria, in fact, schooling has a very low priority for girls and most of the teachers are men. Sex differences in favor of boys even increased from second to sixth grades in Nigeria and England.[71]

The fact that girls generally read better than boys in North American elementary schools is one of the facts that has been offered in support of the view that elementary schools, far from giving support to males and fostering masculine stereotypes, actually are environments that are more compatible with the temperament of girls and have a "feminizing effect" on boys. One group of educators states the matter this way:

There is little doubt that the character of American education is feminine, either by design or as a comfortable acceptance unintentionally adopted by the teachers and administrators developing the structure of the program. Standards of conduct, restricted environments for learning, the majority members of the instructional staff, academic and social expectations, and the physical setting for the school are all substantially feminine, with little regard for the male culture presented within the societal structure outside of the schools.[72]

These authors then present two sets of adjectives, one set describing societal expectations for boys and one set for girls. Boys are expected to be "active, adventuresome, brave, curious, dirty, imaginative, robust, outspoken, disheveled, rough," while girls are expected to be "neat, quiet, mannerly, pretty, clean, artistic, studious, sensitive, obedient, gentle."[73] They believe that the second list of characteristics "more aptly describes the type of child readily accepted in the classroom" and that girls will indeed fit that list better than will boys. Schools do, however, in their view, press boys toward becoming more neat, quiet, mannerly, and so on, thus exerting a "feminizing" effect.

Peer Games

The extent to which children create variations in their relationships independent of the adult world is at this time still a very open question. A case in point is the relationship of children's games to the larger society. Two psychologists have reviewed four surveys of children's games conducted between 1896 and 1959. Children studied were mostly between nine and fifteen years old. The researchers conclude that:

> Perhaps the most important generalizations arising out of this study concern the changing relationships between boys and girls.... the responses of girls have become increasingly like those of boys as the sixty years have passed.... [This] is not unexpected, in the light of the well-known changes in woman's role in American culture during this period.[74]

They suggest that it is more deviant today than sixty years ago for a boy to play such things as dolls, hopscotch, jump-rope, and other specifically girls' games. Though the authors do not delineate the societal changes, it may be pointed out that coeducation has increased greatly during this period and, in general, there is freer mingling between boys and girls. But insofar as there has been "acculturation" in games, the change has been largely in one direction.[75]

SEX ROLES AND IDENTITIES

Boys and girls are born into a society that expects them to become different kinds of people and to occupy different statuses because they are either male or female. As Betty Yorburg states, "In all societies, even those in which sex-typing is not extreme, a person's basic status is that of male or female, and this basic status determines what other statuses the person can or cannot have."[76] In our society, many social institutions have been organized on the assumption that girls would grow up to become mothers and homemakers and boys would grow up to become economic providers. Some women have always departed from this assumption and have worked; increasing numbers are doing so, as we have pointed out in Chapter 5. The aspirations of girls and boys are directed toward different occupations, which differ not only in their content but in their status. Men's occupations tend to be considered higher status than women's.

The fact that boys and girls are prepared for distinctive statuses and social roles means that they also tend to develop distinctive masculine and feminine identities. While there are different analyses of how and why these identities differ, there is widespread agreement that the masculine identity in our society emphasizes an orientation toward achievement, restraint in emotional expression, and a great deal of self-reliance.[77] The female identity emphasizes being helpful and supportive of children, men, bosses—what sociologist Jessie Bernard called "the all-pervading function—stroking."[78] It appears that some girls and women who develop an identity that emphasizes independence and achievement rather than that of pleasing and comforting others often fear they have formed an inappropriate identity. According to some research, even talented girls and women develop a "wish to fail" or a "fear of success" as a way of preserving a more traditional feminine identity.[79] One line of research that seems to give some support to "success-avoidance" as a motive is that girls lose their early superiority over boys in reading ability, so that by the sixth grade boys tend to be equal. Also, whereas there have been no differences between the sexes in mathematical performance during the elementary school years, boys tend to perform significantly better than girls in mathematics during the high school years.[80]

The differences in masculine and feminine identities are manifested not only with regard to the ways in which males and females participate in schools, occupations, and other organized institutional settings. They are also manifested in behaviors that are relatively independent of specific organizational settings. For example, anthropologist Ray L. Birdwhistell has found that in several societies, including American, there are distinctive masculine and feminine ways of moving. These differ somewhat from one society to another, but each society distinguishes masculine and feminine forms of body movement.[81]

Differences between the sexes in the use of language is a growing area of research investigation. Several studies show that women's speech is more "correct," "proper," and polite than men's speech. Women do not swear as much as men, are less likely to use slang, and are more likely to use correct pronunciation (for example saying -ing rather than -in' at the end of a word). These differences have been found consistently in many settings—among children in a New England Village; among both blacks and whites in Detroit and in North Carolina; in Chicago and New York City; in Norwich, England; and in Norway. Women's use of the higher prestige forms of language has often been placed in the context of male dominance and explained as an expression of the greater care that subordinate persons must exercise; or as an effort to compensate for their subordination by using language to indicate higher status; or as due to women's need to use appearances as indicators of morality or prestige, since they lack(ed) occupational status. The Norwich study, carried out by sociolinguist Peter Trudgill, suggests that

> working-class, nonstandard speech has positive connotations for male speakers of all social classes. On the one hand, males expressed the greater value attached to more correct forms (e.g., making comments such as "I talk horrible"), but on the other hand, they indicated in various ways that they were favorably disposed to nonstandard speech, which has strong connotations of masculinity, and may signal male solidarity.[82]

The findings concerning body movement and language usage point to some interesting questions that lie beyond the issue of dominance and subordination. While the pervasiveness of male dominance has been amply documented, the growing tendency to interpret all aspects of male and female sex roles and masculine and feminine identities as nothing more than manifestations of discrimination or power relationships, or both, rests on an apparent assumption that there is nothing sexual in the relations between the sexes, or, alternatively, that sexuality is only another form of power.[83] These interpretations do not inquire into the nature of sexuality and how it might figure in sex differences. For example, the fact that there are characteristic masculine and feminine ways of moving in each society, but that these characteristic differences vary from one society to another, suggests the possibility that both men and women *want* to create distinctions of masculinity and femininity. If this is so, then it is by no means certain that such differences would disappear if women were to gain authority and power fully equal to that of men. Only by adopting "an oversocialized view" of human functioning is it possible to interpret masculinity and femininity as entirely imposed from without. Such a view fails to take account of the gratifications that come from differences and the sources of separateness and autonomy within each person—his or her experience of bodily sensations; and thoughts, fantasies, and speculations about oneself and the world outside oneself. Such subjective experiences may be shared and may become the basis of distinctive conceptions of masculinity and femininity and of male and female sex roles; and they may, of course, change in the course of history. At any given time more than one conception of masculinity and femininity is current and available in a diverse and heterogeneous society.[84] In sum, the analyses of sex roles and sex identities in terms of power make clear that these phenomena can be shaped by power, but they do not demonstrate that the social organization of the sexes can be reduced to nothing but a power relationship.

EGALITARIAN IDEOLOGIES AND THE FUTURE

The differential socialization of boys and girls reflects the fact that adults anticipate that the children of each sex will, when they reach adulthood, occupy statuses that are different. While some advanced thinkers, as long as 200 years ago, considered that these statuses were unequal as well as different, it is only in modern times that concerted efforts have been made consciously to achieve equality of status for the two sexes. In concluding this chapter, we shall turn attention briefly to some of these efforts.

As we indicated above, Sweden since 1962 has sought to offer girls and boys equal access to all educational opportunities. The school curriculum provides that students, during their eighth-grade year, will have a three-week period of practical occupational experience in settings of their own choice. A study in one middle-sized Swedish town during the 1965–1966 school year revealed that the most frequently chosen placements by the boys were with auto mechanics, electricians, bakers, laboratory assistants, photographers, IBM data machine operators, draftsmen, salesmen, and jobs with the railroad, air force, and with the local military regiment. The girls chose placements with primary school teachers, kindergarten teachers, child nurses, saleswomen, hairdressers, office girls, nursing assistants, store decorators, travel bureau assistants, and in animal care. In Sweden as a whole for 1965 and 1966, the most popular work areas selected by girls were in public health and nursing. Swedish sociologist Rita Liljestrom notes that:

> The social changes in the Scandinavian countries up to the present time have meant, in effect, that a legal and formal equality has not been met by a corresponding equalization of roles. In spite of the fact that many *outward* obstacles have been removed, there remain obstacles that are partly of another type having to do with deeply-rooted ideas, role expectations, role ideals, values, and habits among, for example, employers, work supervisors, fellow workers, husbands, and, not least, among women themselves.[85]

It would appear from this evidence that the socialization Swedish boys and girls received before becoming eighth-graders influenced them to select typically sex-stereotyped vocational settings despite the opportunity to make non-stereotyped choices.

The Soviet Union has long encouraged women to participate in the economic activity of the country. As two specialists in Soviet studies report:

> There is little doubt, from a perusal of the Soviet sources, that the woman who deliberately chooses to become a housewife and mother and to restrict her activities to husband, children and hearth is not considered a "complete" Soviet woman because she is not participating fully in the building of the new society and because her position and "dependence" are too strongly reminiscent of the bourgeois housewife of a former stigmatized past.... The woman who chooses to participate and earn her independence on the basis of her occupational and other achievements is likely to be defined as exemplary, *provided* she does not totally neglect her other functions.[86]

But despite the fact that the Soviet Union lost great numbers of men during World War II, so that in 1959, fourteen years after the war ended, women constituted 55 percent of the population, women have not attained occupational equality with men. "While women are engaged in practically all types of work, they are underrepresented in the occupations that embody directive, managerial, decision-making and executive functions, and they tend to be overrepresented in the subordinate and junior positions and in the menial jobs."[87]

A third example is the Israeli kibbutz (plural: kibbutzim). These are settlements that were established, mostly between 1910 and the late 1940s, under the inspiration of socialist ideology, by Jews from eastern Europe and the Middle East who made a determined effort to establish a society of equals. All property was held in common (although today there is private ownership of small personal items). Emancipation of women was (and is) a prominent ideal. Collective rearing of children from birth, and other collective institutions, freed women from traditional household confinement, and they took their place as full-time workers. Efforts were made to abolish all sex distinctions in role and identity that were not directly related to reproduction. The educational system, for example, minimizes sex distinctions: "There is ... little evidence of direct sex-role instruction in Kibbutz childhood ... a deemphasis of any juxtaposition of masculinity and femininity are part of the education process in the Kibbutz."[88] But the effort to minimize sex-role differences has not worked out as anticipated. Men have ended up in most of the jobs in agriculture, management, and other income-producing activities, while women predominate in child care, nursing, clothes supply store work, and kitchen work. Women have become discontented because "the promised equality of opportunity and freedom of occupational choice never materialized." But also,

> many women began to have second thoughts about their "liberation" from the household, especially from the care of their children. The need to be more with their children has been asserting itself very strongly among the mothers who were themselves born outside the Kibbutz as well as among those *sabras* born and reared in the Kibbutzim.... Counteracting the feminine discontent is the increased amount of time women in Kibbutzim are spending with their offspring. Concomitant with this trend is a consolidation of the nuclear family unit. According to many, such a course is endangering the very existence of the Kibbutz, for it may tend to weaken its collectivist foundations.[89]

In the United States today, and somewhat less prominently in other countries, a new effort is under way to change the prevailing conceptions of masculinity and femininity, as well as the prevailing distributions of men and women in various occupations and the disparity between men and women in authority and status. These new efforts are based on the view that equality between the sexes cannot be achieved so long as stereotypical conceptions of masculinity and femininity divide humankind into two kinds of beings based on their morphological sex. Perhaps the best-known modern statement of this view was made by sociologist Alice S. Rossi:

> we need to reassert the claim to sex equality and to search for the means by which it can be achieved. By sex equality I mean a socially androgynous conception of the roles of men and women, in which they are equal and similar in such spheres as intellectual, artistic, political and occupational interests and participation, complementary only in those spheres dictated by physiological differences between the sexes. This assumes the traditional conceptions of masculine and feminine are inappropriate to the kind of world we can live in in the second half of the twentieth century. An androgynous conception of sex role means that each sex will cultivate some of the characteristics usually associated with the other in traditional sex role definitions. This means that tenderness and expressiveness should be cultivated in boys and socially approved in men, so that a male of any age in our society would be psychologically and socially free to express these qualities in his social relationships. It means that achievement need, workmanship and constructive aggression should be cultivated in girls and approved in women so that a female of any age would be similarly free to express these qualities in her social relationships. This is one of the points of contrast with the feminist goal of an earlier day: rather than a one-sided plea for women to adapt a masculine stance in the world, this definition of sex equality stresses the enlargement of the common ground on which men and women base their lives together by changing the social definitions of approved characteristics and behavior for both sexes.[90]

This is a more ambitious program for change in sex-role socialization than has yet been attempted anywhere. In proposing "institutional levers for achieving sex equality," Rossi proposes new child-care arrangements that would enable mothers to pursue their careers. But these substitute child-care arrangements seem to assume that this would be largely a female occupation: "If a reserve of trained practical mothers were available, a professional woman could return to her field a few months after the birth of a child, leaving the infant under the care of a practical mother until he or she reached the age of two years . . . "[91] Would not a fully androgynous conception of the sexes provide equally for men or women to serve in child care, since there is no indication that Rossi is thinking of the reserve mother as also a wet-nurse? Clearly, something kept this possibility from being worked into Rossi's concept. But she is not alone. The ambitious programs attempted in Sweden, the Soviet Union, and the Israeli kibbutz also do not seem to have opened up child care as a male occupation, at least not on a very wide scale. Nor has the People's Republic of China, like the Soviet Union a revolutionary society, defined child-care work as a male occupation, so far as can be discerned from very fragmentary evidence.[92]

A truly androgynous concept of sex roles would contemplate all occupations equally open to and perhaps equally chosen by both sexes. Clearly this is hard to contemplate and harder to achieve. Sumner, in his classic *Folkways,* said "The mores can make anything right." Sociologist Robert E. Park agreed but added, "But they have a harder time making some things right than others."[93] The evidence seems to indicate that even drastic changes in social organization and socialization cannot readily *reduce inequality* between the sexes let alone *attain equality.* Revolutionary societies that succeed in drastically altering many prerevolutionary institutions seem not to succeed in equally drastically altering sex roles. This failure cannot be clearly attributed to hormonal differences between the sexes; the available evidence cannot be stretched to justify this conclusion. It is possible to argue that the failure lies in the "incorrigible" beliefs developed in an earlier time and carried over into revolutionary societies. This argument is plausible enough as far as it goes, but it does not explain why beliefs about sex roles should be more resistant to change than beliefs about other social institutions. At the present time, there is no explanation that is adequately supported by convincing evidence.

The most conservative among sociologists and the most radical among them agree that men have been dominant in virtually all, if not all, societies. Feminists argue that the fact of male dominance is a long-enduring injustice, one that can and should be brought to an end. Others affirm that the fact itself requires explanation; it has been an enduring fact that cannot be wished away. Many would go on to add that the fact has been used to create injustices that cannot be defended. Socialization processes have certainly helped to strengthen—indeed help create—societal beliefs that males and females are different, and these processes continue to play a significant part in preparing males and females for different identities and different patterns of social participation. There is sharp disagreement, however, on the outer limits of possible change in sex-role socialization. Certainly, the total pattern of sex-differentiated behavior to be found in one particular society at one particular period cannot be taken as evidence of a biologically based "natural" difference between the sexes. There are too many variations among societies, and too many changes in the history of our own society, to justify such a view. Throughout all these changes and variations, however, persists the irreducible fact of absolute difference between the sexes in reproductive role. The difference can be magnified or minimized in a society, but it cannot be abolished. But the persistence of difference does not necessarily predict the persistence of inequality.

7 Conclusion: Socialization in Later Life

Socialization continues throughout life. After childhood one continues to enter new groups, to attain new statuses, to learn new roles and thereby to elaborate one's ways of participating in society. A freshman is socialized into the patterns of a college, an immigrant into the life of a new country, a recruit into the army, a new resident into a suburb, a medical student into the profession, a new patient into a hospital ward, and a bride into a life of marriage.

In some respects later socialization is continuous with that of childhood, in other respects discontinuous.[1] The ways in which adult socialization differs from that in childhood will receive our attention later in this chapter. Let us briefly note some continuous aspects. In the home, at school, with the peer group, and through the mass media children acquire their "native language." They learn to speak and to write. Having developed this foundation in early socialization, they later acquire the capacity to issue commands to an army platoon, to preach sermons, or to write love letters, legal briefs, newspaper articles, or sales reports. They thus learn to use their native language in new and specialized ways, consonant with the particular adult statuses they attain and the expectations of their adult roles. Further, the general symbolic capacities that children begin to develop in infancy as they begin to acquire their human nature eventuate in their being able also to use special nonverbal symbol systems. They can learn to read music or blueprints—or, for that matter, tea leaves, smoke signals, or tarot cards.

Children's symbolic capacities are not merely cognitive in nature. These capacities combine with sentiments in particular ways, so that people with whom the child has never actually interacted can come to represent aspects of himself or herself. Popes, presidents, and prime ministers can become dear to the child as representatives of some valued ideal or cause. (And so, of course, can other distant figures who do not hold formal office.) This ability to utilize other persons as symbols of oneself (or parts of oneself) and by this means to become attached to large segments of society—church, nation, social movement—does not arise for the first time in adulthood. It is essentially a development from and a refinement of a capacity that first showed itself when the child was attracted to role models outside the family. The child's imagining himself or herself as police officer, heroic rescuer, or star athlete are the precursors.

Other examples of continuity readily come to mind. In the early games of childhood, children learn to pursue a goal within a framework of rules. Their later ability to play bridge, chess, or tennis is built on their earlier experiences with such games as hide-and-seek. The later rules are more elaborate, but the orientation to rules is a refinement of the childhood orientation.

Other basic elements of the adult socialization process are also similar to those in childhood. There are socializing agents who teach, serve as models, and invite participation. Through their ability to offer gratifications and deprivations they induce cooperation and learning, and they endeavor to prevent disruptive deviance. The persons being socialized, on their part, through observation, participation, and role taking, learn and internalize new expectations and develop new self-conceptions.

The continuities in socialization from childhood to adulthood are significant because there is reason to believe that childhood socialization sets limits to what may be accomplished through adult socialization, even though we are not yet able to define those limits with any precision.[2] Nevertheless, there do appear to be limits. The human organism has great plasticity, as we discussed in Chapter 2, but that plasticity is not infinite. For example, it would appear virtually impossible for a person who never learned to read to begin, at age twenty-five, to prepare to become a physician. This degree of discontinuity between childhood and adult socialization seems insurmountable.

Although certain aspects and certain kinds of adult socialization presuppose continuity with childhood socialization, it is nevertheless equally true that adult socialization, even in the ordinary course of events, is often discontinuous from that of childhood. Before we turn to these aspects we must say something about the period between childhood and adulthood—adolescence.

SOCIALIZATION IN ADOLESCENCE

We cannot do full justice to the literature on adolescence in the brief space available. We shall therefore confine ourselves to a discussion framed generally by this book and this chapter. We shall try to answer this question: Assuming socialization throughout the life cycle to be both continuous and discontinuous, how does adolescence fit into this cycle?

We may begin by noting that the delineation of adolescence as a distinct period of life is not simply derived from observing the biological organism's maturation but is, like childhood, a social invention. Many societies do not identify a distinct period of life as adolescence, and even Western societies did not do so before industrialization. Frank Musgrove goes so far as to claim that:

> The adolescent was invented at the same time as the steam-engine. The principal architect of the latter was Watt in 1765, of the former Rousseau in 1762. Having invented the adolescent, society has been faced with two major problems: how and where to accommodate him in the social structure, and how to make his behaviour accord with the specifications.[3]

This author further argues that the creation of the concept of adolescence as a distinct period was accompanied by the development of a special psychology of adolescence that largely created its own subject matter. He is claiming that the phenomena associated with adolescence are, in effect, the result of a large self-fulfilling prophecy—that is, because people started believing that there was such a stage of life as adolescence, with distinctive characteristics and problems, and started treating adolescents with such expectations, they elicited the behavior they had come to expect. There seems little doubt that in a general sense Musgrove is substantially correct. If the people we now call teen-agers were still allowed to marry, participate fully and actively in the labor force, and otherwise function as adults instead of being set off as a distinct age group and kept in school, socialization in adolescence would not loom as a topic of discussion. In the American colonies, until the Revolution, fourteen-year-old boys could serve as executors of wills; at sixteen they became men, paying taxes and serving in the militia. Marriages in the middle teens were common. The age at which a young person went to work depended on the family's financial situation and the youth's own physical capacity.[4]

The exclusion of youth from adult employment statuses and roles in the United States was accomplished gradually over the period of about 150 years from the Revolution to the New Deal, and it reflected various social and economic forces. During this period there was increasing awareness of youth as a special age group (whose upper-age limit generally came to be legally defined as eighteen for some purposes, twenty-one for others), and there was a correspondingly increased awareness of "youth problems." Marie Jahoda and Neil Warren report that in 1930, 12 percent of the publications summarized in *Psychological Abstracts* dealt with adolescence, delinquency, and juvenile misbehavior. By 1950 the percentage had risen to 59 percent, and in 1960 to 68 percent.[5] The authors suggest that awareness of adolescent problems has grown concomitantly with the increasing tendency of adolescents to remain in school until graduating from high school, where they remain assembled in a distinctive institution rather than being dispersed in the labor force among people of diverse ages. (As educational aspirations and expectations continue to increase, the period of adolescence tends to be prolonged, so that in the middle class, at least, adolescence is sometimes thought to last until graduation from college. The term "youth" is increasingly used to refer to the age period roughly spanning ages sixteen to twenty-four or so.)[6]

A full treatment of socialization during adolescence merits a volume by itself. Here we shall only delineate in a few broad strokes[7] the central issue of whether adolescent socialization should be regarded as fundamentally continuous or discontinuous with the preceding socialization of childhood and the succeeding socialization of adulthood. The argument for discontinuity has gone through several cycles of enunciation and refutation. In recent times it gained notable support from an influential paper by Talcott Parsons, first published in the early 1940s and widely disseminated during the 1950s as an interest in the sociology of adolescence spread.[8] In this essay Parsons introduced the term "youth culture," whose most notable characteristics he considered to be an emphasis on irresponsibility and pleasure seeking—exemplified by concern with "having a good time," heterosocial activities, and athletics—which he contrasted with the emphasis on responsibility in adulthood. Evidence that this emphasis on discontinuity was exaggerated has been presented by Frederick Elkin and William Westley.[9]

The argument in favor of discontinuity was reinvigorated during the 1960s with the publication of a study by James S. Coleman of ten widely varying high schools in Illinois.[10] Coleman starts with the assumption that adolescents constitute a small society of their own, one that "maintains only a few threads of connection with the outside adult society." He does not examine the quantity or the nature of the "threads of connection," even though much of his argument is built upon this assumption. By means of questionnaires administered to the several thousand boys and girls in these high schools, Coleman found that they placed much greater value on athletics and popularity than on academic performance and that intellectual values generally had little to do with popularity among peers (although there were variations among schools in the importance attributed to scholarship by the students). He found further evidence of the "irresponsibility" pattern noted by Parsons—for example, great interest in cars (and activities and paraphernalia related to cars). He found, in effect, that adolescents are socialized into a subculture, a special society of their own peers dominated by their own values. And since the schools are identified by Coleman as society's established agency for preparing adolescents to participate in the adult world, he argues that the activities and values of adolescents are discontinuous with, and in opposition to, the world of adults.

Coleman acknowledges that what constitutes a subculture depends partly upon definition. But despite numerous qualifications that he makes in the course of reporting many data, his basic position is quite clear.

Although there is no doubt that adolescents are in the process of becoming more independent of their parents and, consequently, are more responsive to their peers than they were at younger ages, and although their interests and values may differ from those ostensibly emphasized by the high school, it does not follow that adolescent socialization is peer-dominated and little influenced by adult values and norms. In reviewing Coleman's study, Bennett Berger argues that most of the adolescent values and interests noted by Coleman are more accurately understood as derivative from adults. For example, high school athletics depend greatly on support by parents and local booster organizations. Further, parents are concerned about popularity and prestige. Emphasizing the continuity of adolescent and adult values, Berger comments, "From Coleman's treatment of the *adolescent* 'subculture' one might think that cars and masculine prowess and feminine glamour and social activities and sex and dating and wearing the right clothes and being from the right family were concerns entirely alien to American adults."[11] He points out that athletics, extracurricular activities, and social affairs are sponsored by the schools and are considered to be training grounds for adult responsibilities. Berger thus argues, with some cogency we believe, that Coleman's data tend to support conclusions nearly opposite from those Coleman himself draws from them and that much of what takes place during adolescence may be regarded as *anticipatory socialization* for adulthood, rather than as evidence for a discontinuous interval. (The concept of anticipatory socialization refers to the rehearsal of feelings, values, and actions that takes place before a person actually enters upon a particular status or adopts a new role.)

In contrast to Coleman's emphasis on the separateness of the adolescent from adult society, Edgar Friedenberg is impressed by the extent of adult control, precisely in the high schools. In a study of nine high schools he found that the first social lesson adolescents learn is that they are subject to compulsory attendance and various other specialized regulations (such as requiring a corridor pass to walk through the halls). Such restrictions, he suggests, teach them—although admittedly some steps are skipped in the analysis—that "they do not participate fully in the freedoms guaranteed by the state, and that, *therefore, these freedoms do not really partake of the character of inalienable rights.*"[12] Friedenberg and Coleman thus both argue that adolescent socialization is not a proper preparation for adulthood; but whereas Coleman finds the cause in the adolescent society, Friedenberg finds it in the restrictive authority system of the high school. Indeed, Friedenberg argues that adolescents are being pressed prematurely into adulthood.[13] Friedenberg and Berger thus agree that adolescence is quite directly preparatory for adulthood—perhaps more directly than it should be.

In summary, as Marie Jahoda and Neil Warren have pointed out,[14] one can find evidence to "prove" the existence of a youth culture, if one wishes; or one can likewise find evidence to bear out the contention that the fundamental fact of adolescent socialization is its continuity with and preparation for adulthood. The argument depends on the groups studied, the data selected, and the conceptual approach adopted.

In our own view, the evidence to date suggests that, with regard to fundamental values, the continuity of adolescent socialization with adulthood outweighs the discontinuity. Adolescent values and behavior have been more reflective of adult values and behavior than either Parsons or Coleman believe to be the case. But today the situation *seems* more in flux than before. It may be, as Margaret Mead argues, that we are on the threshold of a new and unprecedented era—one in which the traditional direction of socialization will be reversed and the young will begin to socialize their elders, because the young will have the most relevant information and ideas about the world as it is coming to be.[15] Whether such an era actually comes to pass remains to be seen.[16]

Other observers, who also perceive that long-established age relationships in our society are changing, do not anticipate socialization *by* the young so much as a greater blurring of age distinctions and freer mingling of people of all ages. Increasingly, adolescence is coming to be regarded as a rather special form of age segregation that was characteristic of a particular historical period that is drawing to a close. Historian John Gillis concludes his study of age relationships in England and Germany from 1770 to the present with a chapter entitled "End of Adolescence: Youth in the 1950s and 1960s." He notes that parental control of middle-class adolescents has declined so that by the 1960s

> Freedoms previously associated with university-age youth were being rapidly appropriated by adolescents, who, having access to larger allowances and greater mobility made possible by the automobile, were gaining something of the autonomy they had lost a century or so before.... In effect, adolescence, while still recognized in medical texts and psychological guides, is losing its status as a separate stage of life among the very class with whom it has been previously associated.[17]

In the United States, an advisory panel to the President reviewed the history of age relationships and made numerous recommendations that, if implemented, would reduce both the sharp segregation of one age group from another (for example, junior high school students from high school students) and also segregation of youth from adults. The main thrust of the report is in the direction of more effective socialization for adult roles of responsibility, particularly adult work roles. The panel was chaired by James S. Coleman, and the report tends to emphasize the idea that there has been a discontinuity between adolescence and adulthood which should now be replaced by greater continuity. Although, unlike Gillis in Europe, the report does not find that segregation of age groups is already decreasing, it does suggest that the time is ripe for a change in age relationships, and that adolescence is no longer particularly valuable as a distinctive period of life in a modern industrial society such as the United States.[18]

SOCIALIZATION IN ADULTHOOD

There are several reasons why socialization does not terminate with childhood or even adolescence. One is that individuals enter into new statuses with new role expectations when they reach adulthood and they must learn how to function in them. Earlier socialization gives some preparation, but much of what one needs to know can only be learned when one is actually in the new situation. Thus, boys and girls receive considerable anticipatory socialization for marriage throughout their lives prior to marriage—by observing their own parents and other married couples, by talking about it with their peers, by vicariously experiencing various kinds of marriages portrayed in the mass media. But it is only when they are actually in the new status and role and have made a *commitment* to marriage that they both need and wish to change themselves to function as actual married partners.[19]

A second reason is that many groups, statuses, and roles become known to us only after we have reached adulthood. This is particularly evident with regard to occupations. Only a relatively small number of occupations are known to children and young adolescents. As we noted earlier, the mass media portray a much smaller array of occupations than exists in the actual world,[20] and this picture is only moderately amplified through the child's personal acquaintance and school learning.

A third reason is that the person continues in adulthood to encounter people who become for him or her new significant others. Some of them may be one's own peers; others may be senior in age or social status or both; they may even be one's own children. Through encounters a woman or man may learn to value skiing, or drug taking, or working in community endeavors, or playing the stock market—or any combination of these or other activities.

Encounters with new significant others may occur in various ways. The mass media of communication provide one avenue. For example, during the 1960s John F. Kennedy was widely believed to have stimulated heightened interest in politics, and many of those attracted to him undoubtedly were reached through the media, especially television. During the 1930s and 1940s, the era of "big stars," film actresses became significant others to many moviegoers, who copied their hair styles and in other ways sought to model themselves after one or another "glamour girl." Indeed, the concept of "glamour" gained currency as a value in living via the films and the array of magazines devoted to accounts of film stars and their doings.

New significant others can be neighbors as well as distant figures. Moving into a new suburb results in new patterns of informal interaction, and new neighbors become important to each other as sources of mutual expectations.[21] The role of neighbor itself may have to be learned anew, especially for the person who previously lived in a big-city apartment and now becomes a homeowner. A norm of casual accessibility, rather than a norm of determined insularity, is likely to govern, and this may entail willingness to borrow and lend (lawn mowers and cups of sugar), as well as routine forms of cooperation, such as participating in a car pool.

One major consideration underlying all the reasons cited for the continuing importance of socialization in adult life is the fact that both maturation and previous socialization present new demands and new opportunities to the person. Generally speaking, childhood socialization endows the child with the capacities for participating in adult society in *some* ways. Adult socialization makes possible one's participation in *specific* ways, through participation in particular institutions of society. Following Erik Erikson, we may say that the period through adolescence ordinarily results in the establishment of the person's core identity. Although his or her identity will be further developed and modified (and, in certain extreme situations, such as battlefield fighting, imprisonment, religious conversion, or hospitalization for mental illness, drastically altered), the establishment of a core identity provides a kind of platform from which a person may *launch himself or herself* into further socialization. The importance of the establishment of a core identity is that it provides the person with the opportunities and the capacities for *choice,* and this is one of the fundamental distinctions between child and adult socialization (recognizing, of course, that external circumstance conditions choice). When they reach biological sexual maturity, people may choose to lead celibate or active sexual lives. They may choose to marry or to remain single or to live in a commune; to become parents or not, to have few children or many. They may choose to pursue a college education or go to work as soon as they can find jobs. When they go to work, they may seek to work for a large bureaucratic enterprise or a smaller more personal organization; or they may remain relatively independent, as taxi drivers, traveling sales representatives, lawyers, or physicians. With all such choices, people are also choosing environments in which they will be further socialized, although they will have no more than a vague idea of what their later socialization experiences will be until they are actually enacting the choices they have made and interacting with others whose choices have brought them into mutual contact.

The Nature of Adult Socialization

At the beginning of this chapter we discussed certain ways in which adult socialization is continuous with childhood socialization. Now we ask: How do they differ? Irving Rosow provides one answer. He begins by observing that socialization involves the effort to inculcate both values and behavior so that "the fully socialized person internalizes the correct beliefs and displays the appropriate behavior." But socialization is not always fully successful. Four different types of people can be identified by asking whether they adopt both the values and behavior to which they are being socialized, neither, or one or the other. The socialized are those who adopt both, the unsocialized those who adopt neither. In between are the "dilettante," who adopts the values but not the behavior, and the "chameleon," who displays the expected behavior but does not subscribe to the values. The most suggestive distinction Rosow makes is between the socialized and the chameleon, since both are similar in behavior but different in their commitment to values. Rosow contends that the chameleon type of outcome to socialization is found in many different relationships:

> the stereotyped complaisance of many Negroes in traditional contacts with whites, in the orientation of prostitutes to clients, in the involuntary union member in a closed shop, in the married homosexual, in the unskilled worker in the marginal labor market who has no occupational or organizational identity but fits tolerably into a diversity of work situations. It is also familiar in the typical adjustment of most draftees to military life, in the adaptation of lower ranks of large-scale organizations ... [22]

Rosow then goes on to argue that "chameleon conformity may be the most common pattern in complex societies." In this view, full socialization is concentrated in a few areas of a person's life. Since people are not fully committed to the various positions they occupy and the groups to which they belong, their socialization types will differ with each of them, so that a person is "a chameleon in one, a dilettante in a second, and fully socialized in a third."

Orville Brim picks up Rosow's analysis and carries it further by stating that the most important change from socialization in childhood to that in adulthood is a shift from emphasis on values and motives to emphasis on overt behavior.[23] Brim also points out other significant differences:

1. "Synthesis of old material" rather than acquisition of new material
2. A shift from an idealistic to a realistic outlook

3. Learning how to handle conflicting demands
4. Socialization for increasingly specific roles[24]

The Contexts of Adult Socialization

Important aspects of adult socialization take place in formally organized settings such as colleges and trade schools, work organizations, professional associations, and the military services. There are also special settings—such as prisons and mental hospitals—for those whose earlier socialization comes to be adjudged so seriously faulty that their behavior is deemed to fall outside the range of socially accepted outcomes of socialization. (In Rosow's terms, they are not good chameleons, although some might be dilettantes.)

Stanton Wheeler has attempted to identify some of the main features of these adult socialization settings, features more or less common to all of them, regardless of type.[25] He also notes some important differences between "developmental" socialization organizations as a type (schools, colleges, work organizations) and "resocialization" organizations (prisons, mental hospitals). The latter merit more extended treatment than can be given them here; we shall therefore consider only the developmental organizations, which ordinarily result in socially acceptable socialization outcomes. Although some aspects of Wheeler's analysis may also apply to such childhood settings as the school, our focus here is on adult socialization and on the aspects of organizations that affect socialization outcomes.

The person who enters an organization may be designated a *recruit*. The organization has goals of its own that lead to its providing goals to the recruit. When these are specific goals, such as teaching typing or engineering, the organization is concerned with role socialization. When they are general, such as teaching liberal arts, the concern is with status socialization—preparing the recruit to occupy a generalized status in life and to enact an associated life style. Some organizations may be concerned with both types of goals.[26]

Recruits move through an organization in a sequence of

steps. Organizations that have great control over entry procedures may be able to provide an adequate period of anticipatory socialization. Even so, recruits often experience "reality shock" upon entry—what they had anticipated was either misleading or seriously incomplete. The situation in which they find themselves is unexpected—as when first-year college students are jolted by the amount of work they are expected to do or graduates of secretarial school, expecting to be executive secretaries, are assigned routine filing.

Usually, there are entry procedures of some kind, in which information is exchanged. The recruits receive "an orientation" and learn somewhat more definitely what is expected of them. The socializing agents, in turn, form initial impressions of the recruits and therefore anticipations of what may be expected from them in the way of performance. Of course, other information about the recruits may have been acquired earlier, information from application forms, tests, letters of recommendation, interviews, and transcripts of school grades.

Organizations generally have definite expectations concerning the length of time the recruit is expected to stay in the socialization program. After that time he or she goes through specified exit procedures: graduation from college, assignment to independent responsibilities in a work organization, qualifying examinations for such professions as law or medicine.

The socialization process in formal organizations is not governed entirely by the organization and its officially designated agents. Recruits respond to the situations presented to them and often develop their own norms. An illustration of this is provided in a study of medical students by Howard S. Becker and his associates.[27] Beginning medical students, they found, enter with the expectation of learning everything that is taught them. In the course of the first few weeks they begin to feel overloaded and realize they have set themselves an almost impossible task, so they shift their perspective to trying to learn "only the things that are important." Before the first year is over, the emphasis has shifted to learning what the students think the faculty wants them to know and will ask about on examinations. Student and faculty perspectives differ as to what students should learn and how to judge how much they have learned.

Wilbert Moore has noted that punishment—in the form of heavy work load, great isolation, or required performance of unpleasant tasks and duties—is a component in all socialization to occupations that have high standards of competence and performance and that exhibit high identification of members with the collectivity of fellow practitioners.[28]

All adult socialization leads to some changes in self-image. The formation of a specific occupational identity results, Moore suggests, from these main factors:

1. Learning the language and skills of an occupation
2. Surviving the ordeals that have punished the recruits and their colleagues
3. Accepting fellow recruits and adult role models as significant others for oneself
4. Internalizing the occupational norms, so that self-respect becomes a powerful constraint on poor performance or violation of standards
5. Continuing to be aware of peers as purveyors of potential sanctions
6. Being aware of formal reinforcements, the most important of which is the lack of a market for the services of poor performers

This is, of course, again in Rosow's terms, a model of full socialization; it does not throw much light on how dilettantes and chameleons are produced or on the fact that some of them even do quite well in the market. Questions raised by such observations, however, have not yet been studied carefully.

Socialization for Growing Old

It is now recognized in sociology and other social sciences that socialization is a lifelong activity. In recent years a new discipline has developed—gerontology—concerned with the basic question: What is aging? The long-accepted answer has been that it was basically a biological process with some secondary psychological aspects ("You're as young as you feel"). Increasingly, however, investigators are asking whether there may not be self-fulfilling prophecies built into the process.

According to one theory, aging individuals are motivated naturally to disengage from and relinquish the active roles for which they have been socialized in earlier life;[29] but Matilda Riley and her associates provide evidence to justify questioning this view. They suggest that aging individuals do not seek disengagement from social participation; rather, society operates in many ways to withdraw roles from aging individuals, roles that they might well wish to continue. They are socialized to accept the withdrawal of roles. This is most easily shown with regard to work roles. Retirement is formally defined in many organizations as occurring at a certain age. Individuals are expected to retire at that age and are socialized to define their leaving work as retirement (though other norms might define it as discriminatory exclusion from the labor market). There is anticipatory socialization for retirement: The person's "work role deteriorates around him." He or she may be by-passed for promotion or barred from retraining programs available to younger workers. Performance expectations may rise to levels unattainable by the older worker, resulting in subtle depreciation of his or her performance.

On the basis of scattered evidence, Riley and coauthors suggest that older people, if healthy and provided with useful social roles, might not withdraw. They note that under present conditions "widespread withdrawal might be entirely predictable from the *social* structure—quite apart from any organic or personality changes in the aging *individual.*[30] In the late 1970s, the entire concept of mandatory retirement was becoming less acceptable; corresponding changes in socialization for growing old may follow.

As society changes, more and more life situations formerly left to chance and to individual adjustment are coming to be defined as situations for which the person should be formally socialized. The replacement of apprenticeship by more formalized training programs for work has long been accepted. Increasingly, marriage and parenthood themselves are thought to require formal socialization.[31] And more recently, with more and more people living to advanced age, the need for education for retirement from mature social roles has become a common cry. In modern industrial societies the concern with the outcomes of socialization does not abate.

Notes and References

Chapter 2: Preconditions for Socialization

1. For an insightful discussion of problems in socializing of the blind, see Robert A. Scott, "The Socialization of Blind Children," in David A. Goslin (ed.), *Handbook of Socialization Theory and Research* (Chicago: Rand McNally, 1969), pp. 1025–1046.
2. Charles Horton Cooley, *Social Organization* (New York: Scribner, 1909), p. 27.
3. W. H. Thorpe, *Animal Nature and Human Nature* (Garden City, N.Y.: Anchor Books, 1974), pp. 300–301. The sixteen attributes of human language, comparing them with various animal communication systems, is found in Table 1, pp. 70–71. On pp. 283–300 the book gives a good summary of the work on chimpanzee communication. A slightly more technical summary that raises somewhat different questions about the work is given by social psychologist Roger Brown, *A First Language: The Early Stages* (Cambridge, Mass.: Harvard University Press, 1973), pp. 32–51. A clear discussion by a primatologist of the relevance of primate behavior to human behavior is Alison Jolly, *The Evolution of Human Behavior* (New York: Macmillan, 1972). The assertion that a chimpanzee had been taught to read is put forth in a popular work by the wife and research collaborator of psychologist David Premack in Ann J. Premack, *Why Chimps Can Read* (New York: Harper and Row, 1976). David Premack's work with the chimpanzee Sarah along with that of Allen and Beatrice Gardner with their chimp Washoe are the main studies discussed by Thorpe and by Brown, who consider the work with chimps to be of great scientific importance. But neither of them goes so far as to conclude that Sarah could "read."

4. Cooley, *op. cit.*, p. 30.
5. Robert L. Fantz, "Visual Perception and Experience in Early Infancy: A Look at the Hidden Side of Behavior Development," in Harold W. Stevenson, Eckhard H. Hess, Harriet L. Rheingold (eds.), *Early Behavior: Comparative and Developmental Approaches* (New York: Wiley, 1967), p. 189.
6. *Ibid.*, p. 190.
7. Helen McK. Doan, "Early Stimulation: A Rationale," *Canada's Mental Health,* 24 (June 1976), 10.
8. Fantz, *op. cit.*, p. 218. Italics in original.
9. Doan, *op. cit.*, p. 9.
10. Thorpe, *op. cit.*, p. 223.
11. Lois Barclay Murphy and Alice E. Moriarty, *Vulnerability, Coping, and Growth: From Infancy to Adolescence* (New Haven, Conn.: Yale University Press, 1976), p. 49.
12. M. P. M. Richards, discussion comment in H. R. Schaffer (ed.), *The Origins of Human Social Relations* (New York and London: Academic Press, 1971), pp. 210–211.
13. A listing of fifty-three recorded cases beginning with the "Hesse wolfchild," discovered in 1344, down to the "Teheran ape-child," discovered in 1961, is given in Lucien Malson, *Wolf Children and the Problem of Human Nature* (New York: Monthly Review Press, 1972), pp. 80–82.
14. Harlan Lane, *The Wild Boy of Aveyron* (Cambridge, Mass.: Harvard University Press, 1976). This book is our source for the material that follows.
15. *Ibid.*, p. 37. This quotation is from one of several reports on the boy, written by different specialists of the time.
16. *Ibid.*, p. 56.
17. *Ibid.*, p. 99.
18. *Ibid.*, p. 101.
19. *Ibid.*, p. 102.
20. *Ibid.*, pp. 155 ff.
21. *Ibid.*, pp. 179–180.
22. *Ibid.*, p. 182.
23. *Ibid.*, p. 153, p. 167. Itard wrote two reports to the Ministry of the Interior on his work with Victor. These are reprinted, in English translation, in Malson, *op. cit.* The French film director, Francois Truffaut, in 1970 made a film, *The Wild Child,* based on Victor's capture and life with Itard.
24. E. H. Lenneberg, *Biological Foundations of Language* (New York: Wiley, 1967), cited in Dan I. Slobin, *Psycholinguistics*

(Glenview, Ill.: Scott, Foresman, 1971), p. 56. In addition to the two explanations for Victor's muteness discussed by Lane, at least two others have been proposed as possibilities. Itard himself noted the presence of a large scar on the child's neck and wondered whether his vocal organs might have been injured, but he concluded that the evidence indicated deeper injury to have been unlikely. See Itard, *loc. cit.,* pp. 119–120. In an unpublished communication Ann Beuf has suggested the possibility that Itard's methods of socialization were traumatic in their effect and thereby made it permanently impossible to overcome the initial absence of speech due to Victor's earlier isolation.

25. Kingsley Davis, "Final Note on a Case of Extreme Isolation," *American Journal of Sociology,* 52 (1947), 432–437.

26. J. A. L. Singh and Robert M. Zingg, *Wolf Children and Feral Man* (New York: Harper, 1939).

27. Bruno Bettelheim, "Feral Children and Autistic Children," *American Journal of Sociology,* 64 (1959), 455–467.

28. René A. Spitz, "Hospitalism," *The Psychoanalytic Study of the Child,* 1 (1945), 53–72; and "Hospitalism: A Follow-Up Report," *ibid.,* 2 (1946), 113–117.

29. H. F. Harlow, M. K. Harlow, R. O. Dodsworth, and G. L. Arling, "Maternal Behavior of Rhesus Monkeys Deprived of Mothering and Peer Associations in Infancy," *Proceedings of the American Philosophical Society,* 110 (February 1966), 58–66; Bill Seay and Harry F. Harlow, "Maternal Separation in the Rhesus Monkey," *Journal of Nervous and Mental Disease,* 140 (1965), 434–441; Harry F. Harlow, "Primary Affectional Patterns in Primates," *American Journal of Orthopsychiatry,* 30 (1960), 676–684; M. K. Harlow, "Affection in Primates," *Discovery* (January 1966).

30. S. J. Freedman, H. U. Grunebaum, M. Greenblatt, "Perceptual and Cognitive Changes in Sensory Deprivation," in Philip Solomon, *et al.* (eds.), *Sensory Deprivation* (Cambridge, Mass.: Harvard University Press, 1965), p. 69.

Chapter 3: The Processes of Socialization

1. Alex Inkeles, "Society, Social Structure and Child Socialization," in John A. Clausen (ed.), *Socialization and Society* (Boston: Little, Brown, 1968).

2. M. Brewster Smith, "Competence and Socialization," *ibid.*

3. Inkeles, *op. cit.,* pp. 87–88.

4. The evidence on nutrition and learning is evaluated in Herbert G. Birch, M.D., and Joan Dye Gussow, *Disadvantaged Children: Health, Nutrition and School Failure* (New York: Harcourt, Brace/Grune & Stratton, 1970). See also Nevin S. Scrimshaw and J. E. Gordon (eds.), *Malnutrition, Learning and Behavior* (Cambridge, Mass.: M.I.T. Press, 1968), and Ruth L. Pike and Myrtle L. Brown, *Nutrition: An Integrated Approach,* 2nd ed. (New York: Wiley, 1975), p. 756.

5. W. Lloyd Warner, Robert J. Havighurst, Martin B. Loeb, *Who Shall Be Educated?* (New York: Harper and Brothers, 1944).

6. Bruno Bettelheim, *Symbolic Wounds: Puberty Rites and the Envious Male* (New York: Free Press, 1954).

7. The concept of the infant as evocative is discussed in Gerald Handel, "Analysis of Correlative Meaning: The TAT in the Study of Whole Families," in Gerald Handel (ed.), *The Psychosocial Interior of the Family* (Chicago: Aldine, 1967; London: G. Allen & Unwin, 1968), pp. 104–106.

8. Bettye M. Caldwell, "The Effects of Infant Care," in Martin L. Hoffman and Lois Wladis Hoffman (eds.), *Review of Child Development Research,* Vol. 1 (New York: Russell Sage Foundation, 1964). Contemporary psychoanalytic views are presented in E. James Anthony and Therese Benedek (eds.), *Parenthood: Its Psychology and Psychopathology* (Boston: Little, Brown 1970).

9. Lois B. Murphy, *The Widening World of Childhood* (New York: Basic Books, 1962), cited in Caldwell, *op. cit.*

10. Leon J. Yarrow, "Separation from Parents During Early Childhood," in Hoffman and Hoffman, *op. cit.,* p. 98.

11. M. Kotelchuk, "The Nature of the Child's Tie to the Father" (unpublished Ph.D. dissertation, Harvard University, 1971), cited in Helen Wortis and Clara Rabinowitz (eds.), *The Women's Movement: Social and Psychological Perspectives* (New York: AMS Press, 1972,) p. 34.

12. M. Ainsworth, "The Development of Infant-Mother Interaction Among the Ganda," in B. M. Foss (ed.), *Determinants of Infant Behavior II* (New York: Wiley, 1963), cited in Yarrow, *op. cit.*

13. The impact of newborn infants on adults is beginning to be studied by psychologists. See Michael Lewis and Leonard A. Rosenblum (eds.), *The Effect of the Infant on Its Caregiver*

(New York: Wiley, 1974). All of the contributions to that volume deal with mother-infant interaction. Studies of the effects of newborn infants on the whole family have not, so far as we know, been carried out. This is a topic that is ripe for development.

14. William Caudill, "Tiny Dramas: Vocal Communication between Mother and Infant in Japanese and American Families," Chap. 3 in William P. Lebra (ed.), *Transcultural Research in Mental Health* (Honolulu: University Press of Hawaii, 1972), p. 43. Caudill believes (p. 47, fn. 15) that although his particular study dealt only with first-born infants in middle-class families his findings apply to the two societies more broadly.

15. Some examples of the different ways in which the infant's cry is symbolically interpreted by mothers are reported in the section "Leaving the Baby to Cry" in John and Elizabeth Newson, *Infant Care in an Urban Community* (London: George Allen & Unwin; New York: International Universities Press, 1963), Chap. 6, "The Roots of Socialization," pp. 87–99.

16. An overview of recent work is given in James J. Jenkins, "The Acquisition of Language," in David A. Goslin (ed.), *Handbook of Socialization Theory and Research* (Chicago: Rand McNally, 1969), Chap. 13.

17. This account of the work of these linguistic scholars is adapted from Jenkins, *op. cit.*

18. *Ibid.,* p. 675.

19. *Ibid.,* p. 679.

20. Sigmund Freud, "Three Contributions to the Theory of Sex," in A. A. Brill (ed.), *The Basic Writings of Sigmund Freud,* Book III (New York: Modern Library, 1938), p. 581.

21. Ernest G. Schachtel, *Metamorphosis* (New York: Basic Books, 1959), Chap. 12, "On Memory and Childhood Amnesia," pp. 287–289.

22. Harold Garfinkel, "Studies of the Routine Grounds of Everyday Activities," *Social Problems,* 11, 3 (Winter 1964). Reprinted in David Sudnow (ed.), *Studies in Social Interaction* (New York: Free Press, 1972), p. 4.

23. Iona and Peter Opie, *The Lore and Language of Schoolchildren* (New York: Oxford University Press, 1959), p. 45.

24. A convenient introduction to the concept of communication modalities is given in an article by one of Bateson's co-workers, Jay Haley, "The Family of the Schizophrenic: A Model System," *Journal of Nervous and Mental Disease,* 129 (1959),

357–374. Reprinted in Gerald Handel (ed.), *The Psychosocial Interior of the Family*, 2nd ed. (Chicago: Aldine, 1972), pp. 251–275.

25. Mead does not himself use these examples. His most influential work is presented in George H. Mead, *Mind, Self and Society* (Chicago: University of Chicago Press, 1934). Interpretation and elaboration of his work are found in Herbert Blumer, *Symbolic Interactionism* (Englewood Cliffs, N.J.: Prentice-Hall, 1969); Jerome Manis and Bernard Meltzer (eds.), *Symbolic Interaction* (Boston: Allyn and Bacon, 1967); and Arnold M. Rose (ed.), *Human Behavior and Social Processes, An Interactionist Approach* (Boston: Houghton Mifflin, 1962).

26. Donald W. Ball, "Toward a Sociology of Toys," *Sociological Quarterly*, 8 (Autumn 1967), 447–458.

27. Mead, *op. cit.*, p. 151.

28. Mead, *op. cit.*, p. 155.

29. Philippe Ariès, *Centuries of Childhood* (New York: Knopf, 1962), pp. 128 and 411. Ariès's thesis has been subjected to intense examination by other scholars. They generally support his basic analysis, although with various qualifications and modifications. See David Hunt, *Parents and Children in History: Psychology of Family Life in Early Modern France* (New York: Basic Books, 1970); John R. Gillis, *Youth and History* (New York and London: Academic Press, 1974); and Lloyd deMause (ed.), *The History of Childhood* (New York: The Psychohistory Press, 1974), particularly Chap. 3, Mary Martin McLaughlin, "Survivors and Surrogates: Children and Parents from the Ninth to the Thirteenth Centuries," and Chap. 5, M. J. Tucker, "The Child as Beginning and End: Fifteenth and Sixteenth Century English Childhood," and works cited therein.

30. Ariès, *op. cit.*, pp. 176–177.

31. The following summary of Erikson's approach is adapted from two of his works, *Childhood and Society* (New York: Norton, 1950) and *Identity: Youth and Crisis* (New York: Norton, 1968).

32. Erikson, *Identity: Youth and Crisis*, p. 124.

33. Erikson, *ibid.*, p. 132.

34. Erikson, *Childhood and Society*, p. 231.

35. Alice S. Rossi, "Transition to Parenthood," *Journal of Marriage and Family*, 30 (February 1968), 26–39.

36. Erikson, *Identity: Youth and Crisis*, p. 139.

37. Erikson, *Childhood and Society*, Chap. 3, "Hunters Across the Prairie." For a different interpretation of identity problems of

Indians—though not of the Sioux specifically—see Ann Beuf, *Red Children in White America* (Philadelphia: University of Pennsylvania Press, 1977).

38. Albert J. Reiss, "Social Organization and Socialization: Variations on a Theme about Generations" (unpublished paper, 1965), cited in Eleanor E. Maccoby, "The Development of Moral Values and Behavior in Childhood," in John A. Clausen (ed.), *op. cit.*

39. Erikson, *Identity: Youth and Crisis,* pp. 257–258.

Chapter 4: Socialization and Subcultural Patterns

1. James J. Flink, *The Car Culture* (Cambridge, Mass.: The M.I.T. Press, 1975), p. 231.
2. *Ibid.,* p. 233.
3. Margaret Mead, in Margaret Mead and Martha Wolfenstein (eds.), *Childhood in Contemporary Cultures* (Chicago: University of Chicago Press, 1955), Chap. 1, p. 10. Copyright 1955 by The University of Chicago. Reprinted by permission.
4. The idea of different cultures is most strongly embodied in Oscar Lewis's notion of a "culture of poverty." This and related ideas are discussed and challenged in a carefully reasoned work by Charles A. Valentine, *Culture and Poverty: Critique and Counter-Proposals* (Chicago: University of Chicago Press, 1968).
5. Valentine, *ibid.,* p. 106.
6. Anne Moody, *Coming of Age in Mississippi, An Autobiography* (New York: Delta, 1970), p. 23.
7. See, for example, Arthur J. Vidich and Joseph Bensman, *Small Town in Mass Society* (Princeton, N.J.: Princeton University Press, enlarged edition, 1969).
8. William Graham Sumner, *Folkways* (Boston: Ginn, 1906), p. 13.
9. Tamotsu Shibutani and Kian M. Kwan, *Ethnic Stratification* (New York: Macmillan, 1965), p. 109.
10. Writings that exemplify this belief include Nelson N. Foote and Leonard S. Cottrell, Jr., *Identity and Interpersonal Competence* (Chicago: University of Chicago Press, 1955); Ronald Lippitt, "Improving the Socialization Process," in John A. Clausen (ed.), *Socialization and Society* (Boston: Little, Brown, 1968); and Eugene A. Weinstein, "The Development of Interpersonal

Competence," in David A. Goslin (ed.), *Handbook of Socialization Theory and Research* (Chicago: Rand McNally, 1969).

11. Celia Stendler, *Children of Brasstown* (Urbana: University of Illinois Press, 1949).

12. Bernice Neugarten, in W. Lloyd Warner, *et al.*, *Democracy in Jonesville* (New York: Harper, 1949), Chap. 5.

13. Hyman Rodman, "The Lower-Class Value Stretch," *Social Forces*, 42 (December 1963), 205.

14. Melvin J. Kohn, "Social Class and Parent-Child Relationships: An Interpretation," *American Journal of Sociology*, 68 (January 1963), 471–480.

15. Robert D. Hess and Gerald Handel, *Family Worlds* (Chicago: University of Chicago Press, 1959), Chap. 5, p. 174.

16. Lynda Lytle Holmstrom, *The Two-Career Family* (Cambridge, Mass.: Schenkman, 1973), p. 17.

17. John R. Seeley, R. A. Sim, and E. W. Looseley, *Crestwood Heights: A Study of the Culture of Suburban Life* (New York: Basic Books, 1956; paperback edition, New York: Wiley, 1963), p. 470.

18. *Ibid.,* p. 306.

19. Kohn, *op cit.;* Leonard I. Pearlin and Melvin L. Kohn, "Social Class, Occupation, and Parental Values: A Cross-National Study," *American Sociological Review*, 31 (August 1966), 466–479, reprinted in Alan L. Grey (ed.), *Class and Personality in Society* (New York: Atherton Press, 1969). Kohn's work receives support from James D. Wright and Sonia R. Wright, "Social Class and Parental Values for Children: A Partial Replication and Extension of the Kohn Thesis," *American Sociological Review*, 41 (June 1976), 527–537. See also the exchange of comments by Kohn and the Wrights, *American Sociological Review*, 41 (June 1976), 538–548.

20. Kohn, *op. cit.;* Lee Rainwater, Richard P. Coleman, and Gerald Handel, *Workingman's Wife: Her Personality, World and Life Style* (New York: Oceana Publications, 1959; paperback, Macfadden Books, 1962).

21. Basil Bernstein, "Social Class and Linguistic Development: A Theory of Social Learning," in A. H. Halsey, Jean Floud, and C. Arnold Anderson (eds.), *Education, Economy and Society* (New York: Free Press, 1961), pp. 288–314. A more recent statement is Basil Bernstein, "A Sociolinguistic Approach to Socialization; with Some Reference to Educability," in John J.

Gumperz and Dell Hymes (eds.), *Directions in Sociolinguistics* (New York: Holt, Rinehart and Winston, 1972).

22. Robert D. Hess, Virginia Shipman, and David Jackson, "Early Experience and the Socialization of Cognitive Modes in Children," *Child Development,* 36 (December 1965), 869–886.

23. Louis Schneider and Sverre Lysgaard, "The Deferred Gratification Pattern: A Preliminary Study," *American Sociological Review,* 18 (April 1953), 142–149, reprinted in Alan Grey, *op. cit.*

24. S. M. Miller and Frank Riessman, "The Working Class Subculture: A New View," *Social Problems,* 9 (1961), 86–97; reprinted in Alan Grey, *op. cit.*

25. Allison Davis, "Socialization and Adolescent Personality," *Adolescence, Forty-Third Yearbook,* Part I (Chicago: National Society for the Study of Education, 1944), Chap. 11.

26. Albert K. Cohen and Harold M. Hodges, Jr., "Characteristics of the Lower-Blue-Collar Class," *Social Problems,* 10 (Spring 1963), 303–334. Our account of lower-class subculture draws mainly on this article, unless otherwise indicated.

27. *Ibid.,* p. 322.

28. Eleanor Pavenstedt, "A Comparison of the Child-Rearing Environment of Upper Lower and Very Lower Class Families," *American Journal of Orthopsychiatry,* 35 (January 1965), 89–98. The quotation is taken from the summary given in Bernard Goldstein, *Low Income Youth in Urban Areas: A Critical Review of the Literature* (New York: Holt, Rinehart and Winston, 1967), p. 11. See also Joseph T. Howell, *Hard Living on Clay Street: Portraits of Blue Collar Families* (Garden City, N.Y.: Anchor Books, 1973).

29. Luther P. Jackson, "Telling It Like It Is!" (Washington: Health and Welfare Council of the Capital Area, 1966), quoted in Elizabeth Herzog, *About the Poor: Some Facts and Some Fictions* (Washington: U.S. Department of Health, Education and Welfare, 1968), Chap. 1, "Problem Populations: 'They' and 'We.' "

30. For example, Kurt Mayer and Walter Buckley, *Class and Society* (New York: Random House, 1970); Bennett M. Berger, *Working Class Suburb* (Berkeley: University of California Press, 1960); Herbert J. Gans, *The Urban Villagers: Group and Class in the Life of Italian-Americans* (New York: Free Press, 1962); Arthur Shostak, *Blue-Collar Life* (New York: Random House, 1969); William M. Dobriner, *Class in Suburbia* (Engle-

wood Cliffs, N.J.: Prentice-Hall, 1963); C. Wright Mills, *White Collar: The American Middle Classes* (New York: Oxford University Press, 1951); Charles H. Page, *Class and American Society* (New York: Schocken, 1969); Alan C. Kerckhoff, *Socialization and Social Class* (Englewood Cliffs, N.J.: Prentice-Hall, 1972).

31. The account that follows is adapted from Harry M. Caudill, *Night Comes to the Cumberlands: A Biography of a Depressed Area* (Boston: Little, Brown, 1962).

32. *Ibid.,* p. 51.

33. *Ibid.,* p. 146.

34. *Ibid.,* pp. 337–338.

35. Richard A. Ball, "A Poverty Case: The Analgesic Subculture of the Southern Appalachians," *American Sociological Review,* 33 (December 1968), 885–895.

36. Jack E. Weller, *Yesterday's People: Life in Contemporary Appalachia* (Lexington: University of Kentucky Press, 1965), pp. 47–48.

37. Rex A. Lucas, *Minetown, Milltown, Railtown* (Toronto: University of Toronto Press, 1971).

38. For an excellent book of readings covering most facets of commune life, see Rosabeth Moss Kanter (ed.), *Communes: Creating and Managing the Collective Life* (New York: Harper and Row, 1973).

39. Bruno Bettelheim, *Children of the Dream* (New York: Macmillan, 1969). Also see Melford E. Spiro, *Children of the Kibbutz,* rev. ed. (Cambridge, Mass.: Harvard University Press, 1975); Yonina Talmon, "The Family in a Revolutionary Movement —The Case of the Kubbutz in Israel," in M. F. Nimkoff (ed.), *Comparative Family Systems* (Boston: Houghton Mifflin, 1965), pp. 259–286; A. I. Rabin, *Growing Up in the Kibbutz* (New York: Springer, 1965).

40. Bennett M. Berger, *et al.,* "Child-Rearing Practices of the Communal Family," Progress Report to the National Institute of Mental Health, 1971. Selections reprinted in Kanter, *op. cit.,* and in Arlene S. Skolnick and Jerome H. Skolnick (eds.), *Family in Transition* (Boston: Little, Brown, 1971), pp. 509–523.

41. Berger, *et al.,* in Kanter, *op. cit.,* p. 358.

42. For a discussion of the difficulties with the concept of race and its abandonment by scientists as no longer useful, see J. Z. Young, *An Introduction to the Study of Man* (Oxford: Oxford University Press, 1971), Chap. 41.

43. Gunnar Myrdal, *An American Dilemma* (New York: Harper & Brothers, 1944), p. 157.

44. The suggestion has been made that *generation* is a less useful concept than *cohort,* which is defined as "the aggregate of individuals (within some population definition) who experienced the same event within the same time interval." See Norman B. Ryder, "The Cohort as a Concept in the Study of Social Change," *American Sociological Review,* 30 (December 1965), 843–861. The implication of this approach in the present context would be that children of immigrants ("second generation") in, say, 1880 had different socialization experiences from children of immigrants in 1975. Although this is undoubtedly true, it does not mean that the fact of being second generation may not have common features regardless of the time at which it occurs. For our purposes here, the notion of "generation" remains useful.

45. Marion Radke Yarrow, "Personality Development and Minority Group Membership," in Marshall Sklare (ed.), *The Jews: Social Patterns of an American Group* (Glencoe, Ill.: Free Press, 1958).

46. Judith D. R. Porter, *Black Child, White Child* (Cambridge, Mass.: Harvard University Press, 1971), p. 86. For a classic study published almost twenty years before, which touched on the same point, see Mary Ellen Goodman, *Race Awareness in Young Children* (Reading, Mass.: Addison-Wesley, 1952).

47. For evidence that this is not an irrelevant question in the United States, or at least in Chicago, see William Kornblum, *Blue Collar Community* (Chicago: University of Chicago Press, 1974).

48. A study of Mexican-Americans presents many of the ways in which particular and local context can affect identity. See Leo Grebler, Joan W. Moore, Ralph C. Guzman, *The Mexican-American People: The Nation's Second Largest Minority* (New York: Free Press, 1970).

49. Gordon Allport, *Becoming* (New Haven, Conn.: Yale University Press, 1955), pp. 36–56.

50. Ernesto Galarza, *Barrio Boy* (Notre Dame, Ind.: University of Notre Dame Press, 1971), pp. 211–212.

51. Kurt Lewin, *Resolving Social Conflicts* (New York: Harper & Row, 1948).

52. Robert Coles, *Children of Crisis* (New York: Little, Brown, 1964); Alvin Poussaint, "The Negro American: His Self-Image

and Integration," in Floyd Barbour (ed.), *The Black Power Revolt* (Boston: Porter Sargent Publishers, 1968). See also the discussion by Joyce A. Ladner, *Tomorrow's Tomorrow* (Garden City, N.Y.: Doubleday, 1971), pp. 72 ff. A similar movement, possibly with similar results, has developed among Mexican-Americans. For a brief review of the *chicano movement* see Alfredo Cuéllar, "Perspective on Politics," Chap. 8, in Joan W. Moore, *Mexican Americans* (Englewood Cliffs, N.J.: Prentice-Hall, 1970).

53. Morris Rosenberg and Roberta G. Simmons, *Black and White Self-Esteem: The Urban School Child* (Washington, D.C.: American Sociological Association, 1971).
54. Shibutani and Kwan, *op. cit.,* p. 357.
55. Reported in Beatrice Griffith, *American Me* (Boston: Houghton Mifflin, 1948), p. 151.
56. Robert K. Merton, *Social Theory and Social Structure* (New York: Free Press, 1968), pp. 281 ff. In the sociological literature, the term "reference group" sometimes has other meanings. See Tamatsu Shibutani, "Reference Groups as Perspectives," *American Journal of Sociology,* 60 (May 1955), 562–569.
57. Hylan Lewis, Foreword to Elliot Liebow, *Tally's Corner: A Study of Negro Streetcorner Men* (Boston: Little, Brown, 1967), p. vii.
58. Walt Wolfram, *Sociolinguistic Aspects of Assimilation: Puerto Rican English in New York City* (Arlington, Va.: Center for Applied Linguistics, 1974), p. 31. As migrants, the Puerto Ricans are unique: they are American citizens, racially mixed, without a native clergy, and have come, and may readily return, by plane. The receiving community, especially in New York, is also very different from communities in the past. Governments provide a once inconceivable range of public services, schools are centers of controversy, and blacks are large and active groups in the immediate areas of settlement. See Joseph P. Fitzpatrick, *Puerto Rican Americans: The Meaning of Migration to the Mainland* (Englewood Cliffs, N.J.: Prentice-Hall, 1971). For an analysis of socialization problems of Italian immigrant families in Toronto that touches on this question, see Kurt Danziger, "The Acculturation of Italian Immigrant Girls in Canada," in C. Beattie and S. Crysdale (eds.), *Sociology Canada: Readings* (Toronto: Butterworth and Co., 1974), pp. 134–145.
59. Richard Gambino, "La famiglia: Four generations of Italian-

Americans" in Joseph Ryan (ed.), *White Ethnics: Their Life in Working Class America* (Englewood Cliffs, N.J.: Prentice-Hall, 1973), p. 45.

60. Mark Zborowski, "Cultural Components in Responses to Pain," *Journal of Social Issues,* 8 (1951), 16–30.
61. Stephen Richer and Pierre Laporte, "Culture, Cognition and English-French Competition," in Jean L. Elliott (ed.), *Immigrant Groups* (Scarborough, Ontario: Prentice-Hall, 1971), pp. 141–150.
62. H. Hawthorn, *A Survey of the Contemporary Indians of Canada,* Vol. II (Ottawa: Queen's Printer, 1968).
63. Fred L. Strodtbeck, "Family Interaction, Values, and Achievement," in Sklare, *op. cit.,* p. 149.
64. Bernard C. Rosen, "Race, Ethnicity and the Achievement Syndrome," *American Sociological Review,* 24 (1959), 47–60.
65. W. Lloyd Warner, *American Life: Dream and Reality* (Chicago: University of Chicago Press, 1953), p. 171.
66. Richard Krickus, *Pursuing the American Dream* (Garden City, N.Y.: Anchor Books, 1976), Chap. 8.
67. Nathan Glazer and Daniel P. Moynihan, *Beyond the Melting Pot: The Negroes, Puerto Ricans, Jews, Italians, and Irish of New York City* (Cambridge, Mass.: M.I.T. Press, 1963), p. 310.
68. Nathan Glazer and Daniel P. Moynihan (eds.), *Ethnicity: Theory and Experience* (Cambridge, Mass.: Harvard University Press, 1975), pp. 1–26.
69. Jean Burnet, "Ethnicity: Canadian Experience and Policy," *Sociological Focus,* 9 (1976), 199.

Chapter 5. Agencies of Socialization

1. David Riesman, with Reuel Denny and Nathan Glazer, *The Lonely Crowd: A Study of the Changing American Character* (New Haven: Yale University Press, 1950).
2. Robert K. Merton, *Social Theory and Social Structure* (New York: Free Press, 1968), enlarged ed., chap. entitled "Manifest and Latent Functions."
3. Allen Kassof, *The Soviet Youth Program: Regimentation and Rebellion* (Cambridge, Mass.: Harvard University Press, 1965), p. 173.
4. Dennis Wrong, "The Oversocialized Conception of Man in Modern Sociology," *American Sociological Review,* 26 (April

1961), 183–193. An enlarged version of this article is printed in *Psychoanalysis and the Psychoanalytic Review*, 49 (Summer 1962), where it is accompanied by a rebuttal from Talcott Parsons entitled "Individual Autonomy and Social Pressure: An Answer to Dennis H. Wrong," pp. 70–79.

5. Jean Evans, *Three Men* (New York: Knopf, 1950), p. 11.

6. Peter Blau and Otis D. Duncan, *The American Occupational Structure* (New York: Wiley, 1967), p. 330.

7. Elaboration of the family's mediating role is presented in Gerald Handel (ed.), *The Psychosocial Interior of the Family*, 2nd ed. (Chicago: Aldine, 1972), Part III, "The Family as Mediator of the Culture."

8. David A. Schulz, *Coming Up Black: Patterns of Ghetto Socialization* (Englewood Cliffs, N.J.: Prentice-Hall, 1969).

9. This analysis is developed by Lee Rainwater, "Crucible of Identity: The Negro Lower-Class Family," *Daedalus, Journal of the American Academy of Arts and Sciences*, 95 (1966), 172–216.

10. Handel, *op. cit.;* Robert D. Hess and Gerald Handel, *Family Worlds* (Chicago: University of Chicago Press, 1959).

11. In one study Harris found that both mothers and fathers "invariably showed evidence of using their parenthood to continue or to resolve, through their children, some aspects of their own growing up, and therefore each of their several children might represent a somewhat different aspect of their past." Irving Harris, *Normal Children and Mothers* (New York: Free Press, 1959), p. 39.

12. Talcott Parsons and Robert F. Bales, *Family, Socialization and Interaction Process* (Glencoe, Ill.: Free Press, 1955), Chap. II, "Family Structure and the Socialization of the Child."

13. Herbert J. Gans, *The Urban Villagers: Group and Class in the Life of Italian-Americans* (New York: Free Press, 1962), pp. 54, 59–60. Italics in original.

14. Jack E. Weller, *Yesterday's People: Life in Contemporary Appalachia* (Lexington: University of Kentucky Press, 1965).

15. Norman W. Bell, "Extended Family Relations of Disturbed and Well Families," *Family Process*, 1 (September 1962), 175–193.

16. Leonard Benson, *Fatherhood: A Sociological Perspective* (New York: Random House, 1968), p. 3.

17. Talcott Parsons, *Social Structure and Personality* (New York: Free Press, 1964), Chap. 2, "The Father Symbol: An Appraisal

in the Light of Psychoanalytic and Sociological Theory." Our account is a necessarily oversimplified version of Parsons' complex argument.

18. Benson, *op. cit.,* p. 50. For another overview of father's importance, see David B. Lynn, *The Father: His Role in Child Development* (Monterey, Calif.: Brooks/Cole, 1974).

19. Bernard C. Rosen, "Social Class and the Child's Perception of the Parent," *Child Development,* 35 (December 1964), 1147–1153.

20. James H. S. Bossard and Eleanor Stoker Boll, *The Sociology of Child Development,* 4th ed. (New York: Harper & Row, 1966), pp. 39–40.

21. Bossard and Boll, *op. cit.,* p. 52. The authors do not identify the source of their census data.

22. Orville G. Brim, Jr., "Family Stucture and Sex Role Learning by Children: A Further Analysis of Helen Koch's Data," *Sociometry,* 21 (1958), 1–15.

23. Paul C. Glick, "A Demographer Looks at American Families," *Journal of Marriage and the Family,* 37 (February 1975), 22.

24. Betty E. Cogswell and Marvin B. Sussman, "Changing Family and Marriage Forms: Complications for Human Service Systems," *The Family Coordinator,* 21 (October 1972), 507. In addition to the four types cited in the text, they estimate that 15 percent of the population live in a nuclear dyad without children and that 5 percent live in "other traditional forms," including aged couples, three-generation families, and groupings of extended kin. Their base is evidently the total population living in some kind of family, rather than the total population of the United States, since they present no figure for those living singly.

25. Benjamin Schlesinger, "The One-Parent Family in Canada: Some Recent Findings and Recommendations," *The Family Coordinator,* 22 (July 1973), 305.

26. Marvin B. Sussman, "Family Systems in the 1970's: Analysis, Policies, and Programs," *Annals of the American Academy of Political and Social Science,* 396 (1971), 40–56. Also, Cogswell and Sussman, *op. cit.*

27. Lucile Duberman, *The Reconstituted Family: A Study of Remarried Couples and Their Children* (Chicago: Nelson-Hall, 1975), p. 109.

28. Irene Fast and Albert C. Cain, "The Step-parent Role: Potential for Disturbance in Family Functioning," *American Journal of*

Orthopsychiatry, 36:485–491, summarized in James Walters and Nick Stinnett, "Parent-Child Relationships: A Decade Review of Research," *Journal of Marriage and Family,* 33 (February 1971), 83.

29. Gerald Handel, "Views of a Changing Interior," in G. Handel (ed.), *The Psychosocial Interior of the Family,* 2nd ed. (Chicago: Aldine, 1972), p. vii.

30. Lois Wladis Hoffman and F. Ivan Nye, with others, *Working Mothers: An Evaluative Review of the Consequences for Wife, Mother and Child* (San Francisco: Jossey-Bass Publishers, 1974), p. 5. Similar documentation based on somewhat different sources, may be found in Jessie Bernard, *The Future of Motherhood* (New York: Dial Press, 1974), p. 367. In Canada, the proportion of mothers who work for pay is somewhat lower than in the United States, but the trends are the same. In 1967, 19 percent of married women with children under age six and 28 percent with children ages six to fourteen were working. For 1973, Statistics Canada presents the figure differently, but the increase is evident: 24 percent of mothers whose youngest child was under age two; 30 percent whose youngest child was between ages two and five; and 43 percent whose youngest child was between ages six and sixteen were working. See Women's Bureau, "Women in the Labour Force: Facts and Figures" (Ottawa: Department of Labour, 1975).

31. Arthur C. Emlen and Joseph B. Perry, Jr., "Child-Care Arrangements," in Hoffman and Nye, *op. cit.,* p. 104.

32. These findings and others in the paragraph are summarized from the discussion by Lois Wladis Hoffman, "Effects on Child," in Hoffman and Nye, *op. cit.,* Chap. 6.

33. Hoffman, *op. cit.,* p. 147.

34. Hoffman, *op. cit.,* p. 165.

35. Robert D. Hess and Judith V. Torney, *The Development of Political Attitudes in Children* (Chicago: Aldine, 1967), p. 217.

36. Edmund J. King, *Education and Social Change* (Oxford: Pergamon Press, 1966), p. 3.

37. David A. Goslin, *The School in Contemporary Society* (Glenview, Ill.: Scott, Foresman, 1965), p. 84.

38. Albert J. Reiss, Jr., Introduction to A. J. Reiss, Jr. (ed.), *Schools in a Changing Society* (New York: Free Press, 1965), p. 2.

39. Patricia Cayo Sexton, *Education and Income* (New York: Viking, 1961) reports on one major North American city.

40. S. John Eggleston, *The Social Context of the School* (London:

Routledge and Kegan Paul, 1967), p. 26. The quotation describes a study carried out and reported by J. W. B. Douglas, *The Home and the School* (London: MacGibbon and Kee, 1964). American studies reporting comparable practices include W. Lloyd Warner, Robert J. Havighurst, and Martin B. Loeb, *Who Shall Be Educated?* (New York: Harper and Brothers, 1944) and A. B. Hollingshead, *Elmtown's Youth* (New York: Wiley, 1949). Urban population changes in the United States are probably reducing the number of schools in which there is a mixture of social classes, but in smaller cities and towns such mixing probably continues.

41. Ray C. Rist, *The Urban School: A Factory for Failure* (Cambridge, Mass.: M.I.T. Press, 1973), pp. 241–242. Italics in original.

42. Robert E. Herriott and Nancy H. St. John, *Social Class and the Urban School: The Impact of Pupil Background on Teachers and Principals* (New York: Wiley, 1966).

43. *Ibid.* Herriott and St. John found that teachers' performance in schools with the lowest-status pupils is judged by principals and fellow teachers to be somewhat less competent than in schools with higher-status pupils.

44. Martin Deutsch, "The Disadvantaged Child and the Learning Process," in Martin Deutsch, *et al., The Disadvantaged Child: Studies of the Social Environment and the Learning Process* (New York: Basic Books, 1967).

45. Robert D. Hess, "Effects of Maternal Interaction on Cognitions of Pre-School Children," unpublished paper cited in Norman E. Freeberg and Donald T. Payne, "Parental Influence on Cognitive Development in Early Childhood: A Review," *Child Development,* 38 (March 1967); R. D. Hess and Virginia C. Shipman, "Early Experience and the Socialization of Cognitive Modes in Children," *Child Development,* 36 (1965), 869–886.

46. Fred L. Strodtbeck, "The Hidden Curriculum of the Middle-Class Home," in A. Harry Passow, *et al.* (eds.), *Education of the Disadvantaged: A Book of Readings* (New York: Holt, Rinehart and Winston, 1967), p. 253.

47. Robert J. Havighurst, "Education and Social Mobility in Four Societies," in A. H. Halsey, Jean Floud, C. Arnold Anderson (eds.), *Education, Economy and Society* (New York: Free Press, 1961), p. 116. For data indicating a similar pattern in Canada, see John Porter, *The Vertical Mosaic* (Toronto: University of Toronto Press, 1965).

48. Natalie Rogoff, "American Public Schools and Equality of Opportunity," in Halsey, *op. cit.*

49. Philip W. Jackson, *Life in Classrooms* (New York: Holt, Rinehart and Winston, 1968), p. 5.

50. *Ibid.,* p. 18.

51. *Ibid.,* p. 20.

52. Rist, *op. cit.,* pp. 85–86.

53. Jackson, *op. cit.,* p. 21.

54. Talcott Parsons, "The School Class as a Social System: Some of Its Functions in American Society," *Harvard Educational Review,* 29 (1959), 297–318, reprinted in Talcott Parsons, *Social Structure and Personality* (New York: Free Press, 1964).

55. Rist, *op. cit.*

56. Merton, *op. cit.*

57. Robert Rosenthal and Lenore Jacobson, *Pygmalion in the Classroom: Teacher Expectation and Pupils' Intellectual Development* (New York: Holt, Rinehart and Winston, 1968), p. vii. This book also includes a summary of other pertinent research on self-fulfilling prophecies.

58. *Ibid.,* p. 70.

59. The evidence relating to the nature of intelligence is analyzed by J. McV. Hunt, *Intelligence and Experience* (New York: Ronald Press, 1961). See also Philip E. Vernon, *Intelligence and Cultural Environment* (London: Methuen, 1969).

60. Eleanor Burke Leacock, *Teaching and Learning in City Schools: A Comparative Study* (New York: Basic Books, 1969).

61. *Ibid.,* p. 205.

62. John U. Ogbu, *The Next Generation: An Ethnography of Education in an Urban Neighborhood* (New York: Academic Press, 1974), p. 97. In original, the emphasis was in boldface.

63. *Ibid.,* p. 98.

64. *Ibid.,* p. 2.

65. *Ibid.,* p. 13.

66. *Ibid.,* p. 143.

67. *Ibid.,* p. 258.

68. For a discussion of age-status participation in sports in Scandinavia, see R. Helenko, "Sports and Socialization," in Neil J. Smelser and William T. Smelser (eds.), *Personality and Social Systems* (New York: Wiley, 1963), pp. 238–247. Also see John W. Loy and Alan G. Ingham, "Play, Games, and Sport in the Psychosocial Development of Children and Youth," in G. Law-

rence Rarick (ed.), *Physical Activity: Human Growth and Development* (New York: Academic Press, 1973), pp. 257–302.

69. Iona and Peter Opie, *Children's Games in Street and Playground* (Oxford: Oxford University Press, 1969), p. 17.

70. *Ibid.,* p. 18.

71. Philippe Ariès, "Games, Fashions and Society," in Ariès, *et al., The World of Children* (London: Paul Hamlyn, 1966), pp. 101–111.

72. Opie and Opie, *op. cit.,* p. 10.

73. Iona and Peter Opie, *The Lore and Language of Schoolchildren* (Oxford: Oxford University Press, 1959).

74. Harry Webb, "Professionalization of Attitudes toward Play among Adolescents," in Gerald S. Kenyon (ed.), *Aspects of Contemporary Sport Sociology* (Chicago: The Athletic Institute, 1969), p. 164.

75. *Ibid.,* p. 178.

76. Janet Lever, "Soccer as a Brazilian Way of Life," in Gregory P. Stone (ed.), *Games, Sport and Power* (New Brunswick, N.J.: Transaction Books, 1972), p. 148.

77. Ariès, *op. cit.,* p. 107.

78. Opie and Opie, *Children's Games,* p. 3.

79. Harry Stack Sullivan, *The Interpersonal Theory of Psychiatry* (New York: Norton, 1953), p. 245.

80. Carlfred B. Broderick and S. E. Fowler, "New Patterns of Relationships between the Sexes among Pre-adolescents," *Marriage and Family Living,* 23 (February 1961), 27–30.

81. Carlfred B. Brôderick, "Sexual Behavior among Preadolescents," *Journal of Social Issues,* 22 (April 1966), 6–21.

82. Boone E. Hammond and Joyce A. Ladner, "Socialization into Sexual Behavior in a Negro Slum Ghetto," in Carlfred B. Broderick and Jessie Bernard (eds.), *The Individual, Sex and Society* (Baltimore: The Johns Hopkins Press, 1969). See also, Carlfred B. Broderick, "Social Heterosexual Development among Urban Negroes and Whites," *Journal of Marriage and Family,* 28 (May 1965), 200–204; Rainwater, *op. cit.;* and Schulz, *op. cit.*

83. Among the general works dealing with mass communications are Charles R. Wright, *Mass Communication: A Sociological Perspective,* 2nd ed. (New York: Random House, 1975); and Lewis Anthony Dexter and David Manning White (eds.), *People, Society and Mass Communications* (New York: Free Press, 1964). See also F. Gerald Kline and Phillip J. Tichenor (eds.), *Current Perspectives in Mass Communication* (Beverly Hills,

Calif.: Sage Publications, 1972), Vol. I, Sage Annual Reviews of Communication Research.

84. Donald Horton and R. Richard Wohl, "Mass Communication and Para-Social Interaction," *Psychiatry* 19 (August 1956), 215.

85. A study by Melvin L. DeFleur, "Occupational Roles as Portrayed on Television," *Public Opinion Quarterly,* 28 (Spring 1964), 57–74, shows that the occupational roles portrayed on television are disproportionately higher status compared to the distribution of occupations in the actual work world. Television thus does not present children with a realistic array of occupational models. See also Melvin L. DeFleur and Lois B. DeFleur, "The Relative Contribution of Television As a Learning Source for Children's Occupational Knowledge," *American Sociological Review,* 32 (October 1967), 777–789.

86. Anthony Comstock, *Traps for the Young* (Cambridge, Mass.: Belknap Press of Harvard University Press, 1967 reissue, p. 13; original publication: New York: Funk & Wagnalls, 1883).

87. Wilbur Schramm (ed.), *Mass Communications* (Urbana: University of Illinois Press, 1960).

88. Wilbur Schramm and David M. White, "Age, Education and Economic Status As Factors in Newspaper Reading," in Schramm, *op. cit.,* p. 439.

89. Psychiatrist Fredric Wertham some years ago gained wide attention for his view that comic books (as distinct from comic strips in newspapers) have a morally depraving effect on children. See his *Seduction of the Innocent* (New York: Rinehart and Company, 1953).

90. This figure is of December 31, 1974. *Statistical Abstract of the United States* (Washington, D.C.: Government Printing Office, 1975), p. 723.

91. *Canada 1976* (Ottawa: Statistics Canada, December, 1975, p. 128).

92. Jack Lyle and Heidi R. Hoffman, "Explorations in Patterns of Television Viewing by Pre-School Age Children," in Eli A. Rubinstein, George A. Comstock, and John P. Murray (eds.), *Television and Social Behavior, Reports and Papers* (Washington, D.C.: U.S. Government Printing Office, 1972), IV, *Television in Day-to-Day Life: Patterns of Use,* 259.

93. Wilbur Schramm, Jack Lyle, and Edwin B. Parker, *Television in the Lives of Our Children* (Stanford, California: Stanford University Press, 1961).

94. Aletha Huston Stein and Lynette Kohn Friedrich, "Impact of Television on Children and Youth," Chap. 4 in E. Mavis Heth-

erington (ed.), *Review of Child Development Research,* V (Chicago: University of Chicago Press, 1975), 186–187.

95. Jack Lyle and Heidi R. Hoffman, "Children's Use of Television and Other Media," in Rubinstein, Comstock, and Murray, *op. cit.,* Table 1, "Projected Total Weekly Viewing Time," p. 132.

96. Schramm, Lyle, and Parker, *op. cit.*

97. Lyle and Hoffman, "Children's Use," pp. 192–193.

98. Lyle and Hoffman, "Children's Use," pp. 137–138.

99. Bradley S. Greenberg and Brenda Dervin, with the assistance of Joseph R. Dominick and John Bowes, *Use of the Mass Media by the Urban Poor. Findings of Three Research Projects, with an Annotated Bibliography* (New York: Praeger, 1970), p. 70.

100. Lyle and Hoffman, "Children's Use," pp. 151–152.

101. Lyle and Hoffman, "Children's Use," p. 138.

102. Lyle and Hoffman, "Children's Use," Table 13, p. 147; and Lyle and Hoffman, "Pre-School Age Children," Table 5, p. 262.

103. Lyle and Hoffman, "Children's Use," pp. 148–149.

104. Gary A. Steiner, *The People Look at Television* (New York: Knopf, 1963), p. 84.

105. Steiner, *ibid.,* p. 95.

106. Schramm, Lyle, and Parker, *op. cit.,* p. 88.

107. Schramm, Lyle, and Parker, *ibid.,* pp. 96–97. The English study is reported in Hilde Himmelweit, A. N. Oppenheim, and Pamela Vince, *Television and the Child* (London: Oxford University Press, 1958).

108. Aletha Huston Stein and Lynette Kohn Friedrich, with Fred Vondracek, "Television Content and Young Children's Behavior," in John P. Murray, Eli A. Rubinstein, and George A. Comstock (eds.), *Television and Social Behavior, Reports and Papers* (Washington, D.C.: U.S. Government Printing Office, 1971), II, *Television and Social Learning,* 212.

109. *Ibid.,* p. 273.

110. Gerald S. Lesser, *Children and Television: Lessons from Sesame Street* (New York: Random House, 1974), p. 206.

111. *Ibid.,* pp. 218–220.

112. *Ibid.,* p. 244.

113. *Ibid.,* p. 260. In a critical review of Lesser's book, Rose K. Goldsen argues that the program teaches the values of commercial society. *Contemporary Sociology: A Journal of Reviews,* 4, 3 (May 1975), 234–236.

114. See, for example, Arnold Arnold, *Violence and Your Child* (Chicago: Regnery, 1969); and Fredric Wertham, *A Sign for*

Cain: An Exploration of Human Violence (New York: Macmillan, 1966).

115. Urie Bronfenbrenner, *Two Worlds of Childhood: U.S. and U.S.S.R.* (New York: The Russell Sage Foundation, 1970), p. 114. The concern with violence in the mass media is also reflected in the volume edited by sociologist Otto N. Larson, *Violence and the Mass Media* (New York: Harper & Row, 1968). This anthology covers movies and printed media as well as TV, although the few empirical studies included deal primarily with TV.

116. From letter of Senator John O. Pastore to H. E. W. Secretary Robert Finch, March 5, 1969, quoted in Douglass Cater and Stephen Strickland, *TV Violence and the Child: The Evolution and Fate of the Surgeon General's Report* (New York: Russell Sage Foundation, 1975), p. 17.

117. The research studies are published in a five-volume work bearing the title *Television and Social Behavior*, with each volume having an individual title. Material from two of the volumes has been cited earlier in this chapter.

118. *Television and Growing Up: The Impact of Televised Violence*, Report to the Surgeon General, United States Public Health Service from the Surgeon General's Scientific Advisory Committee on Television and Social Behavior (Washington: U.S. Government Printing Office, 1972).

119. *Ibid.*, p. 186. Also in summary chapter, pp. 18–19. For an account of the committee's problems in reaching its conclusions, see Cater and Strickland, *op. cit.*, especially Chap. 7.

120. L. Zusne, "Measuring Violence in children's cartoons," *Perceptual and Motor Skills*, 27 (1968), 901–902, summarized by Harold W. Stevenson, "Television and the Behavior of Preschool Children," *Television and Social Learning*, II, 350.

121. Robert M. Liebert, John M. Neale, and Emily S. Davidson, *The Early Window: Effects of Television on Children and Youth* (New York: Pergamon, 1973), p. 157.

122. *Ibid.*, p. 151.

123. *Television and Growing Up: The Impact of Televised Violence*, *op. cit.*, pp. 23–24. See also the more detailed account given by Cater and Strickland, *op. cit.* One of the seven persons barred from membership on the Surgeon General's Advisory Committee has written his own analysis of the committee's effort. His conclusions are similar to those of Liebert, Neale, and Davidson, but he arrives at them through another line of

reasoning. See Leo Bogart, "Warning: The Surgeon General Has Determined that TV Violence is Moderately Dangerous to Your Child's Mental Health," *The Public Opinion Quarterly,* XXXVI (Winter 1972–1973), 491–521.

124. Liebert, Neale, and Davidson, *op. cit.,* pp. 152 ff.

125. Dennis Howitt and Guy Cumberbatch, *Mass Media Violence and Society* (New York: Wiley, 1975), p. 106.

126. *Ibid.,* p. 116.

127. Grant Noble, *Children in Front of the Small Screen* (London: Constable; Beverly Hills, Calif.: Sage, 1975), p. 157. For a recent statement explaining research in mass communication from this point of view, see Elihu Katz, Jay G. Blumler, and Michael Gurevitch, "Uses of Mass Communication by the Individual," in W. Phillips Davison and Frederick T. C. Yu, *Mass Communication Research: Major Issues and Future Directions* (New York: Praeger, 1974).

128. As this book was going to press, a nationwide survey of 2200 children between the ages of seven and eleven reported that the majority of them are fearful of some aspect of the world around them. Two-thirds are afraid that "somebody bad" might get into their houses; a quarter of them are afraid that somebody might hurt them when they go outside; and nearly a quarter said they felt afraid of "TV programs where people fight and shoot guns." The study is reported as saying that "heavy watchers—four or more hours a weekday—were twice as likely to feel 'scared often.' However, it was not clear whether heavy watching caused the fear or was the result of being fearful about going out." The report stated that the majority of children who say they are afraid to go outside also said they have been bothered by adults or children while playing. Thus, there is some evidence that viewing TV violence arouses anxiety rather than instigating the viewer to be aggressive. Anxiety is damaging to children, but it is a somewhat different form of damage than a readiness to be violent. So far as we know, no effort has been made to investigate whether viewing TV violence more often or more readily stimulates anxiety than it stimulates aggressive behavior. The actual report of the survey mentioned above was not available to us; our account and the quotations are from the newspaper account by Richard Flaste, "Survey Finds That Most Children are Happy at Home but Fear World," *The New York Times,* March 2, 1977, p. A12.

129. Richard Maxwell Brown, *Strain of Violence: Historical Studies of American Violence and Vigilantism* (New York: Oxford University Press, 1975), p. vii. Also see his summary essay, "Historical Patterns of Violence in America," in Hugh Davis Graham and Ted Robert Gurr (eds.), *Violence in America: Historical and Comparative Perspectives* (New York: Bantam, 1969), as well as Richard Hofstadter and Michael Wallace (eds.), *American Violence: A Documentary History* (New York: Knopf, 1970).

130. Eleanor E. Maccoby, "Effects of the Mass Media," in Martin L. Hoffman and Lois Wladis Hoffman (eds.), *Review of Child Development Research,* I (New York: The Russell Sage Foundation, 1964), 323–348.

131. Lotte Bailyn, "Mass Media and Children: A Study of Exposure Habits and Cognitive Effects," *Psychological Monographs,* 73 (1959), No. 1. George Gerbner argues that TV "shapes the common consciousness of . . . what is important, what is right, and what is related to what . . ." He sees this as more influential than any particular attitude change. Yet he finds that dramatic programs *follow* conventional values and morality. George Gerbner, "Communication and the Social Environment," *Scientific American,* 227, 3 (September 1972), 152–160.

132. Maccoby, *op. cit.,* pp. 341–342.

133. Ira O. Glick and Sidney J. Levy, *Living with Television* (Chicago: Aldine, 1962), p. 206.

134. Ralph Garry, "Television's Impact on the Child," in *Children and TV* (Washington: Association for Childhood Education International, 1967), p. 9.

135. George A. Comstock, "The Effects of Television on Children and Adolescents: The Evidence So Far," *Journal of Communication,* 25 (Autumn 1975), 27.

136. Liebert, Neale, and Davidson, *op. cit.,* p. 109.

137. Liebert, Neale, and Davidson, *op. cit.,* p. 131.

138. We make this statement on the basis of having read the descriptive summaries of the sixty studies for the Surgeon General's report presented in Liebert, Neale, and Davidson, *op. cit.,* Appendix A, pp. 172–185.

139. Herbert Hyman, "Mass Communication and Socialization," in W. Phillips Davison and Frederick T. C. Yu, *Mass Communication Research: Major Issues and Future Directions* (New York: Praeger, 1974).

140. Howitt and Cumberbatch, *op. cit.,* p. 121.

141. Noble, *op. cit.,* pp. 237–238.
142. Liebert, Neale, and Davidson, *op. cit.,* pp. 169–171.
143. Noble, *op. cit.,* pp. 237–240. Noble also feels that the media are controlled by too few people and that more viewpoints should have access than is now the case. He favors a system of public broadcasting rather than commercially sponsored broadcasting, in contrast to Liebert, Neale and Davidson who favor the retention of commercially sponsored broadcasting, provided there is increased government regulation and consumer boycotting of products advertised on violent programs. Noble, *op. cit.,* pp. 240–241. Liebert, Neale, and Davidson, *op. cit.,* pp. 165 ff.
144. Howitt and Cumberbatch, *op. cit.,* p. 121.
145. Joan Swift, "Effects of Early Group Experience: The Nursery School and Day Nursery," in Hoffman and Hoffman, *op. cit.,* pp. 249–288.

Chapter 6: Sex and Socialization

1. Jean Lipman-Blumen and Ann Tickameyer, "Sex Roles in Transition: A Ten-Year Perspective," in *Annual Review of Sociology,* 1 (Palo Alto, California: Annual Reviews, 1975), pp. 302–303.
2. John Money and Anke A. Ehrhardt, *Man & Woman, Boy & Girl* (Baltimore: The Johns Hopkins University Press, 1972). Another useful summary, placing sexual reproduction in the framework of evolutionary biology, is that of anthropologists M. Kay Martin and Barbara Voorhies, *Female of the Species* (New York: Columbia University Press, 1975), Chap. 2.
3. Money and Ehrhardt, *op. cit.,* pp. 1 and 4.
4. *Ibid.,* p. 7.
5. Money and Ehrhardt write, "Normal differentiation of genital morphology entails a dimorphic sex difference in the arrangement of the peripheral nerves of sex which, in turn, entails some degree of dimorphism in the representation of the periphery at the centrum of the central nervous system, that is to say, in the structures and pathways of the brain." *Ibid.,* p. 8. See also Money and Ehrhardt, *op. cit.,* p. 49.
6. Joan Vernikos-Danellis, "Effects of Hormones on the Central Nervous System," in Seymour Levine (ed.), *Hormones and Behavior* (New York: Academic Press, 1972), pp. 12–13.
7. *Ibid.,* p. 50. A more skeptical view is taken by neuroanatomist Ruth H. Bleier, "Brain, Body, and Behavior," in Joan I. Roberts

(ed.), *Beyond Intellectual Sexism. A New Woman, A New Reality* (New York: David McKay, 1976).

8. Robert W. Goy, "Early Hormonal Influences on the Development of Sexual and Sex-Related Behavior," in F. O. Schmitt (ed.), *The Neurosciences: Second Study Program* (New York: Rockefeller University Press, 1970), reprinted in Rhoda Kesler Unger and Florence L. Denmark (eds.), *Woman: Dependent or Independent Variable?* (New York: Psychological Dimensions, 1975), p. 468. On this topic, also see Anke A. Ehrhardt and Susan W. Baker, "Fetal Androgens, Human Central Nervous System Differentiation, and Behavior Sex Differences," in Richard C. Friedman, Ralph M. Richart, and Raymond L. Vande Wiele (eds.), *Sex Differences in Behavior* (New York: Wiley, 1974), Chap. 3.

9. Psychologist David Tresemer has noted that not all societies are as insistent upon two morphological sexes: ". . . nearly half a per cent of the population (a 'conservative' estimate, Overzier, 1963) is markedly intersexual (biologically hermaphroditic). Other cultures treat these challenges to a bipolar system quite differently from ours: the Navaho revered them as possessed of some special power (Hill, 1935); the Potok [sic] of Kenya were somewhat indifferent to them because they did not fit into their bride-price system of exchange (Edgerton, 1964). Interestingly, though Levi-Strauss (1962) and Piaget (1970) consider binary thinking the most primitive, it is our more advanced civilization that treats the intersexual as an unclassifiable monster and tries, through surgical and/or behavioral engineering (Laub and Fisk, 1974; Barlow et al., 1973), to fit the person into one role *or* the other. Thus bipolarity better describes what we think about sex differences rather than what they necessarily are." David Tresemer, "Assumptions Made About Gender Roles," in Marcia Millman and Rosabeth Moss Kanter (eds.), *Another Voice: Feminist Perspectives on Social Life and Social Science* (Garden City, N.Y.: Anchor Books, 1975), pp. 314–315. Tresemer seems to be saying that only a primitive form of thinking prompts people in our society to try to fit morphologically intersexed people into "one role *or* the other." His entire article argues against considering sex and gender as bipolar phenomena, and he does not seem to exclude morphological sex. At the same time, he fails to consider the absolute difference in reproductive function between the sexes.

Anthropologists Martin and Voorhies also discuss anthropological accounts about hermaphrodites. They discuss the same report by Edgerton on the Pokot of Kenya as does Tresemer. Contrary to Tresemer's report of indifference, they state: "Edgerton has reported the Pokot's treatment of intersexes. Such individuals, called *sererr,* are considered to be neither male nor female. Their genitals are too underdeveloped to be circumcised either in the male or female fashion. A Pokot's failure to be circumcised is equivalent to the denial of any adult gender status.

"Some parents respond to the birth of a *sererr* by immediately killing it. This reaction is acceptable among the Pokot, who resort to infanticide whenever a malformed child is born. *Sererr* are thus one type of physical deviant who are diagnosed by that society as defective and undesirable.

"Sometimes, however, *sererr* are permitted to live. Surviving *sererr* can never pass as legitimate males or females and their ambiguous condition is public knowledge. They live on the fringes of their society without a mandate for either gender status. Often they win some social approval by excelling in economic activities, yet their lives are ruthlessly limited in other respects." Martin and Voorhies, *op. cit.,* pp. 88–89.

10. Martin and Voorhies, *op. cit.,* p. 10.
11. *Ibid.*
12. *Ibid.,* pp. 10–11.
13. *Ibid.,* pp. 406–408. Martin and Voorhies change terms—from "sex categories" to "gender categories"—with no explanation.
14. Steven Goldberg, *The Inevitability of Patriarchy* (New York: William Morrow, paperback edition, 1974), p. 30.
15. *Ibid.,* p. 33.
16. *Ibid.,* p. 98.
17. Steven Goldberg, "Response to Leacock and Livingstone," *American Anthropologist,* 77 (March 1975), 69–73.
18. Goldberg, *Patriarchy,* pp. 136–138.
19. John Money and Patricia Tucker, *Sexual Signatures: On Being a Man or a Woman* (Boston and Toronto: Little, Brown, 1975), Chap. 3, "Sex Hormones on the Brain," pp. 78–80.
20. Elina Haavio-Mannila, "Sex Roles in Politics," in Constantina Safilios-Rothschild, *Toward a Sociology of Women* (Lexington, Mass.: Xerox College Publishing, 1972), p. 166, Table 13.

21. These problems are particularly evident when we consider the issue of power and authority among the Iroquois Indians, one of the societies most often cited as demonstrating the dominance that women can have. Women occupying the position of matron—head of household or work group—controlled the economic organization of the Iroquois, and this control gave them much power, but not ultimate authority. According to anthropologist Judith K. Brown, who has reviewed the available evidence: "In the political sphere, Iroquois matrons had the power to raise and depose the ruling elders, the ability to influence the decisions of the Council, and occasional power over the conduct of war and the establishment of treaties. Although women could not serve on the Council of Elders, the highest ruling body of the League, the hereditary eligibility for office passed through them, and the elective eligibility for office was also largely controlled by them." The combination of great power with ineligibility for the highest office is paradoxical; it may be no more than a historical instance that has no bearing on the future of any society. Still, the Iroquois case does seem congruent with Goldberg's theory rather than an exception to it. See Judith K. Brown, "Iroquois Women: An Ethnohistoric Note," in Rayna R. Reiter (ed.), *Toward an Anthropology of Women* (New York and London: Monthly Review Press, 1975).

22. Steven Goldberg, personal communication, December 1976.

23. Roy G. D'Andrade, "Sex Differences and Cultural Institutions," in Eleanor E. Maccoby (ed.), *The Development of Sex Differences* (Stanford, Calif.: Stanford University Press, 1966), pp. 177–178.

24. Valerie K. Oppenheimer, "The Sex-Labeling of Jobs," in Martha T. Mednick, Sandra Schwartz Tangri, and Lois Wladis Hoffman (eds.), *Women and Achievement: Social and Motivational Analyses* (Washington, D.C.: Hemisphere Publishing, 1975), Chap. 19.

25. Jane E. Prather, "When the Girls Move In: A Sociological Analysis of the Feminization of the Bank Teller's Job," *Journal of Marriage and the Family*, 33 (November 1971), 777–782.

26. Richard Flaste, "The Frustrating Battle Against Sex Stereotyping," *The New York Times*, November 12, 1976, p. B5.

27. Ann Beuf, "Doctor, Lawyer, Household Drudge," *Journal of Communication*, 24:142–146 (1974), 143–144.

28. Helen Mayer Hacker, "Women as a Minority Group," *Social*

Forces, 30 (October 1951), 60–69. This paper has been reprinted in many anthologies. The notion that women are discriminated against in ways paralleling discrimination against blacks was set forth a few years earlier by the noted Swedish social scientist Gunnar Myrdal in "A Parallel to the Negro Problem," in his monumental study, *An American Dilemma: The Negro Problem and Modern Democracy* (New York: Harper & Brothers, 1944), Appendix 5.

29. Lipman-Blumen and Tickameyer, *op. cit.* pp. 313–314. This article presents the most comprehensive summary known to us of the literature on sex roles. Also valuable in the present context is the briefer summary by Arlie Hochschild, "A Review of Sex Role Research," *American Journal of Sociology,* 78 (January 1973), 1011–1029.

30. C. D. Spinellis, Vasso Vassiliou, and George Vassiliou, "Milieu Development and Male-Female Roles in Contemporary Greece," in Georgene H. Seward and Robert C. Williamson, *Sex Roles in Changing Society* (New York: Random House, 1970), p. 313.

31. Rita Liljestrom, "The Swedish Model," in Seward and Williamson, *op. cit.,* pp. 205–206.

32. Spinellis, Vassiliou, and Vassiliou, *op. cit.*

33. The literature on the history of sex-role and sex-status changes in the United States is large. One valuable discussion is Peter Gabriel Filene, *Him/Her/Self: Sex Roles in Modern America* (New York: Harcourt, Brace, Jovanovich, 1974).

34. Leo Kanowitz, *Sex Roles in Law and Society: Cases and Materials* (Albuquerque: University of New Mexico Press, 1973).

35. For Canada, see the *Report of the Royal Commission on the Status of Women* (Ottawa: Queen's Printer, 1971) and subsequent reports of the Women's Bureau, Canada Department of Labour.

36. Irene Hanson Frieze and Sheila J. Ramsey, "Nonverbal Maintenance of Traditional Sex Roles," *Journal of Social Issues,* 32 (Summer 1976), p. 136.

37. *Ibid.,* p. 139. For a classic discussion of how such restrictions were experienced by a talented and creative woman, see Virginia Woolf, *A Room of One's Own* (New York: Harcourt, Brace, 1929).

38. Betty Yorburg, *Sexual Identity: Sex Roles and Social Change* (New York: Wiley, 1974), p. 1.

39. *Ibid.,* pp. 1 and 4.

40. Lois W. Hoffman, "Early Childhood Experiences and Women's Achievement Motives," in Martha T. Mednick, Sandra Schwartz Tangri, and Lois Wladis Hoffman, *op. cit.*, pp. 129 and 136. Hoffman's contention gains some cross-cultural support from an earlier study of eighty-two societies that found that 85 percent of them socialized boys to self-reliance to a greater extent than girls. Also, 85 percent of them socialized only boys to be achievers, and only 15 percent showed no significant differences in the treatment of girls and boys in this regard. See Herbert A. Barry, Margaret K. Bacon, and Irvin L. Child, "A Cross-Cultural Survey of some Sex Differences in Socialization," *Journal of Abnormal and Social Psychology*, 55:327–332, findings summarized in Martin and Voorhies, *op. cit.*, pp. 68 and 76.

41. *Ibid.*, p. 136.

42. Lenore J. Weitzman, "Sex-Role Socialization," in Jo Freeman (ed.), *Women: A Feminist Perspective* (Palo Alto, Calif.: Mayfield Publishing, 1975), pp. 108–109.

43. Some of the problems of carrying out such research are discussed by Howard A. Moss, "Early Sex Differences and Mother-Child Interaction," in Friedman, Richart, and Vande Wiele, *op. cit.*, Chap. 8. Conflicting results of various studies are noted by Michael Lewis and Marsha Weinraub, "Sex of Parent x Sex of Child: Socioemotional Development," in Friedman, Richart, and Vande Wiele, *op. cit.*, pp. 170–171. See also Anneliese F. Korner, "The Effect of the Infant's State, Level of Arousal, Sex, and Ontogenetic Stage on the Caregiver," in Michael Lewis and Leonard A. Rosenblum (eds.), *The Effect of the Infant on Its Caregiver* (New York: Wiley, 1974), pp. 110–114.

44. Hoffman, *op. cit.*, p. 139.

45. W. E. Lambert, A. Yackley, and R. N. Hein, "Child Training Values of English Canadian and French Canadian Parents," *Canadian Journal of Behavioral Science*, 3:217–236 (1971), as summarized in Maccoby and Jacklin, *op. cit.*, p. 321.

46. Hoffman, *op. cit.*, pp. 140–141; Weitzman, *op. cit.*, pp. 116 and 118.

47. Hoffman, *op. cit.*, pp. 143–144. For a slightly different emphasis, see the interpretation in Aletha Huston Stein and Margaret M. Bailey, "The Socialization of Achievement Orientation in Females," *Psychological Bulletin*, 80:5 (1973), 345–366 and 358 ff.

48. Ruth E. Hartley, "Sex Role Pressures and the Socialization of the Male Child," reprinted from *Psychological Reports* (1959), in Judith Stacey, Susan Bereaud, and Joan Daniels (eds.), *And Jill Came Tumbling After: Sexism in American Education* (New York: Dell, 1974).

49. Evelyn Goodenough Pitcher, "Male and Female," in Stacey, *et al., op. cit.,* p. 81.

50. Eleanor Emmons Maccoby and Carol Nagy Jacklin, *The Psychology of Sex Differences* (Stanford, Calif.: Stanford University Press, 1974), p. 278.

51. *Ibid.,* p. 279.

52. Janet Saltzman Chafetz, *Masculine/Feminine or Human? An Overview of the Sociology of Sex Roles* (Itasca, Ill.: F. E. Peacock Publishers, 1974), p. 81.

53. Louis Wolf Goodman and Janet Lever, "Children's Toys and Socialization to Sex Roles" (Yale University, 1972, mimeographed). Summarized in Nancy Lyon, "A Report on Children's Toys and Socialization to Sex Roles," *Ms.,* December 1972, reprinted in Diane Gersoni-Stavn, *Sexism and Youth* (New York: R. R. Bowker, 1974), also reprinted in Stacey, Bereaud, and Daniels, *op. cit.,* with authorship attributed to *Ms.* Title of the Goodman-Lever paper is not given in either anthology but is cited only in the briefer summary given in Martin and Voorhies, *op. cit.,* p. 68.

54. Charles Winick, Lorne G. Williamson, Stuart F. Chuzmir, and Mariann Pezzella Winick, *Children's Television Commercials: A Content Analysis* (New York: Praeger, 1973), p. 27.

55. Janet Saltzman Chafetz, *op. cit.,* p. 82.

56. *Ibid.,* p. 85. See also Linda J. Busby, "Sex-Role Research on the Mass Media," *Journal of Communication,* 25 (Autumn 1975), pp. 107–131.

57. Information from Alleen Pace Nilsen, "Women in Children's Literature," *College English* (May 1971), reprinted in Gersoni-Stavn, *op. cit.,* and from Lenore J. Weitzman, Deborah Eiffler, Elizabeth Hokada, and Catherine Ross, "Sex-Role Socialization in Picture Books for Pre-School Children," *American Journal of Sociology,* 77:6 (May 1972), also reprinted in Gersoni-Stavn, *op. cit.*

58. Nilsen in Gersoni-Stavn, *op. cit.,* p. 168.

59. *Ibid.,* p. 169.

60. Weitzman, *et al., op. cit.,* pp. 179–180. This study also included other works in addition to Caldecott winners and runners-up;

the other works were substantially similar in their portrayals of sex roles.

61. Sarah Lawrence Lightfoot, "Sociology of Women: Perspectives on Women," in Millman and Kanter, *op. cit.,* p. 136.

62. L. A. Serbin, K. D. O'Leary, R. N. Kent, and I. J. Tonick, "A Comparison of Teacher Response to the Pre-Academic and Problem Behavior of Boys and Girls," *Child Development,* 44 (1973), 796–804, summarized in Eleanor Emmons Maccoby and Carol Nagy Jacklin, *The Psychology of Sex Differences* (Stanford, Calif.: Stanford University Press, 1974), p. 579. For a study of a nursery school that seeks to minimize sex-role socialization, see Carole Joffe, "Sex Role Socialization and the Nursery School: As the Twig is Bent," in *Journal of Marriage and the Family,* 33 (August 1971), 467–475.

63. Betty Levy, "The School's Role in the Sex-Role Stereotyping of Girls: a Feminist Review of the Literature," in Gersoni-Stavn, *op. cit.,* p. 58.

64. *Ibid.,* pp. 59–60.

65. *Ibid.,* p. 53.

66. *Ibid.,* p. 54.

67. Women on Words and Images, "Look Jane Look. See Sex Stereotypes," in Stacey, Bereaud, and Daniels, *op. cit.,* p. 169. This is an excerpt from a report entitled "Dick and Jane as Victims: Sex Stereotyping in Children's Readers." Somewhat different excerpts from it are reprinted in Gersoni-Stavn, *op. cit.*

68. Sara Goodman Zimet, "Males and Females in American Primers from Colonial Days to the Present," in Sara Goodman Zimet (ed.), *What Children Read in School: Critical Analysis of Primary Reading Textbooks* (New York: Grune & Stratton, 1972), p. 83.

69. *Ibid.,* pp. 83 and 121. See also the discussion in Clarice Stasz Stoll, *Female & Male: Socialization, Social Roles, and Social Structure* (Dubuque, Iowa: William C. Brown, 1974), pp. 102–104. As Stoll notes, different studies have used different categories for assessing how the two sexes are presented in textbooks.

70. For feminist evaluations of diverse categories of children's literature, see Gersoni-Stavn, *op. cit.,* "Books: Propaganda and the Sins of Omission," Part 3.

71. Eleanor J. Gibson and Harry Levin, *The Psychology of Reading* (Cambridge, Mass.: The M.I.T. Press, 1975), p. 270.

72. David E. Austin, Velma B. Clark, and Gladys W. Fitchett, *Reading Rights for Boys: Sex Role in Language Experience* (New York: Appleton-Century-Crofts, 1971), p. 1.

73. *Ibid.,* p. 2.

74. B. Sutton-Smith and B. G. Rosenberg, "Sixty years of Historical Change in the Game Preferences of American Children," in R. E. Herron and Brian Sutton-Smith (eds.), *Child's Play* (New York: Wiley, 1971), p. 48.

75. A similar conclusion is reached by Charles Winick, *The New People: Desexualization in American Life* (New York: Pegasus, 1968), pp. 217 ff.

76. Yorburg, *op. cit.,* p. 153.

77. This summary draws on Joseph H. Pleck, "The Male Sex Role: Definitions, Problems, and Sources of Change," *Journal of Social Issues,* 32: 3 (1976), 155–164; Deborah S. David and Robert Brannon (eds.), *The Forty-Nine Percent Majority: The Male Sex Role* (Reading, Mass.: Addison-Wesley, 1976); Ruth E. Hartley, "American Core Culture: Changes and Continuities," in Seward and Williamson, *op. cit.;* and Yorburg, *op. cit.,* Chap. 5.

78. Jessie Bernard, *Women and the Public Interest: An Essay on Policy and Protest* (Chicago: Aldine-Atherton, 1971), Chap. 5.

79. Some of the recent literature on this subject is reviewed by Maccoby and Jacklin, *op. cit.,* pp. 140–141.

80. Eleanor E. Maccoby, "Sex Differences in Intellectual Functioning," in Eleanor E. Maccoby (ed.), *The Development of Sex Differences* (Stanford, Calif.: Stanford University Press, 1966); Alice S. Rossi, "Women in Science: Why So Few?," *Science,* May 28, 1965, pp. 1196–1202, reprinted in Constantina Safillos-Rothschild (ed.), *Toward a Sociology of Women* (Lexington, Mass.: Xerox Publishing, 1972), pp. 149 ff.

81. Ray L. Birdwhistell, *Kinesics and Context: Essays on Body Motion Communication* (Philadelphia: University of Pennsylvania Press, 1970), "Masculinity and Femininity as Display," Chap. 6.

82. The information on language differences in this paragraph is taken from Barrie Thorne and Nancy Henley, "Difference and Dominance: An Overview of Language, Gender, and Society," in Thorne and Henley (eds.), *Language and Sex: Difference and Dominance* (Rowley, Mass.: Newbury House Publishers, 1975). The quotation is from p. 18.

83. For discussions of various interpretations of relations between

the sexes as power relationships, see Lipman-Blumen and Tickameyer, *op. cit.*, pp. 313–321; Hochschild, *op. cit.;* and Hans Peter Dreitzel (ed.), *Family, Marriage and the Struggle of the Sexes.* Recent Sociology No. 4 (New York: Macmillan, 1972).

84. Filene, *op. cit.;* David and Brannon, *op. cit.;* Yorburg, *op. cit.*
85. Liljestrom, *op. cit.,* pp. 205 ff.
86. Mark G. Field and Karen I. Flynn, "Worker, Mother, Housewife: Soviet Woman Today," in Seward and Williamson, *op. cit.,* pp. 270–271.
87. *Ibid.,* p. 262.
88. Albert I. Rabin, "The Sexes: Ideology and Reality in the Israeli Kibbutz," in Seward and Williamson, *op. cit.,* Chap. 13. See also Melford Spiro, *Children of the Kibbutz,* 2nd ed. (Cambridge, Mass.: Harvard University Press, 1975), pp. 236–248.
89. Rabin, *op. cit.,* p. 305. See also Martha Mednick, "Social Change and Sex-Role Inertia: The Case of the Kibbutz," in Mednick, Schwartz, and Tangri (eds.), *op. cit.,* Chap. 6.
90. Alice S. Rossi, "Equality Between the Sexes: An Immodest Proposal," *Daedalus,* 93 (Spring 1964), 608. While this book was in press, Rossi published an important modification of her views. Alice S. Rossi, "A Biosocial Perspective on Parenting," *Daedalus,* 106 (Spring 1977), 1–31.
91. *Ibid.*
92. William Kessen (ed.), *Childhood in China* (New Haven: Yale University Press, 1975). An interesting sidelight in this report is that kindergarten children are segregated by sex for seating and for participation in races and other activities, much as in North American classrooms. See p. 110. See also Sheila Rowbotham, *Women, Resistance, and Revolution* (New York: Pantheon, 1972), pp. 195 and 196.
93. Margaret Park Redfield (ed.), "The Universally Human and the Culturally Variable," in *Human Nature and the Study of Society: The Papers of Robert Redfield,* I (Chicago: University of Chicago Press, 1962), 451–452.

Chapter 7: Conclusion: Socialization in Later Life

1. The dual character of socialization throughout the life cycle was first enunciated in what became a classic paper by anthropologist Ruth Benedict, "Continuities and Discontinuities

in Cultural Conditioning," *Psychiatry,* 1 (1938), 161–167, reprinted in Clyde Kluckhohn, Henry A. Murray, and David Schneider, *Personality in Nature, Society and Culture* (New York: Knopf, 1953).

2. George Bernard Shaw's play *Pygmalion,* in which a professor of linguistics teaches a Cockney flower girl to become a "lady," dramatizes an effort to explore the limits of adult socialization. Since the girl had not merely to learn new things for which her previous experience had not prepared her, but also had to forget some things she had learned thoroughly, the play is, strictly speaking, about resocialization, the term commonly used to describe socialization that requires the abandonment of previous socialization.

3. Frank Musgrove, *Youth and the Social Order* (Bloomington: Indiana University Press, 1964), p. 33.

4. Beatrice Vulcan, "American Social Policy Toward Youth and Youth Employment," in Melvin Herman, Stanley Sadofsky, and Bernard Rosenberg (eds.), *Work, Youth and Unemployment* (New York: Crowell, 1968), p. 8.

5. Marie Jahoda and Neil Warren, "The Myths of Youth," *Sociology of Education,* 38 (Winter 1965).

6. This trend is discussed by Kenneth Keniston, "Youth: A New Stage of Life," *American Scholar,* 39 (Autumn 1970), 631–654.

7. A more detailed recent summary may be found in Ernest Q. Campbell, "Adolescent Socialization," in David A. Goslin (ed.), *Handbook of Socialization Theory and Research* (Chicago: Rand McNally, 1969), Chap. 20.

8. Talcott Parsons, "Age and Sex in the Social Structure of the United States," *American Sociological Review,* 7 (1942), 604–616, reprinted in Talcott Parsons, *Essays in Sociological Theory,* 2nd ed. (New York: Free Press, 1954).

9. Frederick Elkin and William A. Westley, "The Myth of Adolescent Culture," *American Sociological Review,* 20 (1955), 680–684; and William A. Westley and Frederick Elkin, "The Protective Environment and Adolescent Socialization," *Social Forces,* 35 (1957), 243–249. Parsons himself tempered his views in a later report. See Talcott Parsons, "Youth in the Context of American Society," *Daedalus,* 41 (1962), 97–123.

10. James S. Coleman, *The Adolescent Society: The Social Life of the Teenager and Its Impact on Education* (New York: Free Press, 1961).

11. Bennett M. Berger, "Adolescence and Beyond," *Social Prob-*

lems, 10 (1963), 394–408. For two somewhat different studies showing continuity between parental values and adolescent values and conduct see Clay Brittain, "Adolescent Choices and Parent-Peer Cross Pressures," *American Sociological Review* (June 1963), 385–391; and Richard Flacks, "The Liberated Generation: An Exploration of the Roots of Student Protest," *Journal of Social Issues,* 23 (July 1967), 52–75.

12. Edgar Z. Friedenberg, *Coming of Age in America* (New York: Random House, 1965), p. 42.

13. Edgar Z. Friedenberg, *The Vanishing Adolescent* (New York: Dell Laurel editions, 1962). Berger's article, cited above, compares this volume with Coleman's and with Paul Goodman's *Growing Up Absurd* (New York: Random House, 1960). See also Friedenberg's *Dignity of Youth and Other Atavisms* (Boston: Beacon Press, 1965).

14. Jahoda and Warren, *op. cit.,* p. 147.

15. Margaret Mead, *Culture and Commitment: Notes on the Generation Gap* (New York: Natural History Press/Doubleday, 1970).

16. What is now called the generation gap—that is, a presumed large difference in outlook between youth and adults—may actually reflect the rising levels of education and therefore the increased influence on youth of certain types of adults (teachers, writers, professors) and a decreased influence of other types (parents, aunts and uncles, neighbors, police, traditional clergy). Between 1940 and 1970 the proportion of people in the United States with one or more years of college education increased from 13 to 31 percent; college graduates increased from 6 to 16 percent of the young adult population. (Figures from "Census Study Finds an 'Education Gap,' " *The New York Times,* February 4, 1971, p. 1.) As the more educated young interact with and differ from the types of adults they knew in childhood, both youth and adult may decide there is a generation gap, overlooking the fact that the young may have simply changed their adult reference groups as they continued their education.

17. John Gillis, *Youth and History: Tradition and Change in European Age Relations, 1770–Present* (New York and London: Academic Press, 1974), pp. 187 and 191.

18. James S. Coleman and others, *Youth: Transition to Adulthood* (Chicago: University of Chicago Press, 1974). The volume is a

Report of the Panel on Youth of the President's Science Advisory Committee.

19. The concept of commitment is discussed in Howard S. Becker, "Personal Change in Adult Life," *Sociometry,* 27 (1964), 40–53.
20. Chap. 5, note 60.
21. Herbert Gans' study, *The Levittowners: Ways of Life and Politics in a New Suburban Community* (New York: Vintage Books, 1969), is written as a community study, but many of his observations bear directly on adult socialization.
22. Irving Rosow, "Forms and Functions of Adult Socialization," *Social Forces,* 44 (September 1965), p. 43.
23. Orville G. Brim, Jr., "Socialization through the Life Cycle," in Orville G. Brim, Jr., and Stanton Wheeler, *Socialization After Childhood: Two Essays* (New York: Wiley, 1966), p. 25.
24. Brim, *op. cit.*
25. Stanton Wheeler, "The Structure of Formally Organized Socialization Settings," in Brim and Wheeler, *op. cit.*
26. Charles E. Bidwell, unpublished paper cited by Wheeler, *op. cit.,* p. 70.
27. Howard S. Becker, Blanche Geer, Everett C. Hughes, and Anselm L. Strauss, *Boys in White: Student Culture in Medical School* (Chicago: University of Chicago Press, 1961). See also Fred Davis, "Professional Socialization as Subjective Experience," in Howard S. Becker, *et al.* (eds.), *Institutions and the Person* (Chicago: Aldine, 1968).
28. Wilbert E. Moore, "Occupational Socialization," in David A. Goslin (ed.), *Handbook of Socialization Theory and Research* (Chicago: Rand McNally, 1969), Chap. 21. See also Dan C. Lortie, "Shared Ordeal and Induction to Work," in Becker, *et al., Institutions and the Person.*
29. Elaine Cumming and William E. Henry, *Growing Old: The Process of Disengagement* (New York: Basic Books, 1961).
30. Matilda White Riley, Anne Foner, Beth Hess, and Marcia L. Toby, "Socialization for the Middle and Later Years," in Goslin, *op. cit.,* p. 952. Italics in original. See also, George L. Maddox, "Retirement As a Social Event in the United States," in B. Neugarten (ed.), *Middle Age and Aging* (Chicago: University of Chicago Press, 1968).
31. An overview of work in this field is given by Reuben Hill and Joan Aldous, "Socialization for Marriage and Parenthood," in Goslin, *op. cit.,* Chap. 22.

Selected Readings

Ariès, Philippe. *Centuries of Childhood.* New York: Random House, 1962.
> The author combines the skills of history, sociology, and art criticism to trace the emergence of the concept of childhood as a distinctive period of the life cycle.

Bronfenbrenner, Urie. *Two Worlds of Childhood: U.S. and U.S.S.R.* New York: Russell Sage Foundation, 1970.
> Bronfenbrenner compares socialization in the societies of the world's two superpowers. He feels strongly that peer groups and television have undue influence in socialization of American children.

Clausen, John A. (ed.). *Socialization and Society.* Boston: Little, Brown, 1968.
> Eight encyclopedic chapters examine the concept of socialization as used in seve several disciplines, cross-culturally, and at various phases in the life cycle.

Dreitzel, Hans Peter (ed.). *Childhood and Socialization.* New York: Macmillan, 1973. Recent Sociology, No. 5.
> Many of the papers in this collection are highly critical of contemporary families and schools and of social science's understanding of socialization. The authors present some challenging ideas, as well as some reckless statements, such as the editor's claim: "Thus the typical nuclear family of today provides a pathogenic milieu for the children . . ."

Erikson, Erik H. *Childhood and Society.* New York: Norton, 1950.
> Erikson employs a modified psychoanalytic approach in discussing stages of development and in analyzing the relationship between childhood training and cultural characteristics. These ideas are further developed in the same author's *Identity: Youth and Crisis.* Norton, 1968.

Goldstein, Bernard. *Low Income Youth in Urban Areas: A Critical Review of the Literature.* New York: Holt, Rinehart and Winston, 1967.

This volume provides both annotated references and integrative summaries of the literature on various aspects of socialization of low-income urban youth.

Goslin, David A. *Handbook of Socialization Theory and Research.* Chicago: Rand McNally, 1969.

This reference work has useful chapters on many aspects of socialization.

Greven, Philip J., Jr. *Child-Rearing Concepts, 1628–1861: Historical Sources.* Itasca, Ill.: F. E. Peacock Publishers, 1973.

This collection of essays and sermons by early American Christian writers documents their emphasis on controlling and suppressing the child's will. The last essay in the collection signals the beginning of a change in 1861.

Hess, Robert D., and Gerald Handel. *Family Worlds: A Psychosocial Approach to Family Life.* Chicago: University of Chicago Press, 1959.

Five midwestern families of different social class levels are analyzed, using data obtained from the children and parents of each family, to show how the family group functions as a socializing agency.

Hobbs, Nicholas. *The Futures of Children.* San Francisco: Jossey-Bass, 1975.

Hobbs examines the practices of classifying and labeling exceptional children, and he discusses the social consequences of such labeling.

Hunt, David. *Parents and Children in History: The Psychology of Family Life in Early Modern France.* New York: Basic Books, 1970.

This critical review of Philippe Ariès's work challenges it in some respects and supports it in others.

Jackson, Philip. *Life in Classrooms.* New York: Holt, Rinehart and Winston, 1968.

After observing many elementary school classrooms, the author analyzes some of their main socializing impacts.

Jaros, Dean. *Socialization to Politics.* New York: Praeger, 1974.

This book, an introduction to the rapidly growing field of political socialization, seeks to understand how children are socialized to participate in the political order.

Jencks, Christopher, *et al. Inequality: A Reassessment of the Effect of Family and Schooling in America.* New York: Basic Books, 1972. Jencks and his associates at the Harvard Center for Educational Policy Research argue that eliminating inequalities of educational opportunity would do little to eliminate differences in adult careers. To achieve greater equality among adults, they say, drastic changes must be made in the existing social order. The thesis is not universally accepted. For a series of reviews by scholars in educational research, see the *Harvard Educational Review* (February 1973).

Kanter, Rosabeth Moss (ed.). *Communes: Creating and Managing the Collective Life.* New York: Harper and Row, 1973. The editor, a specialist in the study of communes, has brought together a wide range of selections covering major facets of commune life.

Keniston, Kenneth. *Young Radicals: Notes on Committed Youth.* New York: Harcourt Brace Jovanovich, 1968. The author traces the development from childhood to young adulthood of a group of radicals, showing how personal life histories become intertwined with broader currents of history.

Kerckhoff, Alan C., *Socialization and Social Class.* Englewood Cliffs, N.J.: Prentice-Hall, 1972. Kerckhoff gives a concise summary of social-class differences in socialization from childhood through early adulthood.

Kessen, William (ed.). *Childhood in China.* New Haven: Yale University Press, 1975. A group of social scientists—"The American Delegation on Early Childhood Development in The People's Republic of China"— report on their twenty-day trip to look at socialization settings and processes. The book is useful as an introduction, but the authors caution that such a brief visit provides no more than a glimpse of a huge society.

Kieffer, Christie W. *Changing Cultures, Changing Lives.* San Francisco: Jossey-Bass, 1974. Kieffer traces the impact of historical changes on values and personality development of three generations of Japanese-Americans in San Francisco.

Kohn, Melvin. *Class and Conformity.* Homewood, Ill.: Dorsey Press, 1969.

This is a widely cited study comparing values and socialization practices of middle-class and working-class parents.

Langmeier, J. and Z. Matejcek. *Psychological Deprivation in Childhood.* New York and Toronto: Wiley, 1975.

Translated from the Czech, this work presents a contemporary Central European discussion of American and Western European as well as Czechoslovakian studies of social isolation and other issues related to the concept of deprivation.

Mantell, David Mark. *True Americanism: Green Berets and War Resistors.* New York: Teachers College Press, 1974.

The author's comparison of two groups of men who chose divergent stances in the Vietnam War indicates that different family socialization experiences in childhood partly explain their responses to the war in young adulthood.

Middleton, John (ed.). *From Child to Adult: Studies in the Anthropology of Education.* Garden City, N.Y.: The Natural History Press, 1970.

This collection of studies by anthropologists discusses the educational systems in small-scale societies around the world.

Parsons, Talcott. *Social Structure and Personality.* New York: Free Press, 1964.

These essays by a leading American sociologist examine various aspects of the social structure as they shape socialization.

Piaget, Jean. *The Language and Thought of the Child.* Rev. ed. London: Routledge and Kegan Paul, 1932.

This is one of the earliest and most significant books by this major figure in the study of child development.

Richards, Martin P. M. (ed.). *The Integration of a Child into a Social World.* London: Cambridge University Press, 1974.

Several British authors present their views of the processes of socialization.

Riesman, David, in collaboration with Reuel Denney and Nathan Glazer. *The Lonely Crowd: A Study of the Changing American Character.* New Haven: Yale University Press, 1950.

This imaginative study became an almost instant classic; it presents a detailed picture of how social change affects socialization agencies and processes.

Schaffer, H. R. *The Growth of Sociability.* Harmondworth and Baltimore: Penguin, 1971.

This volume by a British psychologist concisely summarizes our current knowledge of how infants learn to distinguish among and become responsive to human beings.

Schulz, David A. *Coming Up Black: Patterns of Ghetto Socialization.* Englewood Cliffs, N.J.: Prentice-Hall, 1969.

This intensive study of ten families living in a problem-ridden public-housing project points up some of the special problems besetting black children from low-income families in the course of their socialization.

Sigel, Roberta S. (ed.). *Learning About Politics: A Reader in Political Socialization.* New York: Random House, 1970.

This anthology, devoted to a topic of growing interest, includes papers dealing with many different institutions and processes that influence the development of political beliefs and actions.

Spiro, Melford E. *Children of the Kibbutz.* Rev. ed. Cambridge, Mass.: Harvard University Press, 1975.

This is a report of a fascinating social experiment. In this Israeli kibbutz, children are reared under a system of collective education; they do not live with their parents and parents have little authority over them.

Strauss, Anselm (ed.). Rev. ed. *George Herbert Mead on Social Psychology.* Chicago: University of Chicago Press, 1964.

This volume consists of selections from the writings of Mead, noted as the originator of the symbolic interactionist view of self and society.

Trudgill, Peter. *Sociolinguistics: An Introduction.* Harmondsworth and Baltimore: Penguin, 1974.

Sociolinguistics is a growing field with great import for socialization. This book is a general introduction.

Vernon, Philip E. *Intelligence and Cultural Environment.* London: Methuen, 1969.

A noted British psychologist weighs and evaluates diverse evidence to assess the impact of culture on the development of intelligence.

Whiting, Beatrice B. (ed.). *Six Cultures: Studies of Child Rearing.* New York: Wiley, 1963.

Six teams of anthropologists and associates, each working separately but following the same basic outline, consider the relationships between child training practices and personality differences in communities in Kenya, India, Okinawa, the Philippines, Mexico, and New England.

Name Index

Ainsworth, M., 246
Aldous, Joan, 279
Allport, Gordon, 102, 253
Anderson, C. Arnold, 250, 259
Anthony, E. James, 246
Ariès, Philippe, 61–62, 156, 248, 261, 281, 282
Ailing, G. L., 245
Arnold, Arnold, 263
Ashe, Arthur, 102
Austin, David E., 275

Bacon, Margaret K., 272
Bailey, Margaret M., 272
Bailyn, Lotte, 178, 266
Baker, Susan W., 268
Bales, Robert F., 124, 256
Ball, Donald W., 248
Ball, Richard A., 93, 252
Barbour, Floyd, 254
Barry, Herbert A., 272
Bateson, Gregory, 54, 247
Beattie, C., 254
Becker, Howard S., 238, 279
Bell, Norman, 125, 256
Benedek, Therese, 246
Benedict, Ruth, 276
Bensman, Joseph, 249
Benson, Leonard, 126–127, 256, 257

Bereaud, Susan, 273, 274
Berger, Bennett, 95–97, 230, 251, 252, 277, 278
Bernard, Jessie, 216, 258, 261, 275
Bernstein, Basil, 82, 250
Bettelheim, Bruno, 27, 39, 95, 245, 246, 252
Beuf, Ann, 201, 245, 249, 270
Bidwell, Charles E., 279
Birch, Herbert G., 246
Birdwhistell, Ray L., 217, 275
Blau, Peter, 120–122, 256
Bleier, Ruth H., 267
Blumer, Herbert, 248
Blumler, Jay G., 265
Bogart, Leo, 265
Boll, Eleanor, 127–128, 257
Bossard, James, 127–128, 257
Bowes, John, 263
Brannon, Robert, 275, 276
Brill, A. A., 247
Brim, Orville, 128, 236, 257, 279
Brittain, Clay, 278
Broderick, Carlfred B., 158, 261
Bronfenbrenner, Urie, 171–172, 176, 264, 281
Brown, Judith, 270
Brown, Myrtle L., 246
Brown, Richard Maxwell, 176, 266

Brown, Roger, 243
Buckley, Walter, 251
Burnet, Jean, 255
Busby, Linda J., 273

Cain, Albert C., 257
Caldwell, Bettye M., 42, 246
Campbell, Ernest Q., 277
Cater, Douglass, 264
Caudill, Harry M., 89–91, 252
Caudill, William, 46–47, 247
Chafetz, Jane Saltzman, 208, 210, 273
Child, Irvin L., 272
Chomsky, Noam, 49
Chuzmir, Stuart F., 273
Clark, Velma B., 275
Clausen, John A., 245, 249, 281
Cogswell, Betty E., 129, 257
Cohen, Albert K., 85, 87, 251
Coleman, James S., 229–232, 277, 278
Coleman, Richard P., 250
Coles, Robert, 253
Comstock, Anthony, 162–163, 167, 262, 263
Comstock, George A., 178, 262, 263, 266
Cooley, Charles Horton, 17, 20–21, 27, 30, 43, 106, 243
Cottrell, Leonard S., Jr., 249
Crysdale, S., 254
Cuellar, Alfredo, 254
Cumberbatch, Guy, 175, 180, 182, 265, 266, 267
Cumming, Elaine, 279

D'Andrade, Roy, 199, 270
Daniels, Joan, 273, 274
Danziger, Kurt, 254
David, Deborah S., 275, 276

Davidson, Emily S., 174–175, 176, 178–179, 181–182, 264, 265, 266, 267
Davis, Allison, 84, 251
Davis, Fred, 279
Davis, Kingsley, 245
Davison, W. Phillips, 265, 266
DeFleur, Lois B., 262
DeFleur, Melvin L., 262
deMause, Lloyd, 248
Denmark, Florence L., 268
Denny, Reuel, 255, 284
Dervin, Brenda, 165, 263
Deutsch, Martin, 259
Dexter, Lewis Anthony, 261
Doan, Helen McK., 244
Dobriner, William M., 251
Dodsworth, R. O., 245
Dominick, Joseph R., 263
Douglas, J. B., 259
Dreitzel, Hans Peter, 276, 281
Duberman, Lucile, 257
Duncan, O. D., 120, 122, 256

Eggleston, S. John, 258
Ehrhardt, Anke, 188–190, 267, 268
Eiffler, Deborah, 273
Elkin, Frederick, 229, 277
Elliott, Jean L., 255
Emlen, Arthur C., 258
Erikson, Erik, 64–69, 106, 205, 234, 248, 249, 281
Evans, Jean, 256

Fantz, Robert L., 244
Fast, Irene, 257
Field, Mark G., 276
Filene, Peter Gabriel, 271, 276
Finch, Robert, 264
Fitchett, Gladys W., 275
Fitzpatrick, Joseph, 254

Flacks, Richard, 278
Flaste, Richard, 265, 270
Flink, James J., 249
Floud, Jean, 250, 259
Flynn, Karen I., 276
Foner, Anne, 279
Foote, Nelson N., 249
Foss, B. M., 246
Fowler, S. E., 158, 261
Freeberg, Norman E., 259
Freedman, S. J., 245
Freeman, Jo, 272
Freud, Sigmund, 37, 51, 124, 247
Friedenberg, Edgar, 231, 278
Friedman, Richard C., 268, 272
Friedrich, Lynette Kohn, 262, 263
Frieze, Irene Hanson, 203, 271

Galarza, Ernesto, 253
Gambino, Richard, 254
Gans, Herbert J., 124–125, 251, 256, 279
Gardner, Allen, 243
Gardner, Beatrice, 243
Garfinkel, Harold, 52–53, 247
Garry, Ralph, 266
Geer, Blanche, 279
Gerbner, George, 266
Gersoni-Stavn, Diane, 273, 274
Gibson, Eleanor J., 274
Gillis, John R., 232–233, 248, 277
Glazer, Nathan, 112, 255, 284
Glick, Ira O., 266
Glick, Paul C., 129, 257
Goldberg, Steven, 194–195, 197–198, 202, 269, 270
Goldsen, Rose K., 263
Goldstein, Bernard, 251, 282
Goodman, Louis Wolf, 273
Goodman, Mary Ellen, 253
Goodman, Paul, 278

Gordon, J. E., 246
Goslin, David A., 243, 247, 250, 258, 277, 279, 282
Goy, Robert W., 268
Graham, Hugh Davis, 266
Grebler, Leo, 253
Greenberg, Bradley S., 165, 263
Greenblatt, M., 245
Greven, Philip J., Jr., 282
Grey, Alan L., 250, 251
Griffith, Beatrice, 254
Grunebaum, H. U., 245
Gumperz, John J., 251
Gurevitch, Michael, 265
Gurr, Ted Robert, 266
Gussow, Joan Dye, 246
Guzman, Ralph C., 253

Haavio-Mannila, Elina, 198, 269
Hacker, Helen Mayer, 202, 270
Haley, Jay, 247
Halsey, A. H., 250, 259, 260
Hammond, Boone E., 261
Handel, Gerald, 246, 248, 250, 256, 258, 282
Harlow, Harry F., 28–29, 245
Harlow, M. K., 245
Harris, Irving, 256
Hartley, Ruth, 207, 273, 275
Havighurst, Robert J., 246, 259
Hein, R. N., 272
Helenko, R., 260
Henley, Nancy, 275
Henry, William E., 279
Herman, Melvin, 277
Herriott, Robert, 259
Herron, R. E., 275
Herzog, Elizabeth, 251
Hess, Beth, 279
Hess, Eckhard H., 244
Hess, Robert D., 250, 251, 256, 258, 259, 282

Parsons, Talcott, 124, 126, 229–231, 256, 257, 260, 277, 284
Passow, A. Harry, 259
Pastore, John O., 264
Pavenstadt, Eleanor, 86, 251
Payne, Donald T., 259
Pearlin, Leonard I., 250
Perry, Joseph B., 258
Piaget, Jean, 284
Pike, Ruth L., 246
Pinel, Philippe, 23
Pitcher, Evelyn Goodenough, 273
Pleck, Joseph H., 275
Porter, John, 259
Porter, Judith, 101, 253
Poussaint, Alvin, 253
Prather, Jane, 270
Premack, Ann J., 243
Premack, David, 243

Rabin, A. I., 252, 276
Rabinowitz, Clara, 246
Rainwater, Lee, 250, 256, 261
Ramsey, Sheila J., 203, 271
Rarick, G. Lawrence, 261
Redfield, Margaret Park, 276
Redfield, Robert, 276
Reiss, Albert J., 68–69, 249, 258
Reiter, Rayna R., 270
Rheingold, Harriet L., 244
Richards, M. P. M., 244, 284
Richart, Ralph M., 268, 272
Richer, Stephen, 255
Riesman, David, 114, 255, 284
Riessman, Frank, 83, 251
Riley, Matilda, 240, 279
Rist, Ray C., 137, 141–142, 147, 259, 260
Roberts, Joan I., 267
Rodman, Hyman, 78, 250
Rogoff, Natalie, 260
Rose, Arnold M., 248

Rosen, Bernard, 111, 255, 257
Rosenberg, B. G., 275, 277
Rosenberg, Morris, 104, 254
Rosenblum, Leonard A., 246, 272
Rosenthal, Robert, 143, 260
Rosow, Irving, 235–237, 239, 279
Ross, Catherine, 273
Rossi, Alice S., 67, 222–223, 248, 275, 276
Rowbotham, Sheila, 276
Rubinstein, Eli A., 262, 263
Ryan, Joseph, 255
Ryder, Norman B., 253

Sadofsky, Stanley, 277
Safilios-Rothschild, Constantina, 269, 275
St. John, Nancy H., 259
Schachtel, Ernest G., 51–52, 65, 247
Schaffer, H. R., 244, 284
Schlesinger, Benjamin, 130, 257
Schmitt, F. O., 268
Schneider, David, 277
Schneider, Louis, 251
Schramm, Wilbur, 169, 262, 263
Schultz, David, 121, 256, 285, 261
Scott, Robert A., 243
Scrimshaw, Nevin S., 246
Seay, Bill, 245
Seeley, John R., 250
Serbin, L. A., 274
Seward, Georgene H., 271, 275, 276
Sexton, Patricia Cayo, 258
Shaw, George Bernard, 277
Shibutani, Tamotsu, 75, 105, 249, 254
Shipman, Virginia, 251, 259
Shostak, Arthur, 251
Sigel, Roberta, 285
Sim, R. A., 250

Whiting, Beatrice B., 285
Wiele, Raymond L. Vande, 268, 272
Williamson, Lorne G., 273
Williamson, Robert C., 271, 275, 276
Winick, Charles, 209, 273, 275
Winick, Mariann Pezzella, 273
Wohl, R. Richard, 160, 175, 262
Wolfenstein, Martha, 249
Wolfram, Walt, 108, 254
Woolf, Virginia, 271
Wortis, Helen, 246
Wright, Charles R., 261
Wright, James D., 250

Wright, Sonia R., 250
Wrong, Dennis, 117, 255

Yackley, A., 272
Yarrow, Leon J., 43, 246
Yarrow, Marion Radke, 253
Yorburg, Betty, 216, 271, 275, 276
Young, J. Z., 252
Yu, Frederick T. C., 265

Zborowski, Mark, 255
Zimet, Sara Goodman, 213–214, 274
Zingg, Robert M., 245
Zusne, L., 264

Subject Index

Achievement
  academic, 114, 136–137, 147–
    150, 155
  athletic, 154, 156
  motivations in, 111, 207
  occupational, 125, 220
  of women, 205, 207
Adolescence, 62, 66, 235
Adolescent socialization, 66,
  227–233
Adults, 61, 66–68, 80, 95–97, 150,
  153–154, 159, 207, 209, 219,
  228, 230
Adult socialization, 6, 225–227,
  231–239
Age grading, 61, 97, 121, 232
Aging, 67, 239
Appalachian subculture, 89–93,
  125
Aspiration levels, 111, 125, 132,
  147, 216, 238
Attitudes, 58, 117, 137, 154, 187,
  209
Authority, 193–197
  parental, 59, 207
  sex and, 192–194, 197, 203
  women in, 197–199, 205, 218,
    222
  see also Power

Biological inheritance, 9, 13, 31,
  97–98
Blacks, *see* Ethnic groups
Body movement, 217–218
Books, children's, 210–212

Childhood, 61–62, 227, 233
China, People's Republic of, 223
Chromosomal sex, 189–191
Churches, 40, 74, 80, 182
Classroom, 62, 133–134, 136, 139–
  143, 145–146, 212; *see also*
  Teachers
Commitment, 37–39
Communes, 94–96, 131
Communication, 44–54, 56
Community, 88, 93, 119, 182
Competence, 35–39, 48, 115, 206,
  239
Counter culture, 84
Culture, 67, 71–73, 75
  ethnic, 97–98, 100, 102, 105–
    108, 111, 113
Curriculum, hidden, 138, 140

Day care, 132
Deferred gratification pattern,
  83–84
Deprivation, 27, 85, 129, 138

Human nature, 9, 17, 19–21, 25–27, 30–31, 43, 126, 225
Hunting societies, 68, 199

Identity, 66, 235
  affective, 102
  ethnic, 68, 97, 100–103, 105, 111–112
  sexual, 141, 204, 216–218, 224
Immigration, 99
Independence, 205–207, 220
Infant, 27, 29, 41–45, 47–49, 56, 96, 133, 206, 208, 225; see also Newborn
Institutions, 11, 14, 35–38, 40, 96, 176, 192, 197, 203, 216–217, 221–224
  educational, 103, 110, 133–150, 228
  ethnic, 107–108, 113
  political, 69
  social class, 79, 85, 154
  total, 27, 94
Intelligence, 144–145, 147, 170
Intermarriage, 112
Internalization, 55–57
Isolated children, 22–27
Isolation, 25, 28–29, 88, 93
Israel, 95, 103, 221, 223

Japan, 46–47

Kibbutz, 95, 221, 223

Labor unions, 88
Language, 19–20, 51–52, 54, 57, 59, 63–64, 153
  acquisition of, 25, 48–50, 55, 225
  ethnic groups, 98–99, 102–103, 109, 111–112

sex differences in, 217–218
and social class, 82, 84, 138, 218
Life cycle, 60–61, 64, 66–68, 227
Life style, 94, 124
Lower class, see Social class

Males, 199, 217, 224; see also Masculinity; Sex roles
Marginality, ethnic, 105–107
Masculinity, 128, 210, 218–219, 221–222
Mass media, 160–182
  as socializing agents, 40, 162, 225, 233
  themes in, 161, 234
  toys and, 208–210
  and violence, 175, 182
  see also Newspapers; Television
Maturation, 15, 25, 28, 60, 63–64, 66, 151, 184, 227, 234–235
Memory, 51–52, 65
Men, see Males; Masculinity; Sex roles
Middle class, see Social class
Minorities, 98, 136, 148–150; see also Ethnic groups
Mobility, 125, 139, 155
Models
  mass media, 108, 161
  parents as, 132, 154, 226
  see also Fathers; Mothers; Significant others
Morphologic sex, 181, 191–192
Mothers, 22, 62, 65–67, 123–124, 126–127, 129, 202, 221, 223
  in communes, 95–96
  lower-class, 86–87, 121
  middle-class, 46, 80–82, 132
  as role models, 55, 58, 205, 216
  working, 131–133

learning from, 168–170, 178
social class differences, 165–166
socialization by, 167–182
violence in, 171–181
Toys, 56, 58, 208–210
Trained incapacity, 38, 75

Upper middle class, *see* Social class
Urbanization, 74

Values, 10–11, 59–60, 66, 68, 71–72, 117, 123, 142, 161, 180–181, 192
achievement, 72, 154
ethnic group, 98, 110–111

peer group, 151, 156, 158, 230–231
social class, 75–82, 87, 137–138, 146
Violence, 143, 171–181
Voluntary groups, children's, 114

White collar workers, 88; *see also* Social class
Women, *see* Female; Femininity; Sex roles
Women's movement, 186
Working class, *see* Social class
Working mothers, 131–132

Youth culture, 229–232

About the Authors

Frederick Elkin is Professor of Sociology at York University, Toronto. Formerly, he taught at the University of Montreal, McGill University, and the University of Missouri. He is on the Professional Advisory Committee of Dellcrest Children's Centre, in Toronto, and served on the committee that established the Vanier Institute of the Family.

In addition to having made numerous contributions to the journal literature and to edited works, Professor Elkin is the author of *Family in Canada* (1964) and *Rebels and Colleagues: Advertising and Social Change in French Canada* (1973).

Gerald Handel is Professor of Sociology at The City College and Graduate Center of the City University of New York. Formerly, he was with the Center for Urban Education; Social Research, Incorporated; and the Committee on Human Development of The University of Chicago. He was associate editor of *Journal of Marriage and Family* from 1969 to 1975.

Professor Handel's published work includes *Family Worlds* (1959) and *Workingman's Wife* (1959), of which he is coauthor; *The Psychosocial Interior of the Family* (1967; 2nd ed., 1972), which he edited; *The School in the Middle* (1969), which he coedited; and several journal articles and contributions to edited works.